Cities, Diversity and Ethnicity

This volume brings together a variety of studies on the question of cities, diversity and ethnicity. Contributions cover various facets of life in contemporary cities, ranging from the role which street markets play in diverse neighbourhoods, to everyday multiculture in a specific street, the role of community and hometown associations amongst migrant communities, expressions of ethnicity in urban neighbourhoods, and the changing dynamics of integration and community cohesion. This book will be of interest to those who are concerned with developing a better understanding of how urban communities are being transformed by the development of new patterns of migration and ethnic mobilisation. With contributions from a wide range of scholarly and national backgrounds, each chapter helps to provide an overview both of current trends, and of historical patterns and processes. Collectively they provide important insights into the shifting patterns of community and identity in increasingly diverse communities and neighbourhoods.

This book was originally published as a special issue of *Ethnic and Racial Studies.*

Martin Bulmer is Emeritus Professor of Sociology at the University of Surrey, Guildford, UK. He is the author and editor of many books.

John Solomos is Professor of Sociology and Head of Department at the University of Warwick, UK. His most recent publications are *Race, Multiculture and Social Policy* (with Alice Bloch and Sarah Neal) and *Theories of Race and Ethnic Relations: Contemporary Debates and Perspectives* (with Karim Murji).

Ethnic and Racial Studies

Series editors: Martin Bulmer, *University of Surrey, UK,* and John Solomos, *University of Warwick, UK*

The journal *Ethnic and Racial Studies* was founded in 1978 by John Stone to provide an international forum for high quality research on race, ethnicity, nationalism and ethnic conflict. At the time the study of race and ethnicity was still a relatively marginal sub-field of sociology, anthropology and political science. In the intervening period the journal has provided a space for the discussion of core theoretical issues, key developments and trends, and for the dissemination of the latest empirical research.

It is now the leading journal in its field and has helped to shape the development of scholarly research agendas. *Ethnic and Racial Studies* attracts submissions from scholars in a diverse range of countries and fields of scholarship, and crosses disciplinary boundaries. It is now available in both printed and electronic form. From 2015 it will publish 15 issues per year, three of which will be dedicated to *Ethnic and Racial Studies Review* offering expert guidance to the latest research through the publication of book reviews, symposia and discussion pieces, including reviews of work in languages other than English.

The *Ethnic and Racial Studies* book series contains a wide range of the journal's special issues. These special issues are an important contribution to the work of the journal, where leading social science academics bring together articles on specific themes and issues that are linked to the broad intellectual concerns of *Ethnic and Racial Studies*. The series editors work closely with the guest editors of the special issues to ensure that they meet the highest quality standards possible. Through publishing these special issues as a series of books, we hope to allow a wider audience of both scholars and students from across the social science disciplines to engage with the work of *Ethnic and Racial Studies*.

Titles in the series include:

The Transnational Political Participation of Immigrants
Edited by Jean-Michel Lafleur and Marco Martiniello

Anthropology of Migration and Multiculturalism
Edited by Steven Vertovec

Migrant Politics and Mobilisation
Exclusion, Engagements, Incorporation
Edited by Davide Però and John Solomos

New Racial Missions of Policing
International Perspectives on Evolving Law-Enforcement Politics
Edited by Paul Amar

Young People, Social Capital and Ethnic Identity
Edited by Tracey Reynolds

Cosmopolitan Sociability
*Edited by Tsypylma Darieva,
Nina Glick Schiller and
Sandra Gruner-Domić*

Retheorizing Race and Whiteness in the 21st Century
*Edited by Charles A. Gallagher and
France Winddance Twine*

Theorising Integration and Assimilation
*Edited by Jens Schneider and
Maurice Crul*

Ethnic and Racial Minorities in Asia
Inclusion or Exclusion?
Edited by Michelle Ann Miller

Diasporas, Cultures and Identities
*Edited by Martin Bulmer and
John Solomos*

Gender, Race and Religion
Intersections and Challenges
*Edited by Martin Bulmer and
John Solomos*

Latino Identity in Contemporary America
*Edited by Martin Bulmer and
John Solomos*

Migration: Policies, Practices, Activism
*Edited by Martin Bulmer and
John Solomos*

Nationalism and National Identities
*Edited by Martin Bulmer and
John Solomos*

Methods and Contexts in the Study of Muslim Minorities
Visible and Invisible Muslims
*Edited by Nadia Jeldtoft and
Jørgen S. Nielsen*

Irregular Migrants: Policy, Politics, Motives and Everyday Lives
*Edited by Alice Bloch and
Milena Chimienti*

Fighting Discrimination in Europe
The Case for a Race-Conscious Approach
*Edited by Mathias Möschel,
Costanza Hermanin and Michele Grigolo*

Responses to Stigmatization in Comparative Perspective
*Edited by Michele Lamont and
Nissim Mizrachi*

Health Care and Immigration
Understanding the Connections
*Edited by Patricia Fernandez-Kelly and
Alejandro Portes*

Gender, Migration and the Media
Edited by Myria Georgiou

Accounting for Ethnic and Racial Diversity
The Challenge of Enumeration
*Edited by Patrick Simon and
Victor Piché*

Methodologies on the Move
The Transnational Turn in Empirical
Migration Research
*Edited by Anna Amelina, Thomas Faist
and Devrimsel D. Nergiz*

Racialization and Religion
Race, Culture and Difference in the Study
of Antisemitism and Islamophobia
Edited by Nasar Meer

Race and Ethnicity in Secret and Exclusive Social Orders: Blood and Shadow
Edited by Matthew W. Hughey

The Language of Inclusion and Exclusion in Immigration and Integration
*Edited by Marlou Schrover and
Willem Schinkel*

Mothering, Mixed Families and Racialised Boundaries
Edited by Ravinder Barn and Vicki Harman

Race Critical Public Scholarship
Edited by Karim Murji and Gargi Bhattacharyya

Migrants and Their Children in Britain
Generational Change in Patterns of Ethnic Minority Integration
Edited by Anthony Heath

New Racial Landscapes
Contemporary Britain and the Neoliberal Conjuncture
Edited by Malcolm James, Helen Kim and Victoria Redclift

Belonging to the Nation
Generational Change, Identity and the Chinese Diaspora
Edited by Edmund Terence Gomez and Gregor Benton-Langland

Race, Migration and Identity
Shifting Boundaries in the USA
Edited by Martin Bulmer and John Solomos

Multiculturalism, Social Cohesion and Immigration
Shifting Conceptions in the UK
Edited by Martin Bulmer and John Solomos

Books, Bodies and Bronzes
Comparing Sites of Global Citizenship Creation
Edited by Peggy Levitt and Pál Nyíri

Cities, Diversity and Ethnicity
Politics, Governance and Participation
Edited by Martin Bulmer and John Solomos

Cities, Diversity and Ethnicity
Politics, governance and participation

Edited by
Martin Bulmer and John Solomos

First published 2016
by Routledge
2 Park Square, Milton Park, Abingdon, Oxon, OX14 4RN, UK

and by Routledge
711 Third Avenue, New York, NY 10017, USA

Routledge is an imprint of the Taylor & Francis Group, an informa business

© 2016 Taylor & Francis

All rights reserved. No part of this book may be reprinted or reproduced
or utilised in any form or by any electronic, mechanical, or other means,
now known or hereafter invented, including photocopying and recording,
or in any information storage or retrieval system, without permission in
writing from the publishers.

Trademark notice: Product or corporate names may be trademarks or
registered trademarks, and are used only for identification and
explanation without intent to infringe.

British Library Cataloguing in Publication Data
A catalogue record for this book is available from the British Library

ISBN 13: 978-1-138-92487-1

Typeset in Times New Roman
by RefineCatch Limited, Bungay, Suffolk

Publisher's Note
The publisher accepts responsibility for any inconsistencies that may have
arisen during the conversion of this book from journal articles to book chapters,
namely the possible inclusion of journal terminology.

Disclaimer
Every effort has been made to contact copyright holders for their permission to
reprint material in this book. The publishers would be grateful to hear from any
copyright holder who is not here acknowledged and will undertake to rectify
any errors or omissions in future editions of this book.

Contents

Citation Information	ix
Notes on Contributors	xi
Introduction *Martin Bulmer and John Solomos*	1
1. Urban markets and diversity: towards a research agenda *Daniel Hiebert, Jan Rath and Steven Vertovec*	5
2. Super-diverse street: a 'trans-ethnography' across migrant localities *Suzanne M. Hall*	21
3. The perception of ethnic diversity and anti-immigrant sentiments: a multilevel analysis of local communities in Belgium *Marc Hooghe and Thomas de Vroome*	37
4. Policy actors' narrative constructions of migrants' integration in Malmö and Bologna *Sarah Scuzzarello*	56
5. Social change and community cohesion: an ethnographic study of two Melbourne suburbs *Val Colic-Peisker and Shanthi Robertson*	74
6. Narratives of ethnic identity among practitioners in community settings in the northeast of England *Judith Parks and Kye Askins*	91
7. Little of Italy? Assumed ethnicity in a New York City neighbourhood *Elisabeth Becker*	108
8. Levelling the playing field: patterns of ethnic philanthropy among Los Angeles' middle- and upper-class Latino entrepreneurs *Jody Agius Vallejo*	124
9. The bi-national road to immigrant rights mobilization: states, social movements and Chicago's Mexican hometown associations *Rebecca Vonderlack-Navarro and William Sites*	140

CONTENTS

10. Back to the Future: revisiting the contact hypothesis at Turkish and
mixed non-profit organizations in Amsterdam   157
Wahideh Achbari

11. The early history of migration and settlement of Yemenis in Cardiff,
1939–1970: religion and ethnicity as social capital   175
Jody Mellor and Sophie Gilliat-Ray

Index   191

Citation Information

The chapters in this book were originally published in *Ethnic and Racial Studies*, volume 38, issue 1 (January 2015). When citing this material, please use the original page numbering for each article, as follows:

Introduction
Introduction
Martin Bulmer and John Solomos
Ethnic and Racial Studies, volume 38, issue 1 (January 2015) pp. 1–4

Chapter 1
Urban markets and diversity: towards a research agenda
Daniel Hiebert, Jan Rath and Steven Vertovec
Ethnic and Racial Studies, volume 38, issue 1 (January 2015) pp. 5–21

Chapter 2
Super-diverse street: a 'trans-ethnography' across migrant localities
Suzanne M. Hall
Ethnic and Racial Studies, volume 38, issue 1 (January 2015) pp. 22–37

Chapter 3
The perception of ethnic diversity and anti-immigrant sentiments: a multilevel analysis of local communities in Belgium
Marc Hooghe and Thomas de Vroome
Ethnic and Racial Studies, volume 38, issue 1 (January 2015) pp. 38–56

Chapter 4
Policy actors' narrative constructions of migrants' integration in Malmö and Bologna
Sarah Scuzzarello
Ethnic and Racial Studies, volume 38, issue 1 (January 2015) pp. 57–74

CITATION INFORMATION

Chapter 5
Social change and community cohesion: an ethnographic study of two Melbourne suburbs
Val Colic-Peisker and Shanthi Robertson
Ethnic and Racial Studies, volume 38, issue 1 (January 2015) pp. 75–91

Chapter 6
Narratives of ethnic identity among practitioners in community settings in the northeast of England
Judith Parks and Kye Askins
Ethnic and Racial Studies, volume 38, issue 1 (January 2015) pp. 92–108

Chapter 7
Little of Italy? Assumed ethnicity in a New York City neighbourhood
Elisabeth Becker
Ethnic and Racial Studies, volume 38, issue 1 (January 2015) pp. 109–124

Chapter 8
Levelling the playing field: patterns of ethnic philanthropy among Los Angeles' middle- and upper-class Latino entrepreneurs
Jody Agius Vallejo
Ethnic and Racial Studies, volume 38, issue 1 (January 2015) pp. 125–140

Chapter 9
The bi-national road to immigrant rights mobilization: states, social movements and Chicago's Mexican hometown associations
Rebecca Vonderlack-Navarro and William Sites
Ethnic and Racial Studies, volume 38, issue 1 (January 2015) pp. 141–157

Chapter 10
Back to the Future: revisiting the contact hypothesis at Turkish and mixed non-profit organizations in Amsterdam
Wahideh Achbari
Ethnic and Racial Studies, volume 38, issue 1 (January 2015) pp. 158–175

Chapter 11
The early history of migration and settlement of Yemenis in Cardiff, 1939–1970: religion and ethnicity as social capital
Jody Mellor and Sophie Gilliat-Ray
Ethnic and Racial Studies, volume 38, issue 1 (January 2015) pp. 176–191

For any permission-related enquiries please visit:
http://www.tandfonline.com/page/help/permissions

Notes on Contributors

Wahideh Achbari is a Research Fellow in the Department of Applied Economics, Vrije Universiteit Brussel, Belgium.

Kye Askins is Lecturer in the Department of Geography at Northumbria University, Newcastle, UK.

Elisabeth Becker is a PhD Candidate in the Department of Sociology at Yale University, New Haven, Connecticut, USA.

Martin Bulmer is Emeritus Professor of Sociology at the University of Surrey, Guildford, UK.

Val Colic-Peisker is Associate Professor in the School of Global, Urban and Social Studies at RMIT University, Melbourne, Australia.

Thomas de Vroome is a PhD candidate in the Ercomer Department at Utrecht University, The Netherlands.

Sophie Gilliat-Ray is a Reader in the School of History, Archaeology and Religion at Cardiff University, UK.

Suzanne M. Hall is a Researcher at LSE Cities in the Department of Sociology at the London School of Economics and Social Science, London, UK.

Daniel Hiebert is Professor of Geography at the University of British Columbia, Vancouver, Canada.

Marc Hooghe is Professor of Political Science at the University of Leuven, Belgium.

Jody Mellor is a Research Assistant in the School of Sociology, Politics and International Studies at the University of Bristol, UK.

Judith Parks is a Lecturer in the Department of Geography at Northumbria University, Newcastle, UK.

Jan Rath is Professor of Urban Sociology and Chair of the Department of Sociology and Anthropology at the University of Amsterdam, The Netherlands.

Shanthi Robertson is a Research Fellow at the Institute for Culture and Society at the University of Western Sydney, Australia.

NOTES ON CONTRIBUTORS

Sarah Scuzzarello is a Swedish Research Council Post-Doctoral Fellow in the Department of Sociology at City University London, UK.

William Sites is Associate Professor in the School of Social Service Administration at the University of Chicago, Illinois, USA.

John Solomos is Professor of Sociology and Head of Department at the University of Warwick, UK.

Jody Agius Vallejo is Assistant Professor of Sociology at the University of Southern California, Los Angeles, USA.

Steven Vertovec is Director at the Max Planck Institute for the Study of Religious and Ethnic Diversity, Göttingen, Germany.

Rebecca Vonderlack-Navarro is a Post-Doctoral Affiliate at the Institute for Migration and International Social Work at Loyola University, Chicago, Illinois, USA.

Introduction

From its foundations as a distinct field of research and scholarship, the study of race and ethnicity has been focused on the interactions between groups in urban communities and cities. Early scholarship in the field, shaped in many ways by the pioneering work of the Chicago School, explored key facets of the development of what came to be called race relations in urban conurbations such as Chicago (Apter et al. 2009; Bulmer 1984). Much of this early research was focused on the evolution and development of racialized urban situations in the USA during the early part of the twentieth century. This was a time of large-scale internal migration within the USA of African Americans from the old South to the large urban conurbations of the North. This was also a time of continuing large-scale immigration from Europe and other parts of the globe to the USA. In this changing environment, many of the large urban conurbations saw the formation of new forms of racialized relations that were to shape and influence the configuration of race and ethnic relations in the USA throughout the twentieth century (Katznelson 1973; Lal 1989).

Although much of the early research in the field was framed around the experience of the USA, it is also important to note that the emphasis on cities and communities was also evident in the scholarly research of European scholars working on questions about immigration and minority formation in the post-1945 period. A good example of this trend can be found in the work of John Rex, which was concerned with the formation of race relations in British cities such as Birmingham in the period from the 1950s onwards (Rex and Moore 1967; Rex 1973). Rex, and other European scholars subsequently, shared some of the same conceptual frames as the American researchers. In particular, the influence of the urban ethnographic tradition helped to shape scholarship in this field through research agendas in a number of national environments (Body-Gendrot and Martiniello 2000).

In this themed issue of the journal we have brought together a selection of eleven papers that deal with various contemporary facets of race, ethnicity and diversity. Although this selection of papers is by no means exhaustive, we hope that they help to highlight key areas of contemporary scholarship and research in this field. The first two papers are linked together by a common concern to understand the changing make-up of localities and cities in the context of evolving ethnic and racial diversities. The first paper by Daniel Hiebert, Jan Rath, and Steven Vertovec seeks to outline a research agenda for exploring the changing morphology of urban street markets in a context of growing ethnic and racial diversity. Drawing on empirical research on street markets in ethnically diverse cities, the paper seeks to explore the impact of diversity on both the role of street markets and their relationship to wider communities. The core arguments of the paper draw on empirical studies of markets in diverse communities, but the main concern of the authors is to lay out a research agenda for future research on markets and communities. The analysis of urban street markets links up well to the second paper by Suzanne Hall, which is an urban ethnography of a street in South London. In a sense, Hall's contribution can be read as an example of the kind of research that is outlined in the opening paper. Drawing on her wider urban ethnography of the neighbourhood of Peckham in South London, Hall seeks to provide an account of the everyday realities of life in multicultural communities. By focusing on the level of the street, she seeks to argue that shifting patterns of migration and growing diversity are creating new ways in which urban spaces are lived and experienced.

These first two papers are followed by three studies that explore the shifting role of ethnic diversities in specific cities and communities. The first of this group of papers is by Marc Hooghe and Thomas de Vroome and is a detailed empirical exploration of the relationship between ethnic diversity and anti-immigrant sentiments. It draws on a multilevel analysis of local communities in Belgium and it seeks to provide a rounded analysis of how the expression of anti-immigrant values cannot be fully understood within a national frame, since anti-immigrant sentiments often link up to the lived realities of particular communities.

This account is followed by Sarah Scuzzarello's comparative analysis of the constructions of migrants' integration in Malmö and Bologna among a range of policy actors. Scuzzarello's research draws out both the differences as well as the similarities between the policy frames used to talk about migrant integration in the two cities. A particular focus of her analysis lies in the way in which she seeks to argue that policy actors draw on a wide range of both local and national narratives in order to make sense of what integration means in diverse urban environments.

The final paper in this group of studies is Val Colic-Peisker and Shanthi Robertson. They seek to extend this part of the issue by providing an urban ethnography of processes of social change and community cohesion in two suburbs of the Australian city of Melbourne. In focusing their analysis on two ethnically diverse suburbs, Colic-Peisker and Robertson seek to address the question of how community cohesion is impacted upon by wider economic, social and cultural transformations in the two localities.

The focus of the following five papers moves on to the question of how ethnicity is mobilized in the context of community formation and identity construction. The first of these papers is by Judith Parks and Kye Askins and draws on research about narratives of ethnic identity among policy practitioners in community settings in the northeast of England. A key strand in Parks and Askins account is that the meanings attached to community are changing through the experiences of migration, community formation and identity construction.

The next paper, by Elisabeth Becker, addresses a theme that has been the focus of much debate in the USA over the past few decades, namely the construction of ethnicity and identity in a multi-ethnic urban environment. Drawing on Goffman's (1990) account of the presentation of self in everyday life, Becker takes up the question of forms of assumed ethnicity in the Little Italy neighbourhood of New York City. Becker's analysis focuses in particular on the ways in which a group of Albanian

CITIES, DIVERSITY AND ETHNICITY

Kosovars in the restaurant trade find it strategically useful to construct an assumed ethnicity by presenting themselves as another ethnic group.

The phenomenon of the mobilization of ethnicity is also the main concern of the paper by Jody Agius Vallejo, which draws on research about shifting patterns of ethnic philanthropy among Los Angeles' middle- and upper-class Latino entrepreneurs. Vallejo's account seeks to show that while both of these groups of entrepreneurs share some values in relation to helping the mobility of their co-ethnics, they also can be seen as adopting divergent strategies of philanthropic action in order to achieve their objectives.

A somewhat different type of ethnic mobilization is analysed by Rebecca Vorderlack-Navarro and William Sites. Navarro and Sites draw on a detailed empirical analysis of binational and immigrant rights mobilization, and they are particularly concerned with the complex relationship between states, social movements and Chicago's Mexican hometown associations. From this perspective, hometown associations provide a mechanism for mobilizations both about specific communities as well as for broader claims to immigrant rights.

The penultimate paper in this issue is by Wahideh Achbari and it is concerned with an exploration of the contact hypothesis in relation to Turkish and mixed non-profit organizations in Amsterdam. Achbari's analysis seeks to question some of the popular assumptions made about participation in both Turkish and mixed voluntary organizations and to provide empirical evidence that can be used to explore this question in more detail.

The concluding paper in this issue is by Jody Mellor and Sophie Gilliat-Ray and can be seen as providing a historical account of the processes that shaped the formation and evolution of the Yemeni community in Cardiff in Wales from the 1930s to the 1970s. This is a relatively long-established minority community and Mellor and Gilliat-Ray seek to explore the role of various forms of religious, personal and cultural networks in shaping the experiences of the Yemeni community.

The papers in this issue of the journal are by no means exhaustive of the range of papers that related to cities, ethnicity and diversity. But we do hope that they are indicative of the exciting and innovative research that is being done in this field in a wide range of national and urban settings.

References

Apter, David E., Herbert J. Gans, Ruth Horowitz, Gerald D. Jaynes, William Kornblum, James F. Short, Gerald D. Suttles, and Robert E. Washington. 2009. "The Chicago School and the Roots of Urban Ethnography." *Ethnography* 10 (4): 375–96. doi:10.1177/14661381093 46982.

Body-Gendrot, Sophie, and Marco Martiniello, eds. 2000. *Minorities in European Cities: The Dynamics of Social Integration and Social Exclusion at the Neighborhood Level.* Basingstoke: Macmillan.

Bulmer, Martin. 1984. *The Chicago School of Sociology: Institutionalization, Diversity and the Rise of Sociological Research.* Chicago: University of Chicago Press.

Goffman, Erving. 1990. *The Presentation of Self in Everyday Life.* Harmondsworth: Penguin.

Katznelson, Ira. 1973. *Black Men, White Cities: Race, Politics, and Migration in the United States, 1900–30, and Britain, 1948–1968.* Chicago: University of Chicago Press.

Lal, Barbara Ballis. 1989. *The Romance of Culture in an Urban Civilisation: Robert E. Park on Race and Ethnic Relations in Cities*. London: Routledge.

Rex, John. 1973. *Race, Colonialism and the City*. London: Routledge & Kegan Paul.

Rex, John, and Robert Moore. 1967. *Race, Community and Conflict: A Study of Sparkbrook*. Oxford: Oxford University Press.

Martin Bulmer and John Solomos

Urban markets and diversity: towards a research agenda

Daniel Hiebert, Jan Rath and Steven Vertovec

In this paper we advocate the study of local street markets to explore fundamental issues about the relationship between economy and society. This relationship evolves over time and we believe that it has been recast in an age of increasing cultural diversity and neo-liberal state regulatory structures. In street markets we can see how diversity and the nature of economic transactions become mutually constitutive. We argue that cultural diversity propels local markets, while everyday interactions in markets influence intercultural relationships. These complex processes are affected by the spatiality of markets and the regulatory environments within which they operate. We conclude by framing a research programme on street markets and discuss a number of methodological complications that would need to be addressed in this endeavour.

The Dappermarkt is a long, broad avenue lined with stalls in the middle of a working-class area in eastern Amsterdam. These are some observations made on a walk on a sunny Saturday morning through the Dappermarkt. The wares for sale are absolutely mundane: no crafts, decorative arts, organic foodstuffs or tourist items, but cheap clothes (blouses for as little as €3, jackets from €5), clothes, socks and underwear, batteries, watches, vegetables, fish, flowers. There is no seeming order of items: after a succession of clothing stalls one finds a cheese stand, then some fashion accessories, then a couple more clothing stalls, a butcher, some boots, and so on. For certain specific, 'traditional' Dutch foods – certain cheeses or brined herring, for instance – the sellers and buyers are exclusively Dutch whites. For practically everything else, there is no apparent correlation between the ethnic or national background of the sellers or buyers and the commodities on sale. Sellers of clothes and textiles, which seem to dominate the market, are a wide mix of Dutch, Hindustani (Indian Surinamese) or Pakistani, Turkish or Arab, Chinese or Vietnamese, Russian or other Eastern Europeans. The throng of shoppers is yet more diverse than the sellers, indeed many times so. A cross-cutting demographic, however, is that the crowd is over-represented by senior citizens and families.

The occasional, loud sales pitches of a few sellers temporarily break the quiet murmur of the crowd. Otherwise, an air of pleasant calm is created by the slow pace of the browsing shoppers, the behaviour of children pacified by eating treats at the sides of their parents, the polite inquiries of shoppers and cheerful responses of stallholders, people excusing themselves as they meander through the crowd with bikes loaded with flowers and bags, acquaintances greeting one another, and small mixed-gender groups giggling at some shared joke. It is an absolutely routine set of activities at the market – albeit one comprised of one of the most diverse populations imaginable.

This vignette of the Dappermarkt in Amsterdam provides a convenient way to think about the age-old question of the relationship between *economy* and *society*, an issue that has generated many theories and thousands of empirical studies over generations of academic scholarship. We explore the economy/society dynamic by focusing on everyday street markets as our site of analysis. We have selected street markets both because they are so prevalent, and because they are a microcosm of a set of processes that we wish to understand. Street markets are places of many kinds of intersections. Obviously these are places where sellers meet consumers, but in this process other types of intersections occur.

These encounters are frequently between people with different identities, a point emphasized in the Dappermarkt vignette. Why is this the case? In an age of technological complexity and high entry barriers for many occupations and forms of entrepreneurship, a wide range of people can participate in street markets, as sellers and buyers. Buyers and, more importantly, entrepreneurs in these markets need not have full command of the local language, tertiary education, or formal training. At the same time, competition between sellers means that profit margins are thin. This combination of low entry barriers and profits means that marginalized populations can participate in street markets to an extent rarely possible in the more formal economy. As a result, these markets are often the most diverse parts of cities, where people who might lead largely separate lives come face to face and interact.

This is where our interest in 'diversity' is focused. We recognize that there is currently an array of meanings attached to this term in both academic and public discourse (see Vertovec 2012). As migration studies scholars, we are concerned with aspects of social differentiation stemming from international migration. We are not addressing modes of difference surrounding age, sexuality and disability, which are topics included in much diversity discourse. In this article we use 'diversity' in a summary sense to refer specifically to configurations of co-present ethnicities, cultures, languages and religions and, when referring below to 'super-diversity' (Vertovec 2007), the ways that these configurations overlap with or entail multi-dimensional complexities with respect to other variables such as gender, class, legal status and human capital.

While there have been scores of studies on particular street markets, we pose a set of much more general, conceptual questions in this paper: what are the impacts of diversity on the nature and operation of street markets; and what are the implications of street markets for diversity? Do street markets play a role in the process whereby people learn to coexist across their differences, or does participation in markets have no influence on inter-group relationships beyond brief moments of interaction, or even a negative influence? How do everyday encounters in markets contribute to (or undermine) this learning process? When people from different backgrounds *get along* in markets, is this indicative of larger social processes of civility or are these encounters specific and somehow exceptional?

Thinking about this issue from the opposite direction, how does increasing diversity contribute to the opportunity structures that underlie street markets and the economy more generally? Certainly, diversity expands the range of products available to consumers. In this sense, diversity also brings new types of highly specialized entrepreneurs and, with them, jobs. That is, street markets can be seen as the point where diversity becomes part of the fabric of the economy and sets new tastes in motion.

We are also interested in two ancillary issues that influence the relationship between diversity and markets: the role of *place* and *regulatory structures*. Street markets arise in specific places and regulatory regimes and they inevitably reflect the qualities of these places and regimes.

Why do we advocate more intense academic inquiry into markets and diversity now? As we argue throughout this paper, a careful look at markets can provide significant insights into several kinds of dynamics surrounding diversity, an issue that has assumed a central position in contemporary scholarship:

- Without a doubt, and for multiple reasons, over the past ten years there has been more and more attention on various forms of 'diversity', not just in academia but also increasingly in public policy and corporate practice. Across the social sciences we are witnessing the rise of a multidisciplinary field of diversity studies. But scholars have poured considerable energy into certain aspects of diversity (e.g. discrimination and anti-discrimination, changing cultural landscapes in cities), but much less into others (e.g. the links between diversity and the economy).
- To a degree, we can account for this intensified interest in 'diversity' as a consequence of relatively recent changes in anti-discrimination legislation and identity politics. However, it is also concomitant with changing social, cultural and demographic configurations around the world, due in significant ways to the growing complexity of global migration patterns (Vertovec 2007).
- In many Western contexts, the recent development of diversity policies has ironically occurred at the same time as a rise in nativist populist movements, especially across Europe, that have even seen anti-immigration parties participate in some governing coalitions, and the so-called 'crisis of multi-culturalism', entailing public debates over the degree to which states should safeguard cultural difference or pursue measures to promote common values and social 'integration' (Rath 2011; Vertovec and Wessendorf 2010).
- Markets also enable us to interrogate an important debate surrounding the development of urban economies. According to Florida (2002) and others, the urban economy in advanced societies today revolves around industries with high levels of cognitive and cultural labour. The success of these creative economies and, consequently, the prosperity of these cities and the socio-economic well-being of their residents are contingent – among other things – on the presence of a diverse population. In this logic, diversity stimulates innovation and contributes to the liveability of cities, which in turn helps attract

high-skilled workers and businesses. It is interesting to explore how urban street markets relate to this new logic (see also Aytar and Rath 2012).

- The current economic/financial crisis has revealed a pressing need to think beyond the traditional understanding of the formal economy and explore new avenues of economic development and job creation. Street markets can be seen, in this light, as places where micro-businesses come into existence and jobs are generated during periods of stubborn unemployment.
- Despite numerous calls for and attempts to promote a 'clean' bureaucratic culture and 'decent' forms of regulation, informalization abounds. Informal practices can be found in all sorts of places, such as in the fields of policing, caregiving, immigration control, environmental pollution and – last but not least – in the economy. The expansion of the informal economy in relation to the proliferation of diversity is a line of research that deserves further exploration (Kloosterman, van der Leun, and Rath 1999).
- Finally, for some years now scholars have been seeking ways to overcome 'Eurocentrism' or similar biases in perspective and understanding. Encouraging an interest in global topics – like markets and diversity, we propose – provides one way of understanding human phenomena and processes not seemingly associated solely with either 'the West', 'the East' or 'the South'. That is, markets exist everywhere, and the nature and degree of diversity is becoming more complex (almost) everywhere. But the relationship between diversity and markets is highly place-specific. Therefore we cannot understand this relationship without investigating markets across many societies, including those in both the more and less developed countries.

The goal of this paper is to help define and provide a sense of coherence to a field of scholarship, by situating it conceptually and offering a set of research directions. We contend that people in their everyday encounters in street markets develop methods of intercultural engagement and learn a repertoire of intercultural skills, and that diversity helps propel markets. We argue that these processes have consequences for both the economy (the ways that markets operate) and society (the ongoing development of social civility and even, more broadly, social cohesion).

Demarcating markets and diversity

Before examining these issues in depth, we briefly discuss a number of key concepts, starting with the *market*. Markets exist in all shapes and sizes. One may refer to very concrete situations such as a farmers' market, or a night market (i.e. open markets with stalls and their concomitant ethnoscapes, aromascapes, soundscapes and so forth), where stallholders sell their wares directly to consumers, versus others that are more abstract, such as the global market or the energy market whereby the market comprises economic exchanges that are not conducted by people in face-to-face situations. Following a Weberian logic, all types of markets are institutions where more or less voluntary, monetary and non-monetary economic exchanges take place. Various forms of involuntary exchange – piracy, conquest, robbery and theft – as well as those activities that constitute production per se fall beyond this definition (Engelen

2001). A wide range of social, cultural, political and other factors interfere in the functioning of markets, varying from formal laws and regulations to informal – 'moral' – prescriptions. These factors help illustrate that the nature of markets are not simply given, but are products of human action.

In the remainder of this paper, we focus on markets in their most concrete form, namely urban street markets. While we focus on open street markets, we are sensitive to the fact that there are numerous other kinds of markets that show interesting 'family resemblances'. They are outside the scope of our interest at this time, as they are either highly formally regulated or highly informal, while we are interested in places that are in between these polarities. We can, for example, think of ambulatory street sellers; impromptu or flea markets, such as car boot sales or places where goods are sold from blankets on the ground; shopping malls and regular shopping streets where goods are sold from shops that are part of permanent buildings; ethnically themed shopping strips or even neighbourhoods such as Chinatowns (Aytar and Rath 2012); permanent highly regulated markets, such as the Camden Market of London, or the Grand Bazaar of Istanbul, which are enclosed by large buildings and where market structures have become firmly established; and 'high-end' markets, such as the diamond market of Amsterdam or, at the extreme, the stock market of any city. Although we will not address these markets per se, we will draw upon the existing academic literature about them (for a discussion of the different kinds of consumer markets and marketplaces, see Plattner 1989). We also believe that the social processes discussed in this paper apply, in many cases, to these other types of markets, but to discuss each type would exhaust the scope of a journal article.

Street markets are non-permanent structures (i.e. stalls) where entrepreneurs do not own the spaces and/or structures that they sell from. They are often, but not always, built in the morning and removed later that day, sometimes on a daily basis, at other times on a semi-weekly or weekly basis. Street markets are typically 'ordinary' places where 'ordinary' products are sold, such as food, clothing, flowers, shoelaces or inexpensive watches. The exchanges usually take place in flexible ways, which could involve bartering, and typically constitute a cash economy. Typically, street markets are characterized by a relatively high level of informality. The longevity of particular shopping outlets tends to be limited and the turnover of entrepreneurs is therefore high. Yet, these open markets continue to be popular, even when mega malls are located nearby (Pardy 2005) and when virtually every product is also available through the Internet. The low entry barriers for vendors and market-goers to attend open street markets, as well as the style of market exchange, means that they appeal to and include many segments of the population and therefore are often associated with various forms of diversity.

Both markets and diversities are *spatially* specific. Place matters, obviously, although not for every product or every market in the same way. While urban street markets may be connected to wider geographical areas, they operate on the lowest level of spatiality: they are placed in urban neighbourhoods. These urban places are not neutral. Products may be considered more 'authentic' or 'cool' if associated with a particular place.

Different social and economic opportunities exist at different levels of spatiality or at different scalar levels. Each level affects the other in some way. Street markets are local, but more often are also connected to other spaces by: (1) vendors who come from different parts of the world and maintain transnational relations with people from their place of origin, and/or with others from their diaspora; (2) consumers (ditto); (3) the products that rightly or wrongly are associated with particular spaces; and (4) the regulatory structure. Seen in such a way, street markets constitute interesting localized places for direct, local encounters with an otherwise global economy. Local residents may meet with an 'immigrant, ethnic other' coming from a different place in the world (and vice versa), and they may taste, test and purchase products with distant origins. The dynamics of these markets are consequently related to larger social, cultural, political and economic processes and structures.

We are particularly interested in spatiality as a factor that structures market exchange and interaction between people (Seligman 2000). These exchanges and interactions obviously do not take place in an institutional vacuum, but are governed by many forms of *regulation*. The regulation of economic exchanges is not reserved to advanced welfare states, but is a key characteristic of any economy. There are a plethora of regulatory instruments varying from taxes, zoning, health and security laws, migrant labour laws, and so on, but also subsidies, support schemes, mediation and so forth. Regulation, in fact, comprises any 'interference' in market exchanges. It is therefore important to keep several things in mind (Engelen 2001; Kloosterman and Rath 2010). First, regulation entails more than just state regulation. A wide array of individuals and institutions play a role in regulation, including local, national or international governmental agents, business associations, unions, voluntary associations, non-profit organizations, as well as individuals and their social networks. Second, regulation entails more than just do's and don'ts. That is, there are legislative do's and don'ts, but also a multitude of incentives and disincentives, and measures of a more persuasive nature. Third, regulation can be imposed (by the state, by regulatory institutions, or by groups or individuals), or may arise out of everyday voluntary action. Fourth, and related to the previous points, regulation can be more formal or more informal. In the 'white' economy, in the 'grey' (where legislation per se seems non-existent or is conveniently put aside), and also in the 'black' economy (where criminal transactions prevail) economic exchanges are still regulated in one way or another. In sum, regulation never exists alone, but always in complex packages that define what is 'required', 'acceptable' or 'preferable' in a market and what is not.

Finally, the interactions between entrepreneurs and consumers in the street market are *public*. Consumers witness transactions and learn the habits/habitus of the market. In a sense this involves a kind of public theatre, often with exaggerated gestures. Information about prices is communicated in public and codes of behaviour are transmitted from seller to seller, consumer to consumer. This does not happen as transparently in one-on-one street sales, for example, where buyers and sellers interact privately. At the other end of the spectrum, when markets become large and more permanent, buyers and sellers become detached and interact in more programmed ways, and sellers are less concerned about their reputation and place in the local social order (Shepherd 2008).

CITIES, DIVERSITY AND ETHNICITY

The intellectual context

Scholars have long been interested in local markets, from a variety of perspectives. Our engagement with this body of work has provided a number of insights, but has also revealed the relatively limited efforts to situate the study of markets within larger conceptual debates. In this section we outline the most prominent concerns in the literature that have developed around local markets and their relationship with society (see Pottie-Sherman 2011).

First, markets are by definition *spaces of contact* that bring people from diverse backgrounds together (e.g. Pardy 2005, on multiple cultures in the Footscray shopping street in Melbourne; Busch 2010, on Polish food vendors in Germany; Liu 2010, on Chinese wholesalers in Ghana).

Second, markets shape the *sociability of exchange*. There is no consensus in the relevant literature on how this unfolds. On the positive side, markets can be places where dominant and subordinate groups can operate as equals; they can also be sites of camaraderie between buyers and sellers where, for example, stories about products become part of the exchange process when consumers begin to appreciate 'authenticity'; and people from different backgrounds 'rub along' in markets and learn tolerance (Watson 2009). Others are more sceptical about the impact of everyday interaction in markets on these kinds of relationships. Smith (1965), for example, argues that people practise 'mutual avoidance' in markets and Maisel (1974) concludes that the quest for profit trumps sociability and the latter only arises when it is compatible with the former. Pardy (2005) encapsulates both sides of this debate when she ponders whether a street market in Melbourne is a site where 'a spectacle of peaceful co-existence exclude[es] a seething and resentful introversion' (119), but later posits that 'this apparent non-celebration of otherness is, nonetheless, an engagement with it' (126). In her terms, street markets may be places of 'indifference to difference' or 'openness to otherness' (or, perhaps, both of these processes may be occurring).

Third, and along the same lines, markets can contribute to stereotypes and *facilitate the cultural subordination of minority groups*. Kipling's shocking description of markets in China provides an early example of this type of orientalizing process (Lysack 2005). Frequently, products circulating in markets can best be described as 'authentic fakes' (Alraouf 2010) that are based upon, and reinforce, stereotypes.

Fourth, researchers have investigated the *impact of regulatory systems on markets*. At the scale of nation states, the accession of Poland to the EU, for example, undermined the opportunity for Russian entrepreneurs to sell cheap products across the border in Poland (Marcinszak and Van der Velde 2008). More locally, planning regulations control many aspects of markets. Recently, there are examples of planners recognizing the potential for markets to enhance the economic viability of distressed neighbourhoods, although their interventions may inadvertently destabilize markets by trying to sanitize and coordinate them (Dines 2007).

Fifth, markets may be places of *economic incorporation for marginalized groups*. Around the world, struggling populations survive by selling cheap goods in markets. This of course includes newcomers, such as unauthorized migrants (L'Hote and Gasta 2007), and groups that face barriers in the regular labour market, such as Pacific

Islanders in Auckland (De Bruin and Dupuis 2000), or Vietnamese migrants to Soviet-era East Germany who face enormous difficulty gaining access to standard forms of employment (Hüwelmeier 2013). In a sense, in some cases markets provide mechanisms for a kind of limited socio-economic inclusion (Watson 2009).

Finally, scholars have addressed the *temporality and spatiality of markets*. On the former, attention has been given to the specialized form of night markets and the ambiences that they create (Pottie-Sherman and Hiebert 2013). On the latter, researchers draw our attention to the interplay between planning bureaucracies and markets (Dines 2007).

The literature, as sampled above, is inconclusive on the relationship between markets and diversity. Interaction across differences in marketplaces may promote understanding and even a sense of commonality and shared identity based on the collective use of space. But in other instances, market interactions can enable dominant cultures to merely consume the products of subordinate groups, reinforce pre-existing animosities, contribute to the circulation of stereotypes, and intensify tension. And, of course, a mix of these positive and negative processes may occur in any given market. It may be possible to theorize the circumstances that lead to these different outcomes, or the balance between these outcomes, but this has not yet been done.

Continuity and change in markets and diversity

Concerning the relationship between markets and diversity, the issues explored in this paper beg an obvious, nevertheless fundamental, set of questions. What is historically 'old' and globally generic to the nature of this relationship? What is arguably 'new' to the relationship, historically and on a global scale? What practices, activities and physical or spatial aspects have stayed the same, what has changed, and how have the differential composition and effects of diversity across these times related to the continuity or change of those practices and activities? These kinds of questions need to be addressed prior to establishing a research agenda on the dynamics of contemporary markets and diversity.

What is historically 'old' and globally generic to the relationship between markets and diversity?

This first question concerns the fundamentals of market activity: *buying and selling*. At all times, one could say that the basic exchange relationship of buying and selling remains the same through time and across places. A range of accompanying actions surround buying and selling, including: sales-pitching or 'hawking' wares, gathering information about competing products and services, decision-making, agreeing a price, paying, evaluating purchases and managing reputations. Many fleeting or non-economic exchange activities generically take place in markets as well: gathering of news, gossip, flirtation, joking, musical or theatrical entertainment, religious preaching and various practices of healing.

The *'rules of engagement'* between participants in markets entail a set of social practices that bear directly on diversity dynamics, and are open to empirical observation and comparative research. Many types of behaviour and social practice in the market are learned and routinized. Indeed, what may appear as generic encounters of buying and selling in markets may, in fact, be locally and culturally 'scripted' or entail a locally embedded 'command of an idiom, a command that is exercised from moment to moment with little calculation or forethought' (Goffman 1959, 74). Such interpersonal modes of interaction in markets are learned by newcomers, situationally adjusted, and reproduced by repeated exercise. The *discursive practices* for market interactions have often comprised modes of interaction that are highly routinized such that both sellers and regular buyers know what to do and expect. Moreover, such discursive practices often entail important linguistic competences – the ability to change languages, code-switch or use pidgin languages that are purposefully constructed for market trade among people of different backgrounds. In these ways common discursive practices, or rules of engagement, can be bridging devices for crossing types of differences and/ or hierarchies of power. This may be inadvertent or non-conscious, or conversely amount to purposefully selective acts of 'tactical cosmopolitanism' (Landau and Freemantle 2010).

Social diversity of some kind is routinely present in urban markets: while buyers tend to be 'local', many sellers may come from outside the locality. Within various societies, many commodities have traditionally been 'captured' by particular groups (in terms of ethnicity and/or social status), a point first articulated by Max Weber in his concept of 'social closure'; accordingly, the markets themselves can be seen as nodes of long-distant, sometimes group-specific, trade networks. Further, diversity is usually present by way of the sheer variety of commodities on sale and their sometimes remote origins.

What is arguably 'new' to the relationship between markets and diversity?

In keeping with arguments made elsewhere in this article, at least four answers to this question arise.

First, *markets have changed*. This is evident especially with regard to the items bought and sold in markets, across the world. As one consequence of globalization, these shifts have meant that a wider range of commodities from afar have reached local markets worldwide. Along with such 'commodity-reach', local tastes and patterns of consumption have changed.

Second, the *nature of diversity has changed* worldwide at the same time. Changing patterns of global migration have meant that a proliferation of immigrants in small group numbers but from more varied points of origin, through more varied migration trajectories, and with more varied legal statuses, have arrived in a more varied set of destinations (in many places resulting in a new presence of people from previously unknown origins). Such patterns have resulted in profound transformations of local configurations of diversity in terms of ethnicity, religion, language, gender, age, legal status, human capital and more (Vertovec 2007; Hiebert 2012). Local socio-economic orders have been transformed as well. At the same time, in many places around the world, public opinion polls such as Eurobarometer and the World Values Survey show shifting – and contradictory – attitudes towards diversity: large segments of national populations the world over simultaneously espouse the views that 'diversity enriches society' and 'there are too many immigrants'. Hence, either way, there seems to be much more heightened public and political attention, again worldwide, to issues surrounding diversity.

Third, there have been key *changes in the spatiality of markets*. As the pace and complexity of migration have increased, the social geography of cities has been reconfigured. This is most evident in the largest metropolitan centres of the Global North but is also the case in the mega-cities of the Global South. In the case of cities in more developed countries, we are accustomed to think of newcomers first settling in distressed inner-city neighbourhoods. But the twin processes of gentrification and mass migration have profoundly shifted the social geography of migrant settlement, which is now a mainly suburban phenomenon (in essence, conforming to long-standing patterns evident in the Global South).

Traditional inner-city street markets 'on the wrong side of the tracks' continue to exist but are now under pressure from gentrification. Many in fact undergo a process of 'upgrading' to serve a more affluent consumer base when gentrification takes hold. At the same time immigrant settlement has expanded to suburbs, and the clientele for street markets specializing in ordinary goods has also shifted outwards. Amsterdam's Dappermarkt, located several kilometres from the core of the city, exemplifies this trend. Street markets have also proliferated in even more distant areas of European cities, where newcomers congregate in social housing on the periphery of mass transportation networks.

The nature of street markets is closely associated with their setting and especially their consumer base. Therefore we should expect that street markets in highly diverse suburbs differ from those of the inner city (Öz and Eder 2012).

Fourth, *regulation has changed*. Over the past few decades, neo-liberal approaches to national economies have entailed a general relaxation of state intervention in private trade. The collapse of communism has witnessed a boom in the growth of markets in former Eastern bloc countries. In more recent years, the local effects of the global economic crisis have wrought forms of re-regulation (especially austerity measures, as in Greece and several other European countries) and arguably spurred a growth in the informal sector – which has also had impacts on markets as sites of trade and employment.

Beyond these major forms of change taking place at the global and national scales, activities and practices in markets have been variously conditioned by matters highly particular to a locality, such as spatial layout, 'regulations' (in the senses outlined earlier in this paper), social characteristics of customers (not least class) and the dominance or distribution of specific ethnic, regional or other groups and their relation to various goods and services. Investigating such contextual factors is a primary exercise in any research on markets and diversity (e.g. Seligman 2000; Pardy 2005).

In our particular moment in time, street markets exemplify the tension between the neo-liberal commitment to erode the regulatory capacity of the state versus the desire to control migration and also the desire on the part of local authorities to maintain order in urban space (Aytar and Rath 2012).

Conceptual and political complications

There is an underlying tension between the fields of diversity and market studies. Generally, scholars who focus on diversity issues tend to appreciate a strong state that is expected to promote social integration through primary institutions such as the public education system. State bureaucracies also attempt to advance the cause of inclusion in their hiring practices, by ensuring that their personnel more accurately represent the diversity of the wider society. Governments in many countries have also enacted legislation to prevent hate speech and discrimination in the housing and labour markets. Whether reactive or proactive, these policies are important practical tools. They are also symbolic, signifying a preferred outcome of intercultural/religious engagement and mutual respect between different groups.

Non-government organizations (NGOs) also play a recognized role in the enhancement of intercultural communication, in myriad ways. For example, interfaith groups have emerged in many cities across the world and some have been instrumental in diffusing tension between members of different religions. Non-profit media have also taken up this challenge. In many countries, NGOs specialize in immigrant incorporation, providing essential welcoming services such as orientation, language training for adults, housing, and help in preparing for the labour market. These services typically include individuals from different groups and are, whether by design or happenstance, tools for intercultural encounter. If governments and NGOs feel motivated to establish policies and practices to bridge cultural difference, this tells us something: these institutions must believe that cultural interaction will not happen 'naturally' in other spheres of society, or will happen insufficiently to maintain social cohesion.

In other words, scholars – and others more generally – have largely ignored the role of the private sector in the process of intercultural engagement, assigning this grand purpose to the state (and ancillary institutions; Rath and Swagerman 2011). We are sceptical of such a view, although we hasten to add that our stance does not reflect a rejection of the welfare state or an apologetic for neo-liberalism. We take a more basic position and emphasize that many of the intercultural dynamics involved in diverse societies occur in sites of work or exchange. These sites may be regulated by labour codes, commercial law and so on, but their role as places where diverse people meet is generally outside the scope of integration policy or the politics of multiculturalism.

Methodological complications

Before we outline more specific research issues, it is instructive to note several important methodological challenges to studying the relationship between markets and diversity. The first is somewhat ironic given what we have written thus far: where do we demarcate the boundary between society and the market? If we begin with the realization that markets are places of intersection, how much do we need to know about society generally to understand what happens in markets? Put another way, how do we legitimately limit studies of markets from becoming infinite (i.e. studying the supply chains underlying markets; city politics that form the basis from which market regulations are derived; the changing configurations of diversity in society; market fragmentation and changing consumption patterns; and a host of wider issues, all of which matter)?

Second, how can we capture in traditional written texts the three-dimensional properties of markets and the complex social interactions within them? The challenge of providing a more comprehensive account of markets necessitates, first and foremost, combinatorial methodologies – but also a 'publications plus' strategy that will include extensive audio recordings and visual images. Websites are the obvious choice to facilitate multimedia documentation of markets, and these need to be built along with more standard academic publications.

Third, markets are often polyglot places and researchers cannot learn all the relevant languages. To some degree this issue can be addressed by bringing local residents into the research process, for example as research assistants, but some of the nuances of market behaviour and interaction will surely be lost in this process.

Fourth, markets, like so many other social processes, are layered in complex ways that include overt behaviour conforming to formal regulations, and covert behaviour that may not. Ethnographic methods are required to understand the interweaving of these forms of behaviour but even with nuanced, sustained study, it is unlikely that researchers will understand the full complexity of markets.

Fifth, this is particularly true of regulations governing markets. Some of these will be formalized, in some cases as legal texts. But markets also incorporate far more subtle forms of regulation that are related to underlying cultural processes that may be opaque to researchers, even those who invest considerable time in fieldwork.

Finally, we acknowledge at the outset of this research agenda one of the most difficult challenges: that of causality. If people interact routinely in markets across markers of difference, and they 'get along' more generally in society despite potential grievances and animosities, how can we know whether interactions in markets contributed to this outcome? This is of course an instance of a general problem of attribution in any social science project, but it represents a formidable challenge given our key research question. The challenge of identifying causality is compounded by another factor: we believe that the direction of causality in the relationship between markets and diversity is constantly shifting – that what appears at one moment to be a straightforward situation of an independent (say diversity) and dependent (say markets) variable, a moment later seems to be the opposite relationship.

Towards a conclusion: street markets and the relationship between economy and society – a research agenda

In this paper we have argued that street markets offer an ideal setting to explore the relationship between economy and society, especially when we consider the ways that these markets reflect, but also shape, the nature and meaning of social and cultural diversity.

Diversity *shapes* markets. While a basic set of actions around buying and selling are fundamental to market exchange, the repertoire of specific behaviours and social practices – or, as we have put it, 'rules of engagement' – between buyers and sellers (as well as between buyers and between sellers) reflects contextual factors such as the modes of social difference among the actors. Various actors in the market adopt

CITIES, DIVERSITY AND ETHNICITY

behavioural mannerisms to communicate common intentions (here, economic exchange) between people from different backgrounds, whether ethnic, linguistic, class-based, gendered, age-related, or other. Further, diversity affects the market materially, since the stylistic and culinary tastes of clientele are incorporated in items on sale. Social distinctions also impact market activities through the influx or growth in the number of socio-economically marginalized people that might lead to an expansion of precarious or informal work in the urban market. In essence, street markets exemplify the global process of space-time compression, juxtaposing people with backgrounds from distant places and distinct cultures together in the same place.

But at the same time *markets shape diversity*. We can think of this process through three dimensions (see Vertovec forthcoming): configurations, representations and encounters. Markets help *configure* social life. They reflect the basic sociocultural and socio-economic diversity of local areas. They bring together people into a public arena who might otherwise remain apart. This happens in settings that are both relatively controlled through 'rules of engagement' and also highly adaptive and dynamic. Markets also come to *represent* the nature of diversity in societies. Different cultural groups come to be *imagined* through association with their commercial districts. We think that we 'know' something about Chinese people by our experience of Chinatowns, for example. That is, commercial districts and street markets become loci of the process of distinguishing between 'us' and 'them'. It is also worth noting that many ethnic stereotypes have arisen from perceived behaviour in markets (e.g. the putative stinginess of certain groups, or that certain groups are disproportionately inclined to engage in dishonesty or petty theft). Street markets also entail *encounters* between people, frequently across lines of social and cultural difference. Again, these encounters may be highly scripted, especially when there are linguistic challenges between entrepreneurs and consumers, or improvisational, in some cases leading to lengthy conversations. For some people, street markets are the primary means by which they encounter people from other backgrounds.

These bidirectional mutual, simultaneous influences of configurations, representations and encounters suggest a number of potentially fruitful research questions, although this list will hardly exhaust the possibilities in this field of research. One of the foremost of these questions relates to the effects of economic engagement: does positive, or at least routine, engagement across modes of difference 'carry over' to positively impact on attitudes towards, and interactions with, the same categories of others outside of the market? This question is obviously akin to that posed in contact theory, here transposed specifically to the setting of urban markets. As already noted, the scant social science literature that has asked this question seems divided on whether there is much effect, either positively or negatively.

A related issue: in bringing people together by creating a spatial concentration of diversity (i.e. what Elijah Anderson (2011) calls a 'cosmopolitan canopy'), do street markets foster cosmopolitan identities (Pardy 2005)?

Another important question is more starkly economic: do street markets provide a vehicle for social mobility for individuals and groups that might otherwise remain marginalized? Conversely, are the competitive pressures within street markets so intense that they offer limited scope for economic advancement; if so, are sellers and workers in street markets participating in a kind of economic cul-de-sac?

If markets promote a kind of economic integration, does it follow that they have an impact on local interethnic perceptions and relations? That is, does a successful market, which highlights heritage goods of particular groups, generate respect for those groups? If street markets may promote mutual respect, they may also work in reverse, exacerbating animosities. This leads to questions about things that are present and absent from markets. On the former issue, under what circumstances are hostilities replicated in the market? When do they promote the *exclusion* of particular groups? This of course leads to the latter issue: which groups are not present in markets, and is their absence socially significant?

The spatiality of street markets suggests a range of questions at different scales. Is there a relationship between the location of street markets and their local effects? For example, does it matter whether markets are proximate to areas of ethnic minority residential concentration? Do the social effects of street markets in inner-city areas differ from those in suburbs? At a larger scale, we anticipate quite different relationships between street markets and society in cities of the Global South versus Global North. Is this a valid conjecture? Similarly, do street markets operate differently, and yield different sociocultural outcomes, in neo-liberal societies as opposed to states that have maintained a greater degree of income redistribution and, presumably, market regulation?

Throughout this article we have noted the complex nature of regulation in street markets, which is based on a combination of formal rules and a host of informal practices and tacit agreements. On the more formal side of the spectrum, how do planning agencies, business associations and other relevant actors 'see' the relationship between street markets and local societies? Are these agencies aware of the intercultural dynamics associated with markets or are they oblivious to them? Do they attempt to intervene in this respect, or to capitalize on the intercultural qualities of street markets (e.g. by celebrating the multicultural character of markets in tourist brochures)? If so, what are the consequences? On the informal side, what is the relationship between 'rules of engagement' in these markets and the changing landscapes of super-diversity of global cities?

This list of key research issues illustrates the potential for street markets to provide insights into the society/economy nexus. We believe that this will arise most productively through a research programme that is at the same time conceptual and empirical. Conceptually, such a research programme must transcend disciplinary constraints, exploring connections between the insights of anthropologists, cultural theorists, economists, geographers, linguists, sociologists and of course the field of urban studies. Empirically, there is a need for sophisticated, innovative and flexible methods and a wide variety of finely grained case studies. These methods must enable researchers to appreciate both the formal structures of social/economic relations in markets and also the complex informal codes that infuse these relations. They must also strike a balance between comparability and place specificity. Throughout this research, the primary goal should be to see the wider *meaning* in the *mundane*.

References

Alraouf, Ali. 2010. "Regenerating Urban Traditions in Bahrain. Learning from Bab-Al-Bahrain: The Authentic Fake." *Journal of Tourism and Cultural Change* 8 (1–2): 50–68. doi:10.1080/14766825.2010.490587.

Anderson, Elijah. 2011. *The Cosmopolitan Canopy: Race and Civility in Everyday Life.* New York: W.W. Norton & Company Incorporated.

Aytar, Volkan, and Jan Rath, eds. 2012. *Selling Ethnic Neighborhoods: The Rise of Neighborhoods as Places of Leisure and Consumption.* New York: Routledge.

Busch, Dominic. 2010. "Shopping in Hospitality: Situational Constructions of Customer–Vendor Relationships among Shopping Tourists at a Bazaar on the German–Polish Border." *Language and Intercultural Communication* 10 (1): 72–89. doi:10.1080/14708470903452614.

De Bruin, Anne, and Ann Dupuis. 2000. "Constrained Entrepreneurship: An Interdisciplinary Extension of Bounded Rationality." *Journal of Interdisciplinary Economics* 12 (1): 71–86.

Dines, Nick. 2007. *The Experience of Diversity in an Era of Urban Regeneration: The Case of Queens Market, East London.* EURODIV Working Paper 48. Milan: Fondazione Eni Enrico Mattei (FEEM).

Engelen, Ewald. 2001. "'Breaking in' and 'Breaking Out': A Weberian Approach to Entrepreneurial Opportunities." *Journal of Ethnic and Migration Studies* 27 (2): 203–223. doi:10.1080/13691830020041570.

Florida, Richard. 2002. *The Rise of the Creative Class: And How It's Transforming Work, Leisure, Community, and Everyday Life.* New York: Basic Books.

Goffman, Erving. 1959. *The Presentation of Self in Everyday Life.* Garden City, NY: Doubleday.

Hiebert, Daniel. 2012. *A New Residential Order? The Social Geography of Visible Minority and Religious Groups in Montreal, Toronto, and Vancouver in 2031.* Citizenship and Immigration Canada, Research and Evaluation Branch, Research Report. http://www.cic.gc.ca/english/resources/research/residential.asp.

Hüwelmeier, Gertrude. 2013. "Postsocialist Bazaars: Diversity, Solidarity, and Conflict in the Marketplace." *Laboritorium* 5 (1): 52–72.

Kloosterman, Robert C., Joanne van der Leun, and Jan Rath. 1999. "Mixed Embeddedness. Immigrant Businesses and Informal Economic Opportunities." *International Journal of Urban and Regional Research* 23 (2): 253–267. doi:10.1111/1468-2427.00194.

Kloosterman, Robert C., and Jan Rath. 2010. "Shifting Landscapes of Immigrant Entrepreneurship." In *Open for Business. Migrant Entrepreneurship in OECD Countries*, 101–123. Paris: OECD. http://www.keepeek.com/Digital-Asset-Management/oecd/social-issues-migration-health/open-for-business_9789264095830-en#page3.

Landau, Loren B., and Iriann Freemantle. 2010. "Tactical Cosmopolitanism and Idioms of Belonging: Insertion and Self-exclusion in Johannesburg." *Journal of Ethnic and Migration Studies* 36 (3): 375–390. doi:10.1080/13691830903494901.

L'Hote, Leland, and Chad Gasta. 2007 "Immigration and Street Entrepreneurship in Alicante, Spain." *International Journal of Iberian Studies* 20 (1): 3–22. doi:10.1386/ijis.20.1.3_1.

Liu, Jing Jing. 2010. "Contact and Identity: The Experience of 'China Goods' in a Ghanaian Marketplace." *Journal of Community & Applied Social Psychology* 20 (3): 184–201.

Lysack, Krista. 2005. "Goblin Markets: Victorian Women Shoppers at Liberty's Oriental Bazaar." *Nineteenth Century Contexts* 27 (2): 139–165. doi:10.1080/08905490500212727.

Maisel, Robert. 1974. "The Flea Market as an Action Scene." *Urban Life* 2 (4): 488–505.

CITIES, DIVERSITY AND ETHNICITY

Marcinszak, Szymon, and Martin Van Der Velde. 2008. "Drifting in a Global Space of Textile Flows: Apparel Bazaars in Poland's Lódz Region." *European Planning Studies* 16 (7): 911–923. doi:10.1080/09654310802163702.

Öz, Özlem, and Mine Eder. 2012. "Rendering Istanbul's Periodic Bazaars Invisible: Reflections on Urban Transformation and Contested Space." *International Journal of Urban and Regional Research* 36 (2): 297–313. doi:10.1111/j.1468-2427.2011.01076.x.

Pardy, Maree. 2005. "Kant comes to Footscray Mall: Thinking about Local Cosmopolitanism." In *Sub Urban Fantasies*, edited by C. Long, K. Shaw, and C. Merlot, 107–128. Melbourne: Australian Scholarly Publishing.

Plattner, Stuart. 1989. "Markets and Market Places." In *Economic Anthropology*, edited by S. Plattner, 171–208. Stanford, CA: Stanford University Press.

Pottie-Sherman, Yolande. 2011. *Markets and Diversity: An Overview*. Göttingen: Max-Planck-Institute, Working Paper 11–03.

Pottie-Sherman, Yolande, and Daniel Hiebert. 2013. "Authenticity with a Bang: Exploring Suburban Culture and Migration through the New Phenomenon of the Richmond Night Market." *Urban Studies*. http://usj.sagepub.com/content/early/2013/11/15/0042098013510954.full.pdf+html.

Rath, Jan. 1999. "The Netherlands. A Dutch Treat for Anti-social Families and Immigrant Ethnic Minorities." In *The European Union and Migrant Labour*, edited by M. Cole and G. Dale, 147–170. Oxford: Berg Publishers.

Rath, Jan. 2011. "Debating Multiculturalism: Europe's Reaction in Context." Harvard International Review. Accessed May 18, 2012. http://hir.harvard.edu/debating-multicultural-ism?page=0,0

Rath, Jan, and Anna Swagerman. 2011. *Promoting Ethnic Entrepreneurship in European Cities*. Luxembourg: Publication Office of the European Union.

Seligman, Linda J. 2000. "Market Places, Social Spaces in Cuzco, Peru." *Urban Anthropology and Studies of Cultural Systems and World Economic Development* 29 (1): 1–68.

Shepherd, Robert J. 2008. *When Culture Goes to Market: Space, Place and Identity in an Urban Marketplace*. New York: Peter Lang Pub Incorporated.

Smith, Michael Garfield. 1965. *The Plural Society in the British West Indies*. Berkeley: University of California Press.

Vertovec, Steven. 2007. "Super-diversity and Its Implications." *Ethnic and Racial Studies* 29 (6): 1024–1054. doi:10.1080/01419870701599465.

Vertovec, Steven. 2012. "Diversity' and the Social Imaginary." *Archives Européennes de Sociologie* LIII (3): 287–312. doi:10.1017/S000397561200015X.

Vertovec, Steven. Forthcoming. "Introduction: Formulating Diversity Studies." In *Routledge International Handbook of Diversity Studies*, edited by Steven Vertovec. London: Routledge.

Vertovec, Steven, and Susanne Wessendorf, eds. 2010. *The Multicultural Backlash: European Discourses, Policies and Practices*. London: Routledge.

Watson, Sophie. 2009. "The Magic of the Marketplace: Sociality in a Neglected Public Space." *Urban Studies* 46 (8): 1577–1591. doi:10.1177/0042098009105506.

Super-diverse street: a 'trans-ethnography' across migrant localities

Suzanne M. Hall

This paper emerges from an ethnography of the economic and cultural life of Rye Lane, an intensely multi-ethnic street in Peckham, South London. The effects of accelerated migration into London are explored through the reshaping and diversification of its interior, street and city spaces. A 'trans-ethnography' is pursued across the compendium of micro-, meso- and macro-urban spaces, without reifying one above the other. The ethnographic stretch across intimate, collective and symbolic city spaces serves to connect how the restrictions and circuits of urban migration have different impacts and expressions in these distinctive but interrelated urban localities. The paper argues for a trans-ethnography that engages within and across a compendium of urban localities, to understand how accelerated migration and urban 'super-diversity' transform the contemporary global city.

Introduction

What understandings might ethnography yield for urban 'super-diversity'; for Vertovec's (2007) encapsulation of the evermore-varied differentiations of migrant identity, connection and stratification within a fluid world? On a kilometre stretch of street on Rye Lane in Peckham, South London, 199 formal units of retail are tightly packed adjacent to one another, forming a dense, linear assemblage of economic and cultural diversity. The majority of these units are occupied by independent proprietors, aligning among them over twenty countries of origin: Afghanistan, England, Eritrea, Ghana, India, Ireland, Iran, Iraq, Jamaica, Pakistan, Kashmir, Kenya, Nepal, Nigeria, Somalia, Sri Lanka, Tanzania, Uganda, Vietnam and Yemen.

The high concentration of diverse countries of origin among the proprietors on this single street is accompanied by remarkable intercultural proficiencies. Almost a third of the proprietors on Rye Lane are able to converse in four languages or more (Hall 2013). Interactions on the street are more than simply lingual, and one in four of the independent shops have been subdivided and sublet into smaller shops, where proprietors from across the globe, each arriving on the street in different migratory rhythms, share space, risk and prospect. Conventional retail economies mix with emerging ones. Rudimentary agreements, including who locks up at night and how toilets are shared, are arranged alongside mercantile ambitions for how retail activities are best co-located. Exchange, a more apt description of these shared, agile practices than 'community cohesion' (Home Office 2001), occurs within and across affiliations of ethnicity and origin.

During the course of 2012, the economic and spatial morphologies of this intensely diverse street received the attentions of our team of sociologists and architects. We too represented a mix of individuals differentiated in discipline and origin, including Chile, South Africa, the UK and the USA. Between us we counted, photographed, drew, filmed, talked and listened, recording dimensions of space and economy on the street. We were versed in the textures of our own cities: parts of Johannesburg, Cape Town, London, New York and Santiago. However, in Rye Lane we were exploring a street that exceeded our familiarities: a 'super-diverse' concentration of languages, origins and goods, and of ambitions and restrictions. As we progressed with our street-level observations, we came across varied registers of the street's value – or perceived lack thereof – in neighbourhood sites (Benson and Jackson 2013), media representations and, in the London Borough of Southwark's (2012) redevelopment plan for Rye Lane included in the working document *Revitalise: Peckham and Nunhead Area Action Plan*.

In formulating a regeneration vision for the street, the expertise within the borough has drawn on planning and economic conventions, highlighting large sites adjacent to the street for market-led development, emphasising the need for more cafes and restaurants, and 'larger shop units to accommodate large multiple chain retailers' (2012, 34). It was as if the economic and cultural diversity of the street as it exists was somehow invisible to those undertaking the planning exercise. Indeed, an officer commented that no detailed survey of the existing retail activity had been undertaken as part of the planning exercise, remarking with perceptible clarity: 'The council has an economic development strategy: to articulate a strong and inclusive economy. There are tensions between large-scale developments versus supporting existing economies to grow. These two things don't always meet well' (fieldwork discussion, 2012).

This apparent mismatch between lived realities within diverse, comparatively deprived, yet economically active inner-city locations and authorized processes of displacement or regeneration are well documented (Zukin 2010). But our research question deviates from questions of gentrification, towards the question of how contemporary super-diversity registers in the lived and regulated realms of an intensely ethnically diverse street and city. Researchers engaging with the practices and spaces of urban super-diversity point to the visible and invisible dimensions of migrants and their lifeworlds (Knowles 2013), profoundly impacting on the politics of what or who is seen, and what or who is valued. The question of how ethnography might contribute to the emerging research field of urban super-diversity (Vertovec 2011; Hall 2012; Berg and Sigona 2013; Keith 2013) is as much a much a political as it is a methodological concern. The aim of this paper is to methodologically engage with the hidden and overt features of super-diversity in two ways. First, is the analytic alignment of the authorized techniques for making migration and diversity officially visible in the city, such as census data, together with the frequently less visible practices of 'being super-diverse', explored through observation. Second, is an exploration of the urban localities of super-diversity by acknowledging the overlap of intimate, collective and symbolic city spaces.

CITIES, DIVERSITY AND ETHNICITY

An ethnography of urban super-diversity

Within the field of contemporary ethnography, explorations have addressed how a practice essentially attentive to particular, local dimensions can equally engage with planetary scales of change and more complex assemblages of analysis. Such methodological pursuits have forged direction for 'global ethnographies' across territorial borders (Burawoy et al. 2000), 'multi-sited' analysis across 'dichotomies of the "local" and the "global", the "lifeworld" and the "system"' (Marcus 1995, 95), as well as an understanding of the more hybrid identities of individuals and groups alongside asymmetrical conditions of power (Hannerz 1997). These ethnographic approaches address the flows within a global, interconnected world and the migrations of people, objects and ideas. But how is a contemporary ethnography equally able to attend to the disconnect between the lived realities and official (mis)recognitions of the intense and evermore-varied differentiations of human association and stratification within a global city?

Glick Schiller and Çağlar's (2009) paper, 'Towards a comparative theory of locality in migration studies: migrant incorporation and city scale', provides an important steer. Their focus on 'locality' challenges an analytic de-territorialization that suggests that allegiance and identity in an increasingly fluid world is primarily formed outside of place (see e.g. Beck and Grande 2010). Rather than evolving notions of 'unbounded social actors' and 'free floating subjectivities', Guarnizo and Smith (1998, 11) argue that migratory practices are 'embodied in specific social relations established between specific people, situated in unequivocal localities, at historically determined times'. While this paper focuses the specific conditions of urban place, or what Soja (2010) refers to as the 'whereness' in the production of space, our ethnography traverses across a series of distinct but interconnected city spaces. The analytic bounds of the neighbourhood or ghetto have defined many canonical ethnographies of race, ethnicity and the stratified city through the lens of the street (e.g. Liebow 1967; Duneier 1999; Anderson 2000). However, the boundaries of either a singular locality or ethnicity are simply too contained to capture the wider impacts of accelerated migration on the transformation of contemporary urban space.

Glick Schiller and Çağlar (2009, 178) further advance the idea of the contemporary city as a space actively remade by global processes of migration, focusing on migrants engaged 'in acts of contemporary place-making' across the city. The transformative if often unrecognized agency of migrants will be explored in this paper, for example in the reshaping of Rye Lane in South London, through the incorporation of the social and spatial textures of markets and bazaars in Ahvaz, Jammu, Morogoro, Hanoi and Tiazz. Critically, these city-making practices or 'modes of incorporation' need to be analysed alongside the different 'hierarchies of power' (Glick Schiller 2005, 48). Migrants are embedded in the structures of economic and political power that assign their emplacement in a city. You will note in the introductory listing of countries of origin among the proprietors of Rye Lane that the USA, Western Europe and Australia, for example, are absent from the street, while places in Africa and South Asia are prominent. This paper seeks to understand what citizenships are produced in the symbolic, collective and intimate spaces of the city, exploring how different kinds of citizenship and city-making are rendered visible or invisible in different urban localities.

Our 'trans-ethnography' across the city engages with three particular urban dimensions: the symbolic city (London), the collective city (Rye Lane) and the intimate city (shop interiors). Each distinctive but interconnected dimension of the city is grounded in an urban locality within which the structures of power and the processes of integration (Glick Schiller 2005) reveal different aspects of urban super-diversity. The *symbolic city* addresses the notion of the city as a 'whole' and the macro forms of representation that depict an overview of accelerated migration and urban change. The *collective city* refers to a recognizable urban area (in our case, the street) within which a shared range of intercultural practices emerge. Finally, the *intimate city* focuses on the microcosmic dimensions of up-close interaction and expression within shop interiors, where forms of identity merge with the imperatives of livelihood.

The symbolic city: macro perspectives

Why is that certain migrant groups come to live or work in certain parts of the city? This question resonated during our first year of fieldwork on Rye Lane, and although we had elements of data from the street to begin to answer this question, it became important to engage with larger data sets that spatialize and visualize where migrants currently locate across London. Working with data sets on population census, indices of deprivation and locality, we observed three discernible patterns of urban change: an 'ethnic spread' across neighbourhoods (CoDE 2012b); differential concentrations and dispersal of migrant groups (Paccoud 2013); and correlations between areas of inequality and ethnic diversity. To begin with, we were aware of dramatic changes in the size, composition and location of 'ethnic minorities' in England and Wales over the past ten years traced through the 2011 census, as explored by the Centre on Dynamics of Ethnicity (CoDE 2012a, 2012b). One in five individuals living in England and Wales identify themselves as other than 'white British', and there has been a significant increase in people identified with 'mixed' and 'other' ethnic categories. Further, one in eight households comprise individuals from more than one ethnic group, and areas too have become more mixed over the past ten years. The CoDE work points to ethnic overlaps in bodies, households and neighbourhoods, indicating that designated ethnic categories are less able to capture emerging mixings that supersede the official categories.

To complement the variation in ethnic categories analysed by CoDE, we mapped the census category of 'country of origin' to respective residential locality (Paccoud 2013). Distinctive patterns of migrant concentration and dispersal occurs across the UK, but most evident is that global processes of migration into the UK manifest primarily as an urban phenomenon. Greater London, with 41.6% of the UK's migrant population, is the most intense concentration. Of the world's 229 nations, 113 have at least 1,000 representatives in Greater London, with the ten largest groups being India (262,247), Poland (158,300), Ireland (129,807), Nigeria (114,718), Pakistan (112,457), Bangladesh (109,948), Jamaica (87,467), Sri Lanka (84,542), France (66,654) and Somalia (65,333). These groups are further highly concentrated in inner London, with 103 of the world's nations represented in thirteen London boroughs, including the London Borough of Southwark in which Rye Lane in Peckham is located. However, migrant concentration is

CITIES, DIVERSITY AND ETHNICITY

differential for particular groups. Not all groups are similarly concentrated: concentration across the UK is most noticeable, for example, with groups from Sri Lanka, Bangladesh and Somalia who are concentrated in cities across the UK, and in inner-city areas within these cities. By contrast, migrants from Germany, Ireland and Poland are more spread across the UK and across rural, metropolitan and inner-city localities.

Finally, economic globalization continues to exacerbate hierarchies and inequalities within urban landscapes, producing particular relationships between ethnicity, poverty and space (Hamnett 2003). We were particularly interested in how ethnic diversity and disparity is spatialized, and we overlayed two existing maps of London's areas of high ethnic minority concentration with a map of officially designated 'deprivation'. (We used the 2001 ethnicity data mapping as fine-grained ward-level analysis was directly comparable with ward-level analysis of deprivation.) The first mapping of ethnic diversity (GLA 2008a) confirms the concentration of ethnic diversity to area, of which migration is one primary contributor. The second mapping of the *Indices of Deprivation* across London (GLA 2008b), is based on 2006 data including indices of household income, employment status, educational attainment and distance from residence to local amenities. In overlaying the two maps (Figure 1), there is a strong

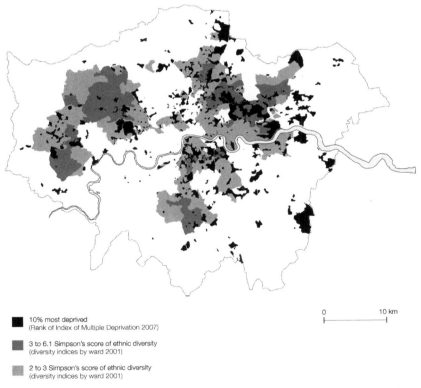

Figure 1. A map of inner London overlaying existing data from the Indices of Multiple Deprivation (2007) and Simpson's score of ethnic diversity (2001). (LSE Cities, Ordinary Streets Project, 2013).

convergence between officially designated 'deprivation' and ethnically concentrated diversity. The map suggests that marginal urban locations are most likely to be the destinations of the majority of less-affluent migrants into London. Urban disparity, marked in locality, contributes to the migrant's emplacement (Smith 2005), embeddedness (Kloosterman, van der Leun and Rath 1999) or 'fit' between the migrant's status and the receiving urban locale.

In 1991, the Peckham ward in which Rye Lane is located was registered as the only ward south of the River Thames to fall among London's locales of the highest concentration of ethnic diversity. A further increase in ethnic diversity in Peckham was registered in 2001 and 2011. Peckham is not simply an ethnically diverse place; it is also officially registered as among the 10% most deprived areas in the UK. Several large social housing estates feature as the most intense areas of deprivation within Peckham such that in one interview, a local officer referred to Rye Lane – the street between social housing estates to the north and east and the gentrifying area of largely privately owned houses to the west – as a 'frontline to gentrification'. If Rye Lane is a frontline of sorts, so too is it a place of reception in the city into which migrants arrive and share space with established residents.

The large data sets and macro-perspectives on ethnicity, origin and deprivation provided a lens on patterns of locality. However, the nuances and dynamics of flows are omitted or invisible. The web of flows from near and far include daily transfers between places of work and home (the census privileges the pinpoint of home), generational succession as economic mobility potentially allows migrant families to acquire more than one local foothold within a city, and transnational interchanges sustained between sending and receiving countries. A real estate agent on Rye Lane articulates how ongoing waves of migration and movement are central to the reshaping of the street:

Interviewer: What do you think will happen to Peckham Rye Lane?
Mark: This is the same thing that's happening all over London. It's similar to Woolwich and Lewisham, where businesses are bought up by Asian people and West Africans. First it was the Irish, then the West Indians took over businesses. And in Lewisham, there were Jewish people, now Indian Sikhs set up shop. ... Any of the long-time residents of the area, white English people, are moving out. They are ageing, dying or moving away. It's not a racial thing. It's about lifestyle. ... Immigrants are the same. After they set up their businesses and once they get established, they'll leave and live somewhere else. They'll keep their business in Peckham, but they'll move out to somewhere quieter.
(interview, 2012)

Understanding migration and the transformation of the city therefore lies in combining the diversity of urban migration patterns with the topological complexity of lives lived within and between a number of urban locales. As highlighted through the analysis of macro-city space, the bounded, official categories of ethnicity, deprivation and territory reveal a trend of urban concentration, where the most ethnically diverse areas have a high correlation with areas of deprivation. However, this is only one view of the city, and the complex, fluid unit of analysis integral to urban migration requires a greater methodological stretch across localities, as well as quantitative and qualitative approaches. If we incorporate ideas of flow (intergenerational as well as daily live–work journeys), exchange (of economies and ideas) and inter-locality (spatial webs of allegiance across space), we obtain a different view of migration and urban change. Both views – of the structural context of increasing urban inequality inscribed in space, and of liminality or fluencies across bodies and spaces – are necessary to engage with urban super-diversity.

The collective city: street perspectives

> Interviewer: Is there any form of management structure for the street as a whole?
> Tim: There is no central management structure for the street... The Council is currently supporting a Business Improvement District [BID]... the idea is to use BIDs to work with traders in southern and central parts of Southwark.
> Interviewer: Can a management structure be developed without a more detailed understanding of the businesses on the street?
> Tim: In large and unwieldy bureaucracies, stereotypes are the tools of discourse. It's easier and quicker to use overarching narratives. Interestingly, we learnt more about businesses in Walworth Road and Rye Lane after the riots.
> (fieldwork discussion, 2012)

The street provides a perspective of the city where shared practices between diverse groups are refined within an area. We focused on the day-to-day practices of exchange on the street, or what Conradson and Latham (2005, 278) refer to as the 'middling' forms of national and cultural interchange: a 'panopoly of mundane efforts'. Methodological challenges at this meso-scale of the city relate to how locality is practised as both a bounded and a connected space. Rye Lane is part of Peckham's designated town centre and is as much a planned and maintained administrative area as it is a dynamic intersection of people, cultures and economies within and beyond the street. We return to the question of why Rye Lane's retail activity remains largely invisible to the officers involved in its replanning, and what a socio-economic survey of the independent shops along the street yields for understanding the role of migration and ethnic diversity in the everyday interactions along an urban high street.

In 2012, we undertook a face-to-face survey of the independent proprietors along Rye Lane. Every permanent unit along the length of street was recorded and linked with a spatial code, so that we could develop a visual and systematic language of the street's composition. Of a total 199 street-level retail properties, 105 were recorded as independent retail, seventy of which were included in a face-to-face survey. We asked each of the proprietors: How long have you traded on this street?; What is your primary trade activity?; Do you live in the surrounding area?; Where were you born?; and How many languages do you speak? The survey took two weeks, and provided us with an important entry point into our fieldwork. At the outset, it provided a record of the array of proprietors' countries of origin, in order of their prevalence on the street: Pakistan (32%), England (16%), Afghanistan (10%), Nigeria (7%), India (6%), Eritrea (4%), Iraq (4%), Iran (3%), Ireland (3%) Jamaica (3%), Sri Lanka (3%), with Ghana, Kashmir, Kenya, Nepal, Somalia, Tanzania, Uganda, Vietnam and Yemen collectively comprising 9%. We subsequently mapped each of the proprietor's country of origin with their shop on the street (Figure 2), drawing a line between the two. In respectively mapping seventy of these links, a dense network of connections and intersections from across the world appears, collectively concentrating on a single street in London (for a comparison, see Hall 2011).

While this map represents a single moment in time, it is important to recognize the migratory rhythms over extensive time periods that accumulate to transform the scale and texture of the street. Our survey revealed that 21% of the traders had been on Peckham Rye Lane for more than twenty years. However, 45% had occupied their shops on the street for five years or less, with 69% for ten years or less, indicating a condensed period of transformation over the last decade. What collections of economic practices emerge on this street? To begin with, 65% of retailers on Peckham Rye Lane operate in independent, non-affiliated retail. Clothing, generally inexpensive (18%) and food including halal meat, fish and ethnically specific foods (17%) predominate, while the presence of beauty products largely in hair and nails (13%), money remittances (12%) and mobile phone products and services (11%) are increasing. Ground-floor retail space is at a premium, testified by the limited number of vacancies (less than 10%) despite the global economic crisis and its impact on the

Figure 2. A map showing the origins of the independent proprietors on Rye Lane, and their respective convergence on the street (LSE Cities, Ordinary Streets Project, 2012).

demise of high streets across the UK. Public activities, such as a host of existing and new mosques and churches, find space to the rear of the street or in basements or above-ground rooms where property prices are cheaper.

The 'locality fit' between Rye Lane and a variety of migrant retailers has been historically assisted by its low entry rents and property values sustained across recent decades, as well as its dense, well-connected urban fabric that has yielded high thresholds of support. Comparatively high residential densities in Peckham (ninety-eight persons per hectare as opposed to London's average of forty-five persons per hectare) combined with numerous bus routes and an overground rail station that sits midway along the length of the street, generate high thresholds of footfall on the street. But its particular vibrancy is not uncontested and the rapidly gentrifying area to the immediate west of Rye Lane supports a different retail compendium. Parallel to and 250 metres to the west of Rye Lane is Bellenden Road, a less active retail street that includes an independent bookstore, cafes and gastro pubs. *The Telegraph* (2006) coarsely sells this as 'the tale of two Peckhams... There is north Peckham... notorious for its sink estates... And then there is Georgian and Victorian Peckham, the conservation area around Bellenden Road.

The question here is how urban change – be it through gentrification in Bellenden Road or migration in Rye Lane – registers in public and official discourse. One local officer gave his opinion:

Interviewer: What is distinctive about Peckham Rye Lane?
Tim: We call it "the inside-out supermarket model". There is a sensory aspect that is distinctive – to some appealing, to others, less so. It is a street with very different business models, one being low entry rents. There is a split set of demands in Peckham in general terms. A large embedded middleclass argue for a "tidying up" and for Rye Lane to sell more things. But "Rye Lane is a mess" is a general attitude together with a wish that Rye Lane has more to offer. There are complaints about butchers, and yet in its own terms it's thriving. Another pressure is the creative types who want to open bars and galleries.
(fieldwork discussion, 2012)

Planning is one way in which authorities organize and enact power, through envisaging a 'better' future, and facilitating a process of redevelopment. The London Borough of Southwark's (2012) regeneration intentions for Rye Lane suggest conserving noteworthy areas of historical distinction, supporting independent shops at the southern end of Rye Lane, and identifying land parcels for redevelopment, including the reintroduction of large-format shops in the northern end of Rye Lane. Both the planning strategies of conservation and renewal will require the removal of existing shops. Yet at the time of undertaking our survey of Rye Lane's shops in 2012, it was evident that no detailed survey of the actual retail activities of the street had been undertaken, although a consumer shopping survey had been done. The emerging forms of retail on Rye Lane, which are arguably pivotal to the future of many high streets across London, remain invisible to the lens of power. It is worth noting, for example, that in London during the period 2000–06, a 78.5% increase in non-affiliated independent retail was reported (Wrigley et al. 2009), and although the connection has not been explicitly made to migration over the same period, this connection warrants further research.

Further, it became clear in mapping the changing economic and cultural activities on Rye Lane that not only different modes of survey and analysis but different forms of notation were required. For example, we started drawing a conventional 'land-use' plan for the street, only to discover that the range of activities within the shop interiors defeated the standard land-use and retail categories. The challenge of understanding and communicating urban change does not only reside with the academic researcher; of concern is how the conventional habits of large bureaucratic planning institutions are able to meet the dynamics and complexities of urban change. The planning default mechanisms of 'conservation' and 'big shop' retail in the redevelopment of inner-city areas like Peckham may not only hasten a certain gentrification trope, but may also be out of sync with the larger urbanization trends where cities and streets will continue to diversify through the processes of city-making by migration, as raised by Glick Schiller and Çağlar (2009).

Our mapping and survey work at the scale of the street provided a sense of the organizational logic of Rye Lane and how a super-diverse amalgam of proprietors and traders individually and collectively respond to Rye Lane's urban locality. While the *Indices of Deprivation* presented in the previous section represents the area around Rye Lane as a place with high unemployment and comparatively lacking in skills and education, zooming into the middle ground offers a different perspective from that of abject deprivation. A dense and diverse economic streetscape is apparent, dominated by independent retail, with vacancies limited to 10% and a core body of retailers who have been active on the street for twenty years or more. On Rye Lane, change on the street is fast, and the street is rapidly being remade as a space of economic opportunity for the diverse, largely immigrant proprietors. Planning institutions have a different organizational logic and are behaviourally slower, tending to rely on long-established conventions and value systems. Surveys, mappings and observations of the street provide an important tier in understanding how migrant proprietors shape the city street. Through our survey data, we continue to engage with local authority officers and members as part of our research. A key question remains as to whether and how migrant forms of city-making can be made legible to the authorities who ultimately regulate and plan the street.

The intimate city: interior perspectives

The intimate city incorporates contact between individuals or small groups, self-expression and micro-scales of organization, through which the city emerges as distinctive or nuanced parts. The different ways in which micro-worlds are textured, divided and amalgamated reveal the mutations of urban migration and diversity as they alter and reform in daily and annual rhythms. The frame for our exploration of economic and cultural hybridity along Peckham Rye Lane is the long, narrow shop. The linear assemblage of shops, whose narrow frontages face the street, is a cadastral inheritance from the mid-1800s when Peckham Rye Lane was formed of suburban villas for the middle class. Each house was accompanied by a generous garden to the front and rear (see e.g. the Dewhirst map of the parish of Camberwell in 1842). As the

CITIES, DIVERSITY AND ETHNICITY

significant momentum of industrialization and urbanization took force in nineteenth-century London, the front and rear gardens along Rye Lane were built over and the street became lined with shopfronts.

The shape and form of these long, narrow shops are currently being put to new mercantile uses, and accommodate a series of interior subdivisions that serve to rearrange floor space, products, services and rental agreements. Economic, cultural and social subdivisions have created a number of hybrid interiors, or what we refer to as 'mutualisms': a reciprocally beneficial coexistence between different entities. One in four shops along Rye Lane have undergone processes of subdivision and several different typologies of 'mutualism' or arrangements of economic and cultural coexistence have emerged.

We mapped several of the interior floor spaces, and combined mapping with observation and interviews to understand the spatial and economic logic of these emerging shop typologies along the street. While the shop interiors along Rye Lane are owned or rented by one owner or head lessee, a host of subdivisions and interior additions belie the simplicity of the primary legal arrangement. The first type of hybrid interior is where a single ownership or lease is upheld by one proprietor, but where the shop interior hosts a variety of diverse retail ensembles. The hybridity follows consumer demand and it is not atypical to find hats, mobile phones, groceries and fresh meat and/or fish all arranged within one long interior. In this first instance, the arrangement is orchestrated by the primary owner/leaseholder, generally in larger stores where the proprietor has been well established on the street for a long period of time.

The second type of mutualism is one where a head proprietor sublets smaller spaces within the shop, but the subletting occurs within close ethnicity or kinship ties. Such shops on Rye Lane have several retail zones within them, each with a separate till point. The boundaries demarking space range from counter-level differentiation to floor-to-ceiling dry walls, particularly in the instances of money remittance services, or hair salons where a higher degree of privacy is required. The third mutualism within one interior relates to the practice of subletting to a variety of tenants across a varied gender and ethnic spectrum, under the curatorial endeavour of the head lessee (Figure 3). Here, for example, one can find a money remittance area run by a proprietor originally from Uganda, adjacent to a seamstress from Ghana, adjacent to a mobile phone and fabric outlet run by a proprietor from Pakistan.

These mutualisms allow the proprietor to respond, on a regular and prompt basis, to the nuances of the market such that adjustments to emerging trends can be immediately attended to. At the core of the hybrid model is an economic imperative, one that has had an increasing impetus over the period of the financial crisis. When Ziyad, a young entrepreneur from Afghanistan who has had a shop on the street for three years, was asked what the most profitable part of his business was, he replied: 'Renting out parts of our store to other people.' The benefit effect works in two directions: Ziyad has a rental income to support his retail business in its early and most vulnerable years, and small entrepreneurs with limited access to start-up funds are able to rent very small spaces on the street. The rescaling of the shop is towards smaller dimensions: one conventional shop footprint subsequently supports several micro-initiatives.

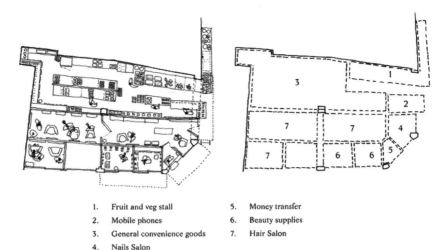

1. Fruit and veg stall
2. Mobile phones
3. General convenience goods
4. Nails Salon
5. Money transfer
6. Beauty supplies
7. Hair Salon

Figure 3. A drawing of a hybrid retail interior, where the primary retail space has been sub-divided and sub-let into several additional spaces (LSE Cities, Ordinary Streets Project 2012).

Ziyad's rental is reportedly approximately £10,000.00 per annum, while he is able to sublet a chair in the hair salon to Abeje for £80 per week. At the another end of the sublet spectrum, money remittance stores and mobile phone shops pay a premium rental for their small spaces. Umesh pays £9600 per annum for his Western Union store located at the back of the shop, his small shop space of approximately 6 m^2 yielding a monthly rental of £130/m^2. Notably, there are several Western Union outlets on Peckham Rye Lane, and a Western Union Consumer trading study of 2008 makes the following claim:

> ...offering a Western Union Service increases the cross-sell opportunity as well as the shopping frequency. 75% of customers making a Western Union Money Transfer transaction also purchased other products and 47% shop more frequently once they know that Western Union is available at the store.[1]

However, the impulse to subdivide, mix and remake these shop interiors is not simply driven by mercantile interests; it is also driven by cultural ones. As Mark, the local real estate agent comments:

> I would say the subdivisions are primarily a cultural thing and secondarily an economic thing. It's a way to create a home away from home.... It appears chaotic but it works. The big owner has multiple streams of income. (interview, 2012)

Certainly the long, hybrid shop interiors have a bazaar-like quality that exhibits a mix of economic dexterity, opportunism and a litmus-like response to the multi-ethnic, less affluent urban population that it serves, with affinities for highly sociable modes of trade. The densely invested interiors are illegible from the pavement and much of the emerging life of the street is therefore invisible to the passers-by. Shop arrangements in more affluent areas in London presumably reflect not only different norms of buying and selling, but also a more stringent interpretation and enforcement of title deeds, subletting and planning regulations.

The planning response on Rye Lane is to revert to established norms and to prevent the practice of subletting in the future. The borough has taken the decision that 'no further subdivisions' will be written into future lease agreements for retail spaces of 500 m^2 and above. However, at the national level of governance, there is broad support for 'pop-up shops' and 'meanwhile spaces' as exploratory ways of allowing new cultural and retail resources to emerge on high streets across the UK, in response to the diminishing presence of the high street (Portas 2011; DCLG 2012). Exploring the city at the scale of interiors and individual recalibrations of retail space and rental provides important cues for understanding retail renewals, migrant entrepreneurs and their transformations of the high street.

Towards a trans-ethnography

What does a trans-ethnography yield for the analysis of the super-diverse city? This paper has explored how the properties of power and practices of adaption evident within different localities of the city render a complex view of urban migration and ethnic diversity. While in each space categories of belonging and practices of exchange appear as visible or masked, what remains crucial is to analyse the macro, meso and micro as distinct *and* connected overlays of the city. To engage with such a complex unit of analysis through the primary orientation of ethnography, this paper has proposed three interconnected perspectives for the analysis of accelerated migration and urban transformation: the macro-perspectives of the symbolic city; the street perspectives of the collective city; and the interior perspectives of the intimate city. We have learnt about important differences in the visibility, regulation and practices of migration and city-making in these different spaces of city, street and shop. Neither the city nor citizenship is singular, and there are multiple and overlapping practices of being an urban inhabitant and migrant, where home, street or shop allows for different cultural repertoires to be tested. Regulatory regimes are similarly diverse, where border agencies, local boroughs and regeneration plans serve to differentially control the contingent. The super-diverse city constantly emerges as the intense place through which migrant citizens are simultaneously integral to and regulated from the past, present and future of the city.

Finally, a note on ethnography and urban change. In seeking to understand the intersections of power, practice and place in the spaces of city, street and shop, it is apparent that analytic conventions and categories – such as ethnicity, deprivation and territory – are officially authorized and re-inscribed by conventions of method. Citizenship, as shown in this paper, is an active phenomenon – vividly made by regulation, compliance and transgression. Understanding it therefore demands attitudes to intersecting concepts, data and methods. In this paper, locality has been a way of understanding the city and how its large and small dimensions are constantly altering through an unprecedented scale, speed and variation of migration processes. Questions that provide the analytic frame are: How is power organized?; What are the practices of integration?; and What are the analytic conventions and can these be productively disrupted? Trans-ethnography traverses across localities, across qualitative and quantitative knowledge, and across verbal and visual communication. Its method, we propose, is to move between the visible and the obscure, the convention and the emergent.

Acknowledgments

This paper is part of the 'Ordinary Streets' project based at LSE Cities. The research has been carried out by an energetic and talented interdisciplinary team, and my thanks extend to Antoine Paccoud, Nicolas Palominos, Sadiq Toffa and Adriana Valdez Young. Thank you to Ricky Burdett for key insights and directions during the project's progress. My colleagues David Madden and Austin Zeiderman provided key comments on an earlier draft of this paper.

Note

1. http://www.westernunion.co.uk

References

Anderson, Elijah. 2000. *Code of the Street: Decency, Violence, and the Moral Life of the Inner City.* New York: W.W. Norton & Company.

Beck, Ulrich, and Edgar Grande. 2010. "Varieties of Second Modernity: The Cosmopolitan Turn in Social and Political Theory and Research." *The British Journal of Sociology* 61 (3): 409–443. doi:10.1111/j.1468-4446.2010.01320.x.

Benson, Michaela, and Emma Jackson. 2013. "Place-Making and Place Maintenance: Practices of Place and Belonging among the Middle Classes." *Sociology* 47 (4): 793–809. doi:10.1177/0038038512454350.

Berg, Mette L., and Nando Sigona. 2013. "Ethnography, Diversity and Urban Space." *Identities: Global Studies in Culture and Power* 20 (4): 347–360.

Burawoy, Michael, Joseph Blum, Sheba George, Zsuzsa Gille, Theresa Gowan, Lynne Haney, Maren Klawiter, Steven Lopes, Séan O' Riain, and Thayer Millie. 2000. *Global Ethnography: Forces, Connections, and Imaginations in a Postmodern World.* Berkeley: University of California Press.

CoDE (Centre on Dynamics of Ethnicity). 2012a. "How Has Ethnic Diversity Grown 1991–2001–2011?" Manchester: CoDe, University of Manchester. http://www.ethnicity.ac.uk/census/869_CCSR_Bulletin_How_has_ethnic_diversity_grown_v4NW.pdf.

CoDE (Centre on Dynamics of Ethnicity). 2012b. *More Segregation or More Mixing?* CoDe, University of Manchester.

Conradson, David, and Alan Latham. 2005. "Transnational Urbanism: Attending to Everyday Practices and Mobilities." *Journal of Ethnic and Migration Studies* 31 (2): 227–233. doi:10.1080/1369183042000339891.

DCLG (Department of Community and Local Government). 2012. *Re-Imagining our Urban Space to Help Revitalise our High Streets.* London: DCLG.

Duneier, Mitchell. 1999. *Sidewalk.* New York: Farrar, Straus and Giroux.

GLA (Greater London Authority). 2008a. *A Profile of Londoners by Country of Birth: Estimates from the 2006 Annual Population Survey.* London: Data Management and Analysis Group, GLA.

GLA (Greater London Authority). 2008b. *Indices of Deprivation 2007: A London Perspective.* London: Data Management and Analysis Group, GLA.

Glick Schiller, Nina. 2005. "Transnational Urbanism as a Way of Life: A Research Topic not a Metaphor." *City and Society* 7 (1): 49–64. doi:10.1525/city.2005.17.1.49.

Glick Schiller, Nina, and Ayse Çağlar. 2009. "Towards a Comparative Theory of Locality in Migration Studies: Migrant Incorporation and City Scale." *Journal of Ethnic and Migration Studies* 35 (2): 177–202. doi:10.1080/13691830802586179.

Guarnizo, Luis E., and Michael Peter Smith. 1998. "The Locations of Transnationalism." In *Transnationalism from Below*, edited by Michael Peter Smith and Luis Eduardo Guarnizo, 3–34. New Brunswick, NJ: Transaction Publishers.

Hall, Suzanne M. 2011. "High Street Adaptations: Ethnicity, Independent Retail Practices and Localism in London's Urban Margins." *Environment and Planning A* 43 (11): 2571–2588. doi:10.1068/a4494.

Hall, Suzanne M. 2012. *City, Street and Citizen: The Measure of the Ordinary.* London: Routledge.

Hall, Suzanne M. 2013. "Multilingual Citizenship." *Discover Society* 1 (1). http://www.discoversociety.org/multilingual-citizenship

Hamnett, Chris. 2003. *Unequal City: London in the Global Arena.* London: Routledge.

Hannerz, Ulf. 1997. "Flows, Boundaries and Hybrids: Keywords in Transnational Anthropology." *Mana* 3 (1): 7–39. doi:10.1590/S0104-93131997000100001.

Home Office. 2001. *The Cantle Report – Community Cohesion: A Report of the Independent Review Team.* London: Home Office.

Keith, Michael. 2013. "Emergent Publics, Critical Ethnography, Scholarship and Race and Ethnic Relations." *Ethnic and Racial Studies* 36 (9): 1374–1392.

Kloosterman, Robert, Joanne van der Leun, and Jan Rath. 1999. "Mixed Embeddedness: (In) formal Economic Activities and Immigrant Business in the Netherlands." *International Journal of Urban and Regional Research* 23 (2): 253–267. doi:10.1111/1468-2427.00194.

Knowles, Caroline. 2013. "Nigerian London: Re-Mapping Space and Ethnicity in Superdiverse Cities." *Ethnic and Racial Studies* 36 (4): 651–669. doi:10.1080/01419870.2012.678874.

Liebow, Elliot. 1967. *Tally's Corner: A Study of Negro Streetcorner Men.* Boston, MA: Little, Brown.

London Borough of Southwark. 2012. "Revitalise: Peckham and Nunhead Area Action Plan, February 2012." http://www.southwark.gov.uk/futurepeckham.

Marcus, George E. 1995. "Ethnography in/of the World Systems: The Emergence of Multi-Sited Ethnography." *Annual Review of Anthropology* 24: 95–117. doi:10.1146/annurev.an.24.100195.000523.

Paccoud, Antoine. 2013. "Country of Birth in the 2011 Census: Local Authorities and London's Extended Metropolitan Region." LSE Cities Working Paper. http://eprints.lse.ac.uk/51152.

Portas, Mary. 2011. *The Portas Review: An Independent Review into the Future of our High Streets.* London: Department for Business, Innovation and Skills.

Soja, Edward. 2010. "On the Production of Unjust Geographies." Chap. 2 in *Seeking Spatial Justice.* Minneapolis: University of Minnesota Press.

Smith, Michael P. 2005. "Transnational Urbanism Revisited." *Journal of Ethnic and Migration Studies* 31 (2): 235–244. doi:10.1080/1369183042000339909.

Vertovec, Steven. 2007. "Super-Diversity and its Implications." *Ethnic and Racial Studies* 30 (6): 1024–1054. doi:10.1080/01419870701599465.

Vertovec, Steven. 2011. *Migration and New Diversities in the Global City. Working Paper.* Göttingen: Max-Planck-Institute.

Wheeler, W. 1842. *Map of the Parish of St. Giles, Camberwell.* Drawn by J. Dewhirst, surveyor. http://www.ideal-homes.org.uk/southwark/assets/maps/peckham.

Wrigley, Neil, Julia Branson, Graham Clarke and Andrew Murdoch. 2009. "Extending the Competition Commission's Findings on Entry and Exit of Small Stores in Britain's High Streets: Implications for Competition and Planning Policy." *Environment and Planning A* 41 (9): 2063–2085. doi:10.1068/a41326.

Zukin, Sharon. 2010. *Naked City: The Death and Life of Authentic Urban Places*. Oxford: Oxford University Press.

The perception of ethnic diversity and anti-immigrant sentiments: a multilevel analysis of local communities in Belgium

Marc Hooghe and Thomas de Vroome

Most of the literature suggests a positive relationship between immigrant concentration and anti-immigrant sentiments. The main goal of this study is to investigate the impact of both perceived and actual size of migrant populations on anti-immigrant sentiments. A representative survey of inhabitants of local communities in the Flemish region of Belgium shows a strong tendency to overestimate the presence of non-nationals. The survey allows us to conclude that respondents living in ethnically diverse communities do not have more negative attitudes towards immigrants. Individuals who perceive more immigrants to be present in their communities are more hostile even after controlling for reported contact with members of immigrant groups. We can therefore conclude that the perceived size of the immigrant group has a stronger impact on anti-immigrant sentiments than the actual presence of ethnic minority groups.

Introduction

In recent decades, migration flows have resulted in an increased level of ethnic and cultural diversity in most societies of Western Europe (Castles and Miller 2003). According to some of the literature, this rise of ethnic diversity has been associated with a rise of anti-immigrant sentiments in at least a number of European countries (Semyonov, Raijman, and Gorofzeisky 2008). A common assumption in the research on this topic is that anti-immigrant attitudes, directly or indirectly, should be seen as a reaction to rising levels of ethnic diversity (Quillian 1995; Scheepers, Gijsberts and Coenders 2002; Schneider 2008; Semyonov, Raijman and Gorofzeisky 2008). The existing body of empirical research, however, does not always support this assumption (Sides and Citrin 2007; Strabac and Listhaug 2008). A prevailing theme in the literature is that anti-immigrant attitudes to a large extent can be understood as a reaction to a real or perceived group threat (LeVine and Campbell 1972; Fossett and Kiecolt 1989; Quillian 1995). As natives assume there is a potential conflict with immigrant groups about the allocation of scarce resources like jobs, housing or cultural hegemony, the most likely outcome could be that they perceive the new groups to be competitors on these markets (McLaren and Johnson 2007). Whether the circumstances favouring inter-group competition and potential threat need to be real

(Bobo 1983; Quillian 1995; Putnam 2007; Sniderman and Hagendoorn 2007; Strabac 2011) or can be imagined is still a matter of debate. Regardless of the threat being real or imaginary, group threat theories where competition for scarce resources contributes to a conflict between minorities and majorities predict a positive correlation between the concentration of minorities and anti-immigrant sentiments among the native population.

The goal of the present study is to contribute to a better understanding of the relation between ethnic diversity, perceived threat and anti-immigrant sentiments, by building on recent community-level data from Belgium. Anti-immigrant sentiments may arise as the result of a combination or an interaction between contextual- and individual- level explanatory characteristics (Bobo and Fox 2003; Pettigrew and Tropp 2006; Schlueter and Scheepers 2010). Controlling for relevant individual background characteristics, our goal is to determine whether the presence of immigrant populations is associated with the development of anti-immigrant sentiments.

We aim to contribute to the literature in three distinct ways. First, while previous studies tend to focus on large geographical units, in this study we focus on small local communities, where real contact between different ethnic groups is still possible. Second, the small scale of the communities under investigation renders it possible to include intergroup contact as a variable in the analysis. We do so because the assumption is that prejudice is being reduced as a result of positive interpersonal contacts between groups and it is difficult to test this assumption at the country level. Third, the survey data we are using also include measurements of perceived ethnic diversity. By comparing this assessment with official population figures, we can ascertain whether actual diversity or the perceived level of diversity contributes most strongly to the development of anti-immigrant sentiments. Previous research has shown that ethnic majority residents do not always have a reliable perception about the presence of ethnic minorities, and therefore it is a straightforward assumption that both measurements could diverge and have different effects (Strabac 2011). Majority group members systematically overestimate the proportion of immigrants in society (Herda 2010).

The survey we use was conducted in the northern Flemish region of Belgium, a country with fairly average levels of ethnic diversity and anti-immigrant sentiments for Western Europe (Semyonov, Raijman and Gorofzeisky 2006). In this article, we first briefly review the literature on social and spatial determinants of anti-immigrant sentiments, before presenting the data and methods. Following the results section, we reflect on whether these findings could be generalized towards other contexts.

Literature

Building on the theoretical assumption that hostility, prejudice and discrimination towards out-group populations can be considered as a reaction to (rises in) their relative size of the population (Williams 1947; Blalock 1967), numerous researchers have claimed that anti-immigrant sentiments, ethnic prejudice and discrimination tend to rise with the relative size of the out-group population (Scheepers, Gijsberts and Coenders 2002; Coenders, Gijsberts and Scheepers 2004; Kunovich 2004; Semyonov,

Raijman and Gorofzeisky 2006). However, the empirical evidence that out-group size is associated with an increase in anti-immigrant sentiments has been judged as inconclusive (Semyonov et al. 2004; Wagner et al. 2006; Semyonov, Raijman and Gorofzeisky 2008). One group of studies has demonstrated a positive relation of out-group size with anti-immigrant attitudes (Fossett and Kiecolt 1989; Quillian 1995; Coenders 2001; Scheepers, Gijsberts and Coenders 2002). Other studies, however, failed to provide such evidence (Evans and Need 2002; Semyonov et al. 2004; Coenders, Lubbers and Scheepers 2005; Strabac and Listhaug 2008). Still another group of authors even documented a negative relation (Hood and Morris 1997). This negative relation can be explained by relying on inter-group contact theory resulting in the claim that a larger out-group size provides more opportunities for positive inter-group contact, which in turn ameliorates anti-out-group attitudes (Allport 1954; Pettigrew 1998;Wagner et al. 2006; Pettigrew, Wagner, and Christ 2010; Schlueter and Scheepers 2010). One of the likely reasons for this pattern of inconclusive evidence might be that two causal mechanisms can lead to opposite results. Supporters of realistic group conflict theory assume that the larger the size of the out-group, the more likely it is that the native population will develop negative attitudes towards these minorities. On the other hand, the contact theory suggests that real-life interaction will lead to positive learning opportunities and will thus reduce anti-immigrant sentiments. Basically, this implies an interaction effect: while the presence of minorities in the community would lead to higher levels of prejudice, this effect could be mitigated if natives interact in a positive manner with the minority group members. In more segregated societies, with little interaction between ethnic groups, we thus expect higher levels of prejudice than in less segregated societies (Semyonov and Lewin-Epstein 2011; Uslaner 2011). It has to be noted, however, that the country level might be less appropriate to investigate the occurrence of contact effects, as the geographical scale of a country is simply too large to allow for real inter-group contact. This kind of contact, however, is still possible at a smaller, community level.

Negative attitudes towards immigrants are not only associated with socio-demographic characteristics of respondents and structural characteristics of the communities, but also by the perception of the size of the foreign population (Semyonov, Raijman, and Gorofzeisky 2008). Research has repeatedly shown that most natives have inflated views of the relative size of the minority population (Sigelman and Niemi 2000; Gallagher 2003; Alba, Rumbaut and Marotz 2005; Semyonov, Raijman and Gorofzeisky 2008). An increase in the population share of a migrant group is often perceived by majority group members as a source of competition over scarce resources, and hence, as a competitive threat to their own interests. Distorted perception is therefore likely to increase negative attitudes towards foreigners and minorities (Semyonov et al. 2004; Semyonov, Raijman and Gorofzeisky 2008).

Group conflict theory and out-group size

Group conflict theory assumes that competition between social groups over scarce resources and values induces conflicts between those groups (LeVine and Campbell

1972). On the other hand, anti-immigrant sentiments may stem from the perception of the (detrimental) impact of minorities and immigrants on the host society (Bobo 1983; Smith and Dempsey 1983; Enoch 1994; Bobo and Zubrinsky 1996; Scheepers, Gijsberts and Coenders 2002). Therefore, group conflict theory relates out-group size as a contextual-level characteristic to individual-level anti-out-group attitudes, proposing that a larger out-group size increases anti-out-group attitudes, and it is assumed that this effect is mediated by perceptions of threatened group interests (Blalock 1967; Quillian 1995; Bobo 1999; Schlueter and Scheepers 2010).

Blalock (1967) introduced an analytical distinction between actual and perceived competition and in his work he linked the group-level phenomenon of inter-group (actual) competition to anti-immigrant attitudes. Within group conflict theory, the proportion of a minority group living within a specific community is of crucial importance. Several researchers have concluded that the size of the out-group is positively associated with the presence of anti-immigrant attitudes (Scheepers, Gijsberts and Coenders 2002; Kunovich 2004; Schneider 2008).

Some of the more recent research, however, has suggested that it is not the actual size of the out-group that contributes to anti-immigrant feelings, but rather the perceived size of this group (Semyonov et al. 2004). In this analysis of German population data, it was shown that the perceived proportion of ethnic minorities is not correlated with the actual proportion, as measured by population statistics; nor is the actual minority proportion related to the majority respondents' attitudes towards ethnic minorities. The only relation that was present in this study was the one between perceived diversity and anti-immigrant feelings. More recent research has confirmed these findings (Weins 2011; Outten et al. 2012).

Hypotheses

This review of the literature leads to the following three hypotheses:

H1: The greater the proportion of migrant groups measured at the community level, the higher the levels of anti-immigrant sentiment among the individuals living in that community.
H2: The greater the number of social contacts with members of migrant groups, the lower the anti-immigrant sentiment.
H3: Perception of the size of the ethnic minority population is more strongly associated with anti-immigrant sentiments than is the actual size of the ethnic group measured at the community level.

Data and methods

These three hypotheses assume that community-level variables have an effect on the level of anti-immigrant sentiments of the individual. Therefore, we need a data set that allows us to connect communitylevel indicators with individual survey data. First, for attitudinal indicators and socio-demographic control variables, we use the results of the Social Cohesion Indicators in Flanders (SCIF) survey that was conducted in 2009 among a representative sample of the population of the Flemish region of Belgium aged eighteen and over by means of 2,085 face-to-face interviews.[1] The response rate of the survey was 54 per cent (Hooghe, Vanhoutte, and Bircan 2009).

In the analysis, only the responses of the Belgian-born respondents were included (n–1,910), as it would require a different question wording to investigate anti-immigrant sentiments among respondents who have an immigrant background. We have deleted cases with missing values listwise. Because missing values on income amount to about 13 per cent, we use a categorical variable for income with 'income missing' as an additional category. All in all, the sample in the analysis includes 1,816 respondents.

The structural variables available for the smallest geographic data unit in Belgium are situated at the municipal level. Given the fact that the average municipality in the Flemish region has 20,000 inhabitants, this can still be considered a real community allowing for interaction with fellow residents. Thus, we will use the community-level statistical data (n–40) (source: National Institute of Statistics 2011), which were collected at the municipal level.

There is no reason to assume that Belgium would be a strongly deviant case for the study of anti-immigrant sentiments in Europe. An analysis of the European Social Survey (ESS) samples for 2008 and 2010 suggests that the level of anti-immigrant sentiments in Belgium (5.04 on a 0–10 scale) is very close to the average in European countries (5.11). For budgetary reasons and for reasons of comparability, we focus on just one language community in the country: the Dutch language community. An analysis of the same ESS data suggests that the difference in ethnocentrism between the Dutch and the French language community in Belgium is not significant.

Anti-immigrant sentiments

In this study, a three-item scale was used to measure anti-immigrant sentiments in exactly the same manner as in the ESS:

(1) Would you say it is generally bad or good for the Belgian economy that people come to live here from other countries?
(2) Would you say that Belgian cultural life is generally undermined or enriched by people coming to live here from other countries?
(3) Is Belgium made a worse or a better place to live by people coming to live here from other countries?

The three items proved to be a one-dimensional scale, with one factor, eigenvalue 1.94, and 64.51 per cent explained variance. The scale is internally coherent with a Cronbach's a of 0.73 (Table 1).

Independent variables

In line with the theoretical arguments, the actual proportion of the immigrant population at the community level is the first main variable of interest. The concentration of immigrants is investigated by using several different measurements. We started with the actual size of the broadest group, that is, non-nationals, and narrowed this group further down in order to explore the possible effect of specific

CITIES, DIVERSITY AND ETHNICITY

Table 1. Characteristics of the anti-immigrant sentiments scale.

Items	Item average (0–10)	Factor loading	Cronbach's α if deleted
Effect on economy (good–0, bad–10)	5.48	0.82	0.61
Effect on cultural life (enrich–0, undermine–10)	4.53	0.82	0.62
Effect on living place (better place–0, worse place–10)	4.87	0.77	0.69
Cronbach's α	0.73		

Extraction method: Principle component analysis.
Source: SCIF Survey 2009 (Hooghe et al. 2009); N–1,816.

immigrant groups: non-EU nationals (Semyonov, Raijman, and Gorofzeisky 2006), EU nationals (Dustmann and Preston 2007) and incoming migrants (Mayda 2006). Non-EU nationals refers to immigrants from countries outside the EU-15 countries (Schneider 2008). We selected this criterion because previous analyses suggest that in the Belgian context, anti-immigrant sentiments are almost exclusively directed towards this group. In order to investigate any possible ethnic bias among natives, the main non-EU migrant groups in Belgium, namely Turkish nationals and Moroccan nationals, are also investigated separately. Because of non-normality, a log transformation of three community-level variables (the size of the non-Belgian, non-EU and EU foreign national population in the community) was used to approximate a normal distribution more closely.[2]

Second, we argue that the perceived size of the immigrant population is also important, in addition to the actual size. Therefore, the perceived relative size of the immigrant population in Belgium is also investigated. This variable was measured by asking respondents how many out of every 100 people in Belgium they think are non-Belgian. Third, we investigate the role of cross-ethnic social contact with a measure of having cross-ethnic friendships. Respondents were asked whether they have any friends with a different ethnic background, so the variable we use distinguishes between people who do and people who do not have friends from a different ethnic background.

Control variables

In the analysis, we control for the individual-level variables age, gender, education, income, religiosity, watching television and generalized trust. Age tends to be positively associated with anti-immigrant sentiments (Citrin et al. 1997; Dustmann and Preston 2007). Anti-immigrant attitudes also tend to be stronger among socio-economically weak and vulnerable populations (Espenshade and Hempstead 1996; Raijman and Semyonov 2004). Regarding education, therefore, we include a dummy variable indicating whether respondents have a relatively low level of education (i.e. maximum lower secondary education) (1) or a relatively higher level of education (i.e. at least higher secondary education) (0). Regarding income, we use a variable with four categories, distinguishing between lower-income households (€0–1,999/month), middle-income households (€2,000–3,499/month) and higher-income households (€3,500 or more/month). The fourth category designates the respondents who refused to provide information on their income.

Generalized trust has been the focus of the social capital school and much of the related work on civic attitudes and behaviours. Previous research has established a strong negative association between generalized trust on the one hand, and ethnocentrism and anti-immigrant feelings on the other (Hooghe, Reeskens and Stolle 2007).

In research on anti-immigrant sentiments, it has been found that mass media are an important factor because of their major role in influencing public opinion about ethnic minorities (Fitzgerald, Curtis, and Corliss 2012). Perceived threats and ethnocentric attitudes are often shaped by negative mass media portrayals of minority groups. Media presentations of immigration-relevant issues can be an important source of social bias (Law 2002). The negative role of television has been attributed especially to commercial stations as being a contributor to the cultivation of a less civic-minded value pattern (Hooghe 2002). We therefore include the number of hours that respondents spend watching television every day and their preference for a commercial station as control variables. On the municipality level, we control for community size (i.e. the number of residents in the municipality) and use a dummy variable indicating whether respondents live in a 'cosmopolitan' city (i.e. one of the two largest cities in Flanders: Antwerpen and Ghent). It is important to take these community-level factors into account, because it is possible that a 'deprovincialization' effect occurs in the larger urban centres (Verkuyten, Thijs and Bekhuis 2010). Descriptive statistics of the available measures are listed in Table 2.

Method

The nested structure of the SCIF survey research design, combined with the community-level data, is addressed by using multi-level models. This allows the simultaneous modelling of the effects of individual-level and community-level predictors (Snijders and Bosker 1999; Hox 2002). With multi-level modelling, variance explained by attributes of the context and variance explained by attributes of the individual can be distinguished and standard errors are estimated correctly. We centred all individual-level variables (but not the dummy variables) on the overall mean. We have tested cross-level interactions to evaluate whether the effects of the perceived proportion of non- Belgians and of having cross-ethnic friendships differ between communities. We therefore included random slopes for the perceived proportion of non-Belgians and for having cross-ethnic friendships in the respective models that test the cross-level interactions.

Results

Actual and perceived diversity

If we want to compare the effect of actual and perceived diversity on the development of anti-immigrant attitudes, it is important to note that both measurements differ

CITIES, DIVERSITY AND ETHNICITY

Table 2. Descriptive statistics of variables used in the analysis (40 municipalities; N–1,816).

	Min.	Max.	M / Proportion	SD
Individual-level parameters				
Anti-immigrant sentiments	0	10	4.96	1.86
Perceived% non-Belgian	1	99	28.03	17.36
Friend with other ethnic background	0	1	0.36	
Age	17	84	47.28	17.96
Female	0	1	0.52	
Lower education level	0	1	0.27	
Income: 0–1,999	0	1	0.28	
Income: 2,000–3,499	0	1	0.34	
Income: 3,500-upwards	0	1	0.26	
Income: Missing	0	1	0.12	
Religious attendance	0	1	0.50	
TV – average hours a day	0	18	2.43	1.58
TV – prefers commercial station	0	1	0.35	
Generalized trust	0	10	5.40	1.79
Valid N (listwise)				
Community-level parameters				
% non-Belgian	0.68	22.86	5.41	5.08
(log)% non-Belgian	−0.39	3.13	1.31	0.85
% non-EU	0.14	8.77	2.05	2.16
(log)% non-EU	−1.99	2.17	0.25	0.98
% EU	0.54	21.94	3.35	3.93
(log)% EU	−0.62	3.09	0.78	0.86
% Turkish	0	2.02	0.38	0.58
% Moroccan	0	2.53	0.36	0.66
% Inflow	0	1.80	0.39	0.32
Community size ($\times$ 1,000 residents)	5	478	68.62	115.71
Cosmopolitan city	0	1	0.12	

Source: SCIF Survey 2009; National Institute for Statistics of Belgium 2009.

strongly. Official figures show that about 6 per cent of the Belgian population does not have Belgian citizenship status. Taking into account that a large group of the immigrant population has acquired Belgian citizenship status, this would suggest that something like 12 per cent of the total population should be seen as belonging to an immigrant group. On average, however, the respondents in the survey estimated that 28 per cent of the Belgian population consists of non-Belgians. In line with previous research (Herda 2010), it can therefore be observed that respondents overestimate the presence of ethnic minorities. Additional analyses show that there is a significant positive relation between actual diversity at the community level and perceived diversity, but the relation is of modest size, and actual diversity does not appear to be a better predictor of perceived diversity than factors such as being younger, being female and having more (commercial) television consumption, which are all related to higher levels of perceived diversity (Table 3).

Table 3. Multi-level model for perceived percentage non-Belgians.

	Model 1		
	B	SE	p
Community-level parameter			
% non-Belgians (log)	3.073	0.739	***
Individual-level parameters			
Perceived% non-Belgians	–	–	
Friend with different ethnic origin	−0.701	0.810	
Control variables			
Age	−0.133	0.025	***
Female	8.575	0.740	***
Lower educational level	2.889	0.926	**
Income (ref.–lower income)			
Middle income	−2.203	0.997	*
Higher income	−3.286	1.143	**
Income missing	−1.519	1.342	
Does attend religious services	0.380	0.755	
TV – hours watched daily	0.981	0.259	***
TV – prefers commercial station	5.770	0.832	***
Generalized trust	−1.288	0.212	***
Community size (× 1,000 residents)	−0.001	0.014	
Cosmopolitan city	−0.684	4.995	
Intercept	29.610	2.310	***
Random part			
Individual-level variance		241.09	
% individual-level variance explained		16.9	
Community-level variance		6.28	
% community-level variance explained		43.5	

Source: SCIF Survey 2009; NIS 2009.
Note: Entries are the result of a multi-level regression analysis in SPSS, with 'perceived% non-Belgians' as the dependent variable.
Significance levels (two-tailed): $*p <.05, **p <.01, ***p <.001$.

Multi-level findings and interpretations

We have already noted that the intention of the current article is to use various community-level indicators in order to assess the impact of diversity on anti-immigrant sentiments. In order to avoid multicollinearity, however, it proved to be impossible to include all these indicators simultaneously. Therefore, these community-level indicators will have to be introduced in distinct models, and we first start with the description of the individual-level model, which will serve as a control for all future multi-level models.

As a starting point, a baseline model of the multi-level regression analysis was fitted (Table 4). The analysis shows that 3.31 per cent of the variance in anti-immigrant sentiments can be attributed to the community level. This limited level of intra-class correlation already suggests that the size of the immigrant group in one's society cannot be the main driving force for levels of anti-immigrant sentiments. It

CITIES, DIVERSITY AND ETHNICITY

Table 4. Multi-level regression null model for anti-immigrant sentiments (40 municipalities; N–1,816).

	B	SE	p
Fixed part			
Intercept	4.985	0.069	**
Random part			
Individual-level variance	3.356	0.113	**
Community-level variance	0.115	0.043	*
Intraclass correlation	3.31%		

Source: SCIF Survey 2009.
Note: Entries are the result of a multi-level regression analysis, with anti-immigrant sentiments as the dependent variable.
Significance levels (two-tailed): *p <.01, **p <.001.

has to be noted, however, that 3.31 per cent cannot be neglected either, and therefore we pursue with the multi-level analysis.

Turning to the results of our main analysis in Table 5, it becomes clear that anti-immigrant sentiments are not significantly related to ethnic diversity at the community level, given conventional levels of significance (Model 1). This is in contrast to our first hypothesis, and with most of the literature on this topic, suggesting a positive association between actual diversity and anti-immigrant sentiments. Interestingly, the second model in Table 5 shows that there is a modest but clearly significant positive association between the perceived percentage of non-Belgians in Belgium and anti-immigrant sentiments. This means that anti-immigrant sentiments are higher among those who provide higher estimates of the percentage of non-Belgians living in the country. Including the perception, there is even a very small negative relation between the actual percentage of immigrants in the community and anti-immigrant sentiments.

In the third model of Table 5, we investigate the possible impact of inter-ethnic contact. The results show that having one or more friends with a different ethnic background is associated with lower levels of anti-immigrant sentiments, as predicted by our second hypothesis.

When we include cross-ethnic friendship in the third (full) model, the negative relation between the actual percentage of non-Belgians in the community and anti-immigrant sentiments is not significant. As already noted, the non-significant relation between diversity and anti-immigrant sentiments is quite unique in the international literature. One of the ways that we could explain our finding is the fact that in diverse communities, the odds are higher that members of the majority group will have positive contacts with members of the minority group, and that especially among those who have positive contacts, levels of prejudice are negatively related to actual diversity. Conversely, the actual size of the non-Belgian population may lead to more anti-immigrant sentiments, especially among those who perceive high levels of ethnic diversity. Therefore, we have tested cross-level interactions between community levels of diversity on the one hand and perceived diversity and inter-group contact on the other, as can be seen in Models 4 and 5 of Table 5. These interactions turn out not to be significant. This means that we do not find any evidence that the relation

Table 5. Multi-level regression models for anti-immigrant sentiments (40 municipalities; N=1,816)

	Model 1			Model 2			Model 3			Model 4			Model 5		
	B	SE	p	B	SE	p	B	SE	p	B	SE	p	B	SE	p
Community-level parameter															
% non-Belgians (log)	−0.111	0.073		−0.141	0.074	γ	−0.103	0.070		−0.096	0.070		−0.147	0.076	γ
Individual-level parameters															
Perceived% non-Belgians				0.010	0.002	***	0.010	0.002	***	0.006	0.005		0.010	0.002	***
Friend with different ethnic origin							−0.666	0.082	***	−0.667	0.082	***	−0.845	0.167	***
Cross-level interactions															
% non-Belgians * Perceived%										0.003	0.003				
% non-Belgians * Friend ethnic origin													0.134	0.105	
Control variables															
Age	0.016	0.002	***	0.017	0.003	***	0.013	0.003	***	0.012	0.003	***	0.013	0.003	***
Female	−0.030	0.076		−0.117	0.079		−0.142	0.078	γ	−0.136	0.077	γ	−0.141	0.078	γ
Lower educational level	0.360	0.096	***	0.330	0.095	***	0.299	0.094	**	0.304	0.094	**	0.298	0.094	***
Income (ref. = lower income)															
Middle income	−0.019	0.103		0.003	0.103		−0.010	0.101		−0.015	0.101		−0.013	0.101	
Higher income	−0.099	0.118		−0.066	0.118		−0.113	0.116		−0.117	0.116		−0.114	0.116	
Income missing	−0.032	0.139		−0.015	0.138		−0.016	0.136		−0.027	0.136		−0.014	0.135	
Does attend religious services	−0.100	0.078		−0.105	0.078		−0.118	0.076		−0.112	0.076		−0.118	0.076	
TV – hours watched daily	0.080	0.027	**	0.069	0.027	**	0.058	0.026	*	0.057	0.026	*	0.059	0.026	*
TV – prefers commercial station	0.632	0.086	***	0.573	0.087	***	0.553	0.085	***	0.547	0.085	***	0.557	0.085	***
Generalized trust	−0.350	0.022	***	−0.336	0.022	***	−0.328	0.022	***	−0.326	0.022	***	−0.327	0.022	***
Community size (x 1,000 residents)	0.000	0.001		0.000	0.001		0.000	0.001		0.001	0.001		0.001	0.001	
Cosmopolitan city	−0.335	0.484		−0.328	0.493		−0.370	0.458		−0.427	0.451		−0.411	0.460	
Intercept	5.879	0.231	***	5.866	0.231	***	6.277	0.230	***	6.255	0.230	***	6.317	0.232	***

Table 5 (*Continued*)

	Model 1			Model 2			Model 3			Model 4			Model 5		
	B	SE	*p*	*B*	SE	*p*	*B*	SE	*p*	*B*	SE	*p*	*B*	SE	*p*
Random part															
Individual-level variance	2.580			2.555			2.469			2.445			2.458		
% individual-level variance explained	23.1			23.9			26.4			27.1			26.8		
Community-level variance	0.055			0.059			0.048			0.046			0.042		
% community-level variance explained	52.2			48.7			58.3			60.0			63.5		
Variance random slope individual parameter										0.000			0.051		

Source: SCIF Survey 2009.
Significance levels (two-tailed): $^{\gamma}p<.010$, * $p<.05$, ** $p<.01$, *** $p<.001$.
Note: Entries are the result of a multi-level regression analysis, with anti-immigrant sentiments scale as the dependent variable.

between the actual size of the non-Belgian population and anti-immigrant sentiments is more negative among those who have cross-ethnic friendships or perceive low levels of ethnic diversity. This suggests that inter-group friendship and perceived diversity do not help us to explain the negative relation between actual diversity and anti-immigrant sentiments.

Turning to the control variables, our analysis mostly confirms the results of previous studies. The level of anti-immigrant sentiments is higher among those who are older, have less education, watch more television and prefer commercial stations, and have lower levels of generalized trust. We do not find evidence for effects of income and religiosity. The media seem to be an important factor, as both the time spent watching television and a preference for commercial television stations are positively related to the level of anti-immigrant sentiments. At the community level, we find no relations between community size or living in a cosmopolitan city and anti-immigrant sentiments. The main finding from the previous model is that there is no significant relation between the percentage of non-Belgians at the community level and anti-immigrant sentiment. To determine whether this is caused by the specific operationalization of the ethnic diversity measure we used, we also test different diversity measures in additional analyses. Table 6 thus shows the results from nine different multi-level regressions in which every model includes all the individual-level variables of the corresponding models (Models 1–3) in Table 4. The results listed in Table 6 provide further evidence that there is no significant (positive) relation between actual diversity and anti-immigrant sentiments. We only find some very small negative relations in the second model, which does not take inter-group contact into account. This allows us to conclude that people living in more diverse communities do not tend to have more negative attitudes towards immigrants, as group conflict theory would predict.

Table 6. Effect of different diversity-related community-level parameters in Models 1–3 (40 municipalities; $N = 1,816$)

	Model 1			Model 2			Model 3		
	B	SE	p	B	SE	p	B	SE	p
% non-Belgians	−0.012	0.012		−0.015	0.013		−0.012	0.012	
% non-Belgians (log)	−0.111	0.073		−0.141	0.074	γ	−0.103	0.070	
% non-EU	−0.026	0.065		−0.053	0.067		−0.006	0.063	
% non-EU (log)	−0.103	0.074		−0.138	0.075	γ	−0.079	0.072	
% EU	−0.013	0.013		−0.016	0.014		−0.014	0.013	
% EU (log)	−0.095	0.066		−0.117	0.067	γ	−0.094	0.063	
% Turkish origin	−0.098	0.141		−0.140	0.144		−0.061	0.136	
% Moroccan origin	0.083	0.129		0.040	0.133		0.099	0.123	
% inflow	−0.083	0.192		−0.088	0.197		−0.096	0.193	

Source: SCIF Survey 2009.
Significance level (two-tailed): [γ]$p<.010$.
Note: Entries are the result of a multi-level regression analysis, with anti-immigrant sentiments scale as the dependent variable. Models include all variables that are also included in Model 3 of Table 5.

As stated in our third hypothesis, one of our main goals in this analysis was to ascertain the difference between the effect of actual and perceived diversity. Our models demonstrate the importance of the perceived size of the migrant group in predicting anti-immigrant sentiments. How people perceive the presence of migrants has an important impact on anti-immigrant sentiments. The relation between the actual concentration of foreigners in the municipality and ethnocentrism is not only less strong, but even absent. The results reveal that higher proportions of foreigners (either non-Belgians, non- EU-15 citizens or EU nationals) in the community are not associated with higher levels of anti-immigrant sentiments among the natives.

Discussion

In this article, we investigated the impact of both perceived and actual ethnic diversity on the level of anti-immigrant sentiments. In line with most proponents of the group conflict theory, it was assumed that both diversity measures could have a positive effect on the level of anti-immigrant sentiments. Somewhat surprisingly, however, this was not confirmed by our results. While the perceived level of diversity is indeed positively related to anti-immigrant sentiments, the actual diversity measures turned out not to be associated with these sentiments. In more diverse communities, natives clearly do not have a more negative outlook on migration and this observation runs counter to most observations based on forms of the conflict approach. A first possibility to explain why levels of anti-immigrant sentiments are not higher in more diverse communities would be to look at the increased potential for inter-group friendship in these diverse communities. However, we did not find evidence for a mediation (suppression) effect or a significant interaction effect between the level of ethnic diversity in one's community and having inter-group friendships. This means that we do not find evidence for a negative indirect relation between actual diversity and anti-immigrant sentiments by increased positive inter-group contact. Neither do we find evidence that the relation between actual diversity and anti-immigrant sentiments is only negative among those who have cross-ethnic friendships and positive among others. Another possibility that remains to be investigated is a self-selection effect. Given the fact that ethnic minorities tend to concentrate in the inner cities, those with high levels of anti-immigrant sentiments are more likely to move out of the inner city, to relocate themselves in mostly homogeneous suburbs. The end result of this process of geographical self-selection is that the natives that do remain in the city centre, or are attracted to inner cities, are characterized by lower levels of anti-immigrant sentiments. As a third possibility, it should be noted that the absence of a positive relation between actual diversity and anti-immigrant sentiments may be related to the size of our communities. The empirical evidence for a positive relation between actual diversity and anti-immigrant sentiments mainly comes from cross-national studies, while other studies that look at diversity at the community level have also found no relation (Semyonov et al. 2004). This suggests that perceived ethnic threat may be more salient at the national level than at the community level. It also implies that, at the national level, interaction with ethnic minority members most likely does not play a role in the development of anti-immigrant sentiments, while it is more likely that this interaction does occur at the level of the municipality.

On the other hand, we could establish a positive effect between the perceived size of the ethnic minority group in Belgium and the level of anti-immigrant sentiments. However, in this case, too, extreme caution is necessary if our goal is to establish any causality. First of all, it has to be remembered that the perception of diversity is only weakly related to actual diversity as most native actors arrive at a huge overestimation of the presence of foreigners in the country. The logic underlying the current analysis was that the perception of reality (even if it is not based on actual facts and figures) could contribute to the development of specific attitudes. Different approaches, however, are just as likely. Actors with a hostile attitude towards ethnic minorities could be more likely to overestimate the presence of non-nationals, because in their perception of what goes on in society they are more likely to be focused on these specific groups. It could even be argued that both measurements refer to the same latent concept, as obviously those who worry about cultural and ethnic diversity in society are more likely to pay more attention to this topic in their day-to-day observations of their community. Actors who are not concerned at all about diversity simply have fewer reasons to focus on this aspect of reality on their observations about the community in which they live. It is important, therefore, that in future studies we should be able to determine more clearly what the conceptual status of this perception is. On the one hand, it is partly reality driven, but simultaneously it does reflect underlying attitudes held by the respondent. While it is clear that the perceived size of minority groups and anti-immigrant sentiments are related, it remains to be investigated how exactly this perception is being constructed.

Conclusion

The current analysis demonstrates that perception is important, and maybe even more important than social reality. The fact that we find a strong relation with media use even might lead in the same direction as actors who spend a lot of time in front of the television set, obviously also use media content to make sense of their society, even if they do not have any direct observations about what goes on in the community they reside in. It has to be noted in this regard that this specific study was limited to the Flemish region of Belgium. While this country is not exceptional with regard to the presence of ethnic minorities, it has to be noted that this region might offer a specific cultural context. Since the 1980s, the extreme right Vlaams Belang party has been quite successful in this region, and it has consistently used a discourse about the negative social impact of the presence of non-nationals. This discourse might be associated with a general outlook where the perception is that Belgian society is being 'flooded' by the arrival of immigrants. It remains to be ascertained, therefore, whether our conclusion ('perception matters more than reality') is also valid in other cultural contexts, where a different discourse on the consequences of ethnic diversity prevails. It is important therefore, to investigate the effect of both real and perceived ethnic diversity also in other cultural contexts.

Notes

1. Following a cluster analysis, forty municipalities in the sample were chosen. For a detailed explanation, see the Technical Report (Hooghe, Vanhoutte and Bircan 2009).
2. It has to be noted that official population records only keep track of current citizenship status. A large proportion of immigrants (and their descendants), however, have acquired Belgian citizenship status and they are therefore no longer present in the official population records. However, a study from the Flemish regional government has demonstrated that these groups live in exactly the same communities as the ones who do not have Belgian citizenship status (correlation is 0.99).

References

Alba, Richard, Ruben G. Rumbaut, and Karen Marotz. 2005. "A Distorted Nation: Perceptions of Racial/Ethnic Group Sizes and Attitudes Toward Immigrants and Other Minorities." *Social Forces* 84 (2): 901–919. doi:10.1353/sof.2006.0002.

Allport, Gordon. 1954. *The Nature of Prejudice*. Reading, MA: Addison-Wesley.

Blalock, Hubert. 1967. *Toward a Theory of Minority-group Relations*. New York: Wiley.

Bobo, Lawrence. 1983. "'Whites' Opposition to Busing: Symbolic Racism or Realistic Group Conflict?" *Journal of Personality and Social Psychology* 45 (6): 1196–1210. doi:10.1037/0022-3514.45.6.1196.

Bobo, Lawrence D. 1999. "Prejudice as Group Position: Micro-foundations of a Sociological Approach to Racism and Race Relations." *Journal of Social Issues* 55 (3): 445–472. doi:10.1111/0022-4537.00127.

Bobo, Lawrence D., and Cybelle Fox. 2003. "Race, Racism, and Discrimination: Bridging Problems, Methods and Theory in Social Psychological Research." *Social Psychology Quarterly* 66 (4): 319–332. doi:10.2307/1519832.

Bobo, Lawrence, and Camille L. Zubrinsky. 1996. "Attitudes on Residential Integration: Perceived Status Differences, Mere In-group Preference, or Racial Prejudice?" *Social Forces* 74 (3): 883–909. doi:10.1093/sf/74.3.883.

Castles, Stephen, and Mark Miller. 2003. *The Age of Migration: International Population Movements in the Modern World*. New York: Guilford Press.

Citrin, Jack, Donald P. Green, Christopher Muste, and Cara Wong 1997. "Public Opinion Toward Immigration Reform: The Role of Economic Motivations." *The Journal of Politics* 59 (3): 858–881. doi:10.2307/2998640.

Coenders, Marcel. 2001. *Nationalistic Attitudes and Ethnic Exclusionism in a Comparative Perspective: An Empirical Study of Attitudes Toward the Country and Ethnic Immigrants in 22 Countries*. Nijmegen: ICS-dissertation.

Coenders, Marcel, Mérove Gijsberts, and Peer Scheepers. 2004. "Resistance to the Presence of Immigrants and Refugees in 22 Countries." In *Nationalism and Exclusion of Migrants*, edited by Mérove Gijsberts, Louk Hagendoorn, and Peer Scheepers, 97–120. Aldershot: Ashgate.

Coenders, Marcel, Marcel Lubbers, and Peer Scheepers. 2005. *Majorities' Attitudes Towards Minorities in Western and Eastern European Societies, Report 4*. Vienna: European Monitoring Centre on Racism and Xenophobia.

Dustmann, Christian, and Ian P. Preston. 2007. "Racial and Economic Factors in Attitudes to Immigration." *The B. E. Journal of Economic Analysis & Policy* 7 (1) doi:10.2202/1935-1682.1655.

Enoch, Yael. 1994. "The Intolerance of a Tolerant People: Ethnic Relations in Denmark." *Ethnic and Racial Studies* 17 (2): 282–300. doi:10.1080/01419870.1994.9993825.

Espenshade, Thomas J., and Katherine Hempstead. 1996. "Contemporary American Attitudes Toward US Immigration." *International Migration Review* 30 (2): 535–570. doi:10.2307/2547393.

Evans, Geoffrey, and Ariana Need. 2002. "Explaining Ethnic Polarization Over Attitudes Toward Minority Rights in Eastern Europe: A Multilevel Analysis." *Social Science Research* 31 (4): 653–680. doi:10.1016/S0049-089X(02)00018-2.

Fitzgerald, Jennifer, K. Amber Curtis, and Catherine L. Corliss. 2012. "Anxious Publics: Worries About Crime and Immigration." *Comparative Political Studies* 45 (4): 477–506. doi:10.1177/0010414011421768.

Fossett, Mark, and Jill K. Kiecolt. 1989. "The Relative Size of Minority Populations and White Racial Attitudes." *Social Science Quarterly* 70 (4): 820–835.

Gallagher, Charles A. 2003. "'Miscounting Race: Explaining Whites' Misconceptions of Racial Group Size." *Sociological Perspectives* 46 (3): 381–396. doi:10.1525/sop.2003.46.3.381.

Herda, Daniel. 2010. "How Many Immigrants? Foreign-born Population Innumeracy in Europe?" *Public Opinion Quarterly* 74 (4): 674–695. doi:10.1093/poq/nfq013.

Hood, Marvin, and Irwin Morris. 1997. "Amigo o Enemigo? Context, Attitudes and Anglo Public Opinion Toward Immigration." *Social Science Quarterly* 78 (2): 133–143.

Hooghe, Marc. 2002. "Watching Television and Civic Engagement: Disentangling the Effects of Time, Programs, and Stations." *The Harvard International Journal of Press/Politics* 7 (2): 84–104. doi:10.1177/1081180X0200700206.

Hooghe, Marc, Tim Reeskens, and Dietlind Stolle. 2007. "Diversity, Multiculturalism and Social Cohesion: Trust and Ethnocentrism in European Societies." In *Belonging? Diversity, Recognition and Shared Citizenship in Canada*, edited by Keith Banting, Thomas Courchene, and F. Leslie Seidle, 387–410. Montreal: Institute for Research on Public Policy.

Hooghe, Marc, Bram Vanhoutte, and Tuba Bircan. 2009. *Technical Report for the Social Cohesion Survey Flanders 2009 (SCIF 2009)*. Leuven: Centre for Citizenship and Democracy.

Hox, Joop. 2002. *Multilevel Analysis: Techniques and Applications*. Mahwah, NJ: Erlbaum.

Kunovich, Robert M. 2004. "Social Structural Position and Prejudice: An Exploration of Cross-national Differences in Regression Slopes." *Social Science Research* 33 (1): 20–44. doi:10.1016/S0049-089X(03)00037-1.

Law, Ian. 2002. *Race in the News*. Basingstoke: Palgrave.

Levine, Robert, and Donald Campbell. 1972. *Ethnocentrism: Theories of Conflict, Ethnic Attitudes and Group Behavior*. New York: Wiley.

Mclaren, Laura, and Mark Johnson. 2007. "Resources, Group Conflict and Symbols: Explaining Anti-immigration Hostility in Britain." *Political Studies* 55 (4): 709–732. doi:10.1111/j.1467-9248.2007.00680.x.

Mayda, Annamaria. 2006. "Who Is Against Immigration? A Cross-country Investigation of Individual Attitudes Toward Immigrants." *Review of Economics and Statistics* 88 (3): 510–530.

National Institute of Statistics. 2011. *Belgian Population Data*. Brussels: National Institute of Statistics.

Outten, H. Robert, Michael T. Schmitt, Daniel A. Miller, and Amber L. Garcia 2012. "Feeling Threatened About the Future: Whites' Emotional Reactions to Anticipated Ethnic Demographic Changes." *Personality and Social Psychology Bulletin* 38 (1): 14–25. doi:10.1177/0146167211418531.

Pettigrew, Thomas F. 1998. "Reactions Toward the New Minorities of Western Europe." *Annual Review of Sociology* 24 (1): 77–103. doi:10.1146/annurev.soc.24.1.77.

Pettigrew, Thomas F., and Linda R. Tropp. 2006. "A Meta-analytic Test of Intergroup Contact Theory." *Journal of Personality and Social Psychology* 90 (5): 751–783. doi:10.1037/0022-3514.90.5.751.

Pettigrew, Thomas F., Ulrich Wagner, and Oliver Christ. 2010. "Population Ratios and Prejudice: Modelling Both Contact and Threat Effects." *Journal of Ethnic and Migration Studies* 36 (4): 635–650. doi:10.1080/13691830903516034.

Putnam, Robert D. 2007. "E Pluribus Unum: Diversity and Community in the Twenty-first Century the 2006 Johan Skytte Prize Lecture." *Scandinavian Political Studies* 30 (2): 137–174. doi:10.1111/j.1467-9477.2007.00176.x.

Quillian, Lincoln. 1995. "Prejudice as a Response to Perceived Group Threat: Population Composition and Anti-immigrant and Racial Prejudice in Europe." *American Sociological Review* 60 (4): 586–611. doi:10.2307/2096296.

Raijman, Rebeca, and Moshe Semyonov. 2004. "Perceived Threat and Exclusionary Attitudes Toward Foreign Workers in Israel." *Ethnic and Racial Studies* 27 (5): 780–799. doi:10.1080/0141987042000246345.

Scheepers, Peer, Me´rove Gijsberts, and Marcel Coenders., 2002. "Ethnic Exclusionism in European Countries. Public Opposition to Civil Rights for Legal Migrants as a Response to Perceived Ethnic Threat." *European Sociological Review* 18 (1): 17–34. doi:10.1093/esr/18.1.17.

Schlueter, Elmar, and Peer Scheepers. 2010. "The Relationship between Outgroup Size and Anti-outgroup Attitudes: A Theoretical Synthesis and Empirical Test of Group Threat- and Intergroup Contact Theory." *Social Science Research* 39 (2): 285–295. doi:10.1016/j.ssresearch.2009.07.006.

Schneider, Silke L. 2008. "Anti-immigrant Attitudes in Europe: Outgroup Size and Perceived Ethnic Threat." *European Sociological Review* 24 (1): 53–67. doi:10.1093/esr/jcm034.

Semyonov, Moshe, Rebeca Raijman, Anat Yom Tov, Peter Schmidt. 2004. "Population Size, Perceived Threat, and Exclusion: A Multiple-indicators Analysis of Attitudes Toward Foreigners in Germany." *Social Science Research* 33 (4): 681–701. doi:10.1016/j.ssresearch.2003.11.003.

Semyonov, Moshe, and Noah Lewin-Epstein. 2011. "Wealth Inequality: Ethnic Disparities in Israeli Society." *Social Forces* 89 (3): 935–959. doi:10.1353/sof.2011.0006.

Semyonov, Moshe, Rebeca Raijman, and Anastasia Gorodzeisky 2006. "The Rise of Anti-foreigner Sentiment in European Societies, 1988–2000." *American Sociological Review* 71 (3): 426–449. doi:10.1177/000312240607100304.

Semyonov, Moshe, Rebeca Raijman, and Anastasia Gorodzeisky. 2008. "Foreigners' Impact on European Societies: Public Views and Perceptions in a Cross-national Comparative Perspective." *International Journal of Comparative Sociology* 49 (1): 5–29. doi:10.1177/0020715207088585.

Sides, John, and Jack Citrin. 2007. "European Opinion about Immigration: The Role of Identities, Interests and Information." *British Journal of Political Science* 37 (3): 477–504. doi:10.1017/S0007123407000257.

Sigelman, Lee, and Richard G. Niemi. 2000. "Innumeracy about Minority Populations: African Americans and Whites Compared." *Public Opinion Quarterly* 65 (1): 86–94. doi:10.1086/320039.

Smith, Tom W., and Glenn R. Dempsey. 1983. "The Polls: Ethnic Social Distance and Prejudice." *Public Opinion Quarterly* 47 (4): 584–600. doi:10.1086/268819.

Sniderman, Paul, and Louk Hagendoorn. 2007. *When Ways of Life Collide*. Princeton, NJ: Princeton University Press.

Snijders, Tom, and Roel Bosker. 1999. *Multilevel Analysis*. London: SAGE.

Strabac, Zan. 2011. "It Is the Eyes and Not the Size that Matter: The Real and Perceived Size of Immigrant Populations and Anti-immigrant Prejudice in Western Europe." *European Societies* 13 (4): 559–582. doi:10.1080/14616696.2010.550631.

Strabac, Zan, and Ola Listhaug. 2008. "Anti-Muslim Prejudice in Europe: A Multilevel Analysis of Survey Data from 30 Countries." *Social Science Research* 37 (1): 268–286. doi:10.1016/j.ssresearch.2007.02.004.

Uslaner, Erik M. 2011. "Trust, Diversity, and Segregation in the United States and the United Kingdom." *Comparative Sociology* 10 (2): 221–247. doi:10.1163/156913311X566571.

Verkuyten, Maykel, Jochem Thijs, and Hidde Bekhuis. 2010. "Intergroup Contact and Ingroup Reappraisal: Examining the Deprovincialization Thesis." *Social Psychology Quarterly* 73 (4): 398–416. doi:10.1177/0190272510389015.

Wagner, Ulrich, Oliver Christ, Thomas F. Pettigrew, Jost Stellmacher, and Carina Wolf. 2006. "Prejudice and Minority Proportion: Contact Instead of Threat Effects." *Social Psychology Quarterly* 69 (4): 380–390. doi:10.1177/019027250606900406.

Weins, Cornelia. 2011. "Gruppenbedrohung oder Kontakt? Ausländeranteile, Arbeitslosigkeit und Vorurteile in Deutschland." *Kölner Zeitschrift für Soziologie und Sozialpsychologie* 63 (3): 481–499.

Williams, Robin. 1947. *The Reduction of Intergroup Tensions*. New York: Social Science Research Council.

Policy actors' narrative constructions of migrants' integration in Malmö and Bologna

Sarah Scuzzarello

Governments have policies explicitly directed at the integration of migrants. This article addresses how policymakers and politicians privilege certain constructions of the social relationship between migrants and the majority society (expressed through narratives of 'integration'), while making it seem as if they were presenting facts in their policies. These constructions provide the justifications for adopting a direction in policy-making over other alternatives. This article sets to analyse comparatively how policy actors in two urban contexts construct migrants' integration through policy narratives and how, within this, they evaluate migrants as 'integrated' and 'non-integrated'. Through narrative analysis, the article sheds light on how migrants are positioned by political institutions within the normative order of the society in which they live. Furthermore, it shows that local policy-making is shaped by national citizenship regimes, models of steering, welfare regimes and stories about the nation and its people.

This article undertakes a comparative analysis of the reasoning and justifications put forward by policy community actors in two urban settings (Malmö in Sweden and Bologna in Italy) to legitimate their respective policies for migrants' integration. Specifically, it addresses two questions. How do policy actors define migrants' integration in the city of settlement? And how, within the identified definitions of integration, do actors in the policy community evaluate migrants as 'integrated' and 'non-integrated'? These reasoning and perceptions are analysed as narratives,[1] understood as 'diagnostic/prescriptive stories that tell, within a given issue terrain, what needs fixing and how it might be fixed' (Rein and Schön 1996, 87).

The analysis aims to add to constructivist debates in policy analysis that advocate the importance of narratives in policy-making (e.g. Kaplan 1986; Roe 1994; Fischer 2003). I aim to show how local integration policies exist in an environment characterized by different and at times competing normative narratives about a political space and its people. Integration policies are a good example to illustrate this. Questions about who is to be 'integrated' in the recipient society and the best ways to do so go to the core of important questions about society and its political system. Policy actors have to relate to these narratives in order to justify and legitimize their policies to the public.

The second contribution of this article concerns the debates about the relation between local and the national levels of policy-making. The analysis will show how local narratives of integration are intertwined with national ones, thus questioning the literature on migrants' integration that emphasizes the local level as being of more decisive importance for migrant integration than the national one (e.g. Penninx et al. 2004; Garbaye 2005).

The comparative element of the analysis will reveal a substantial range of possible narratives that are used by policy communities to address the social relationship between migrants and the majority society, expressed through a definition of 'integration'. Although both traditionally left wing, the two cities are characterized by different typologies of migration and they are embedded in different national contexts insofar as migration and integration regulations are concerned. The variations between the cases ensure that I have a relatively broad, albeit not exhaustive, range of narratives that could be used to justify the adoption of specific integration policies. A comparative approach is particularly useful for teasing out the often taken-for-granted assumptions about the criteria used by local state authorities for including or excluding migrants.

In the following, I argue that the study of narratives is important for understanding how policy community actors form integration policy agendas and thereby shape the political space available for migrants to be part of the society of settlement. Second, I introduce the case-study municipalities and outline the article's analytic framework. Then I present how policy community actors in Malmö and Bologna have perceived and constructed migrants' integration between 1997 and 2008. Finally, these narratives are analysed in relation to local developments and national politics.

Narratives and policy communities

People weave perceptions of social situations and observable facts together through narratives in order to make sense of reality and of their position in society. Since the late 1980s, several scholars working in public policy analysis have advocated that narratives are also elements of the policy process (e.g. Kaplan 1986; Roe 1994; Fischer 2003; Boswell, Geddes, and Scholten 2011). For example, Fischer (2009, 192) argues that 'when we examine communication in their everyday realm of politics and policymaking, we find people largely explaining things by telling stories'.

Policy actors' narratives about a policy problem tell citizens stories about the relations between citizens, between citizens and the state, between states, and so on, in politically selective ways that impact back decisively on the set of social relations that they describe. Through processes of selective appropriation of a few salient features and relations of an otherwise complex reality, actors in a policy community describe what is wrong with the present situation in a way that shapes its future transformation. Policy solutions are affected by how actors specify a set of claims about a policy problem that needs addressing, the causes of that problem, and the extent to which the problem should be addressed. In so doing, stories position groups or individuals at the core of such a problem description *vis-á-vis* each other and can depict one part as being responsible for the identified problem, while supporting another (Stone 1989; Schön and Rein 1994). This means that narratives are used, intentionally or not, by policy community actors to legitimize the existence of particular opportunities and define the boundaries of a community, where it begins and ends, who populates it, and which of their concerns are to be included and which are to be excluded.

Stories of integration

This article focuses on narratives about the relation between migrants and the recipient society expressed through stories about 'integration' constructed and made public by policymakers and politicians. I analyse how policy actors narratively construct migrants' integration, duties and rights, and what consequences these constructions have for the evaluation of migrants as more or less integrated in society. The space in which migrants operate is shaped by how integration is conceptualized. For instance, if policy actors emphasize the sociocultural dimension of integration, it is likely that migrants' claims to cultural group rights will have visibility and resonance in the public domain.

Narratives involve the positive or negative demarcations of the target population (Schneider and Ingram 1993). These constructions often resonate with deeply held perceptions by the public. While it is part of human cognition to value positively one's group and to attach negative valence to an out-group (Tajfel 1982), governments' attempts to make political capital out of group categorizations has political and democratic consequences. The entitlements provided to those whose electoral support is most needed and who are constructed as deserving of support, need not be distributed equally among the population. In the context of diverse societies, it is important to understand how the 'integrated' and the 'non-integrated' migrants are constructed through narratives because this sheds light on how migrants are placed by political institutions within the normative order of society. It informs groups of people of their status as citizens and of how they are likely to be treated by the government and the local state. This affects their understanding of what it means to be a citizen, that is, their rights, duties and obligations; it influences their perception of whether their claims and interests are relevant to society; and it shapes how they participate in society.

Malmö, Bologna and their national contexts

Malmö, a former industrial city, was the destination of labour migration until the 1970s, when it was ended by a governmental decision. Since then immigration to the city has been characterized by family reunifications and refugees. The financial crisis in the 1990s hit Malmö's non-Swedish population particularly hard. Migrants' unemployment, urban segregation and poor housing conditions in areas densely populated by migrants became major issues for the council, and are still highly prioritized. Currently, 40% of the total population of 305,033 (as of 2012) is either born abroad or has one parent who is born abroad.[2] Migrants tend to live in rented accommodations in the south-east part of the city. Unemployment in migrants is higher than in the general population, 27.6% compared to 14.1% for 2012, and the percentage of school dropouts is higher for young migrants than for their Swedish counterparts.

Bologna has been a destination of labour migration since the early 1980s. In the past fifteen years the migrant population has settled down, demonstrated by an increase in the permits given for family reunification and by the growing number of children born of non-Italian mothers. As of 2011, Bologna had a total population of 382,784, of which 14% are migrants.[3] The main problems faced by migrants are poor living conditions in allocated accommodation and the complicated national regulations to obtain a permit of stay. This forces thousands of migrants to live clandestinely for long periods, something that they can be prosecuted and repatriated for. Because of this, tension has grown between migrants and the police and social services.

Malmö is embedded in a national context of integration policies that is considered a model of a multicultural welfare society (Castels and Miller 2001). Sweden officially introduced the notion of multiculturalism in its immigrant policies in 1974 (Proposition 1975: 152). Following the principles of equality, freedom of cultural choice and cooperation, Sweden guarantees migrants extensive political and socio-economic rights, including voting rights at local elections and generous regulations for naturalization. Notwithstanding the emphasis on corporatism, migrants (as a group) have never achieved the same level of influence on the decision-making process as traditional corporatist actors, such as the trade unions. Migrants are not perceived as representing any social class or organization, and associations that work with immigration and integration have only been able to affect policies through public opinion formation (Spång 2008).

Since the mid-1990s, the Swedish model of welfare has undergone significant changes. It now promotes business-friendly policies that mobilize human capital, foster entrepreneurial spirit, and maximise regional and local comparative advantages (Schierup 2010). These changes have impacted on integration policies that now stress the importance of employability, entrepreneurship and ethnically run small companies, and see migrants as a flexible resource for regional economic growth. The onus of integration has shifted from being the state's responsibility in securing equal outcomes to one where the state provides equal opportunities for individuals to participate in society.

In Italy, Law 286/1998 regulates both the entry and the integration of migrants. Introduced in 1998, it opens up public education and health provisions to all migrants, regardless of their legal status in the country. It does not guarantee voting rights or ease naturalization procedures. Law 189/2002 on immigration and integration, which amends Law 286/1998, cuts the funding that the regions responsible for the management of social policies – including integration policies – can benefit from. It therefore restricts migrants' opportunities for integration, particularly in those regions that do not prioritize it as a policy area. Migrants are the target of hostile rhetoric used by prominent public figures that has given legitimacy to anti-immigration sentiments by parts of the Italian population (Ambrosini 2013). The region Emilia Romagna, where Bologna is located, is an exception in the Italian context. It has established regional representative bodies for migrants and promoted the formation of similar bodies at the municipal level. The region has also advocated the introduction of voting rights for non-EU nationals and shorter naturalization procedures.

Method

In order to reconstruct which narratives about integration are adopted by policy actors and how, within this, they construct the 'integrated' and the 'non-integrated' migrant, I conducted fifteen semi-structured interviews in each city with key politicians and policymakers.[4] All the interviewees were important actors in the development and implementation of integration policies in each city between 1997 and 2008, the time span of this article. In addition, for each municipality I have analysed policy papers issued between 1997 and 2008 concerning migrants' integration. This comprehensive material allows me to identify a substantial range of possible narratives of integration. The long time span ensures that the narratives presented are characterized by a significant continuity and that they have potentially played an important role in shaping policy measures.

To identify and analyse systematically the narratives in the data, I rely on an interpretative approach, meaning that the present inquiry aims at interpreting intentions and meaning in context (Fischer 2003; 2009). Narratives are forms of discourse with a plot presenting a beginning, middle and end, and which order events chronologically. To structure instances of stories that I have identified in the data, I was inspired by Franzosi's (1998) idea of 'semantic grammar' and Kaplan's (1993) understanding of narrative structure. I have broken down the structures of narratives into six elements: *agent* (who utters the narrative); *act* (what is narrated); *scene* (when and where is the narrative expressed); *agency* (how is the narrative used in public forums); *purpose* (why – the justification of the narrative); and *object* (for/against whom is the narrative expressed). These elements bestow narratives with an evaluative dimension that enables the speaker to selectively appropriate elements of the sociopolitical environment to construct a certain narrative. When speaking about 'integration', policy actors (*agents*) will selectively appropriate happenings in society (*act and scene*, e.g. ageing population; need to replenish sectors of the labour market), arrange them in some order (*agency and purpose*, e.g. because of ageing population and labour shortages there is a need for increased migration) and normatively evaluate these arrangements (*purpose and object*, e.g. migrants employed in specific sectors are beneficial to society but, in order to avoid animosity with the majority society, policymakers may depict some migrants as problematic and non-integrated).

The article wants to shed light on norms and relations of power expressed in stories, for instance the inclusion of the concerns of some and the exclusion of others; and the distribution of responsibility, causality and blame. These are more clearly expressed in narratives that have informed policy interventions. I focus on these stories and I do not include counter-narratives (Andrews 2007) or negative cases (Flick 2002). This does not mean that the narratives presented are static, however. Policy actors contest narratives and emphasize different plots, or aspects, of a narrative. For instance, while policy actors in Malmö narratively construct 'integration' as participation in the labour market, they provide different justifications for this narrative. Employment is seen as a way of establishing bridging social capital, as an expression of the Swedish welfare state regime, or as a necessity to ensure tax revenues. The analysis will highlight the different plots within each narrative to bring forward their dynamic character.

Malmö

Policy actors in the municipality of Malmö adopt mainly two narratives to present the issue of migrants' integration. One depicts the 'integrated migrant' as participating in the labour market. The second presents migrants as an economic resource and as a comparative advantage for the city's development.

The 'employed migrant' narrative

The documents issued by Malmö council emphasize that paid employment is a means to foster migrants' integration in society. The 1999 Strategy Paper for Integration states that people's participation in the labour market is crucial for successful integration (Malmö Stad 1999a, 20).

Six years later, the strategy paper for increased welfare, *Välfärd för alla*,[5] underlined that the first objective to be met in order to oppose segregation and social exclusion is that 'everyone who is able to work should do so' (Malmö Stad 2004, 1). Because employment 'has a pivotal significance for migrants' integration' (Malmö Stad 2004, preface), participation in the labour market is a key requirement that migrants have to meet if they are to be considered full members of Malmö. Unemployment is depicted as curtailing migrants' opportunities to participate in society and integrate:

> There are groups of people who are socio-economically deprived and who are strongly dependent on social benefits to make ends meet. Many are concentrated in particular areas of Malmö. The issue has therefore a clear geographic dimension. It has also a strong ethnic dimension because several migrant groups are particularly affected by this. ... Through economic independence... one obtains freedom, increased self-esteem and the opportunity to become engaged in several different social issues.... Paid work is a precondition for economic self-sufficiency, housing and safety. (Malmö Stad 2004, 1–2, 6)

The former councillor for employment and integration clarifies how employment benefits integration:

> The idea is that employment, and the autonomy that follows from it, provides a number of choices – you can choose where to live, which cultural expressions you want to adopt etc. ... If you give people autonomy, they can choose how to integrate... and they are then not pushed around by politicians. ... A lot of integration politics is traditional class politics, it is about having access to employment, education, material resources, contacts. (interview M2)

Policy actors not only justify this narrative by reference to autonomy and interaction with the Swedish society; economic reasons are also important:

> The low employment rate in Malmö is the main reason why the city has the highest level of benefit dependency. The high costs for this... constrain the possibilities for the municipality to make important investments in education and health care. (Malmö Stad 1999b, 4)

A policy officer reiterates this: 'Of course, there are financial reasons [for emphasizing employment in integration policies]. We need to do something to reduce the costs that the municipality faces. Employment is part of this' (interview M3).

The 'employed migrant' narrative relies on an understanding that employment leads to autonomy, self-sufficiency and well-being. However, full participation in the labour market is not presented only as socially positive. Some actors emphasize a strictly economic evaluative plot of this narrative and refer to unemployment as untenable for the municipality's finances. This juxtaposes employed and unemployed migrants. The former are constructed as active individuals, who can take care of themself and their family. Unemployed migrants are described as not contributing to Malmö, at least not in the way that a citizen is supposed to contribute to it, and they constitute a financial burden to the municipality. When migrants fail to enter the labour market, and thus fail to integrate, they are narratively positioned at the periphery of Malmö's society. This is expressed in the council's perceptions of the problems faced by young migrants:

> Today we see that migrants' children are overrepresented among those who drop out of school. Research has shown that these young people could face more difficulties than their parents in entering the labour market. The reason for this is that many of them do not have parents in employment to act as role models. They have also ended up in-between two cultures, their parents' culture and the Swedish culture, and find it difficult to identify themselves with any of them. (Malmö Stad 2004, 3)

Unemployed parents act as a negative role model in both socio-economic and cultural terms, making their children unable to break through the glass ceiling and become fully fledged members of Malmö's society. The opportunities for many young migrants to exit a situation of socio-economic deprivation are prevented not only by the fact that their parents are unemployed; they are also stuck in between two cultures and confused by the different values and mores of the Swedish culture and their own.

This narrative has given legitimacy to two types of policies (Scuzzarello 2010). The first tries to increase contact between migrants and Swedes through mentorship programmes. The municipality's urban planning strategy also aims to create public areas where migrants and Swedes can interact. The second type of policy relates to the economic aspects of this narrative. Since the end of the 1990s, the municipality has introduced a range of activities to get migrants into employment, at times as part of national regeneration strategies (e.g. the 'Policies for Metropolitan Cities'). These initiatives aim at creating new jobs by supporting the private sector and by providing educational and training programmes targeting the long-term unemployed, in particular migrants.

The 'cosmopolitan entrepreneurial migrant' narrative

The second narrative adopted by policy actors in Malmö presents migrants as an economic resource and as a comparative advantage to the city. Migrants who are in employment, who can easily negotiate between the Swedish culture and their own, and who have a large international network – and are in this sense 'cosmopolitan' – can

CITIES, DIVERSITY AND ETHNICITY

make Malmö more attractive to investors. The former head of the council's trade and industry office exemplifies this:

> The big advantage here is that we have a very young city... many migrants came here when they were very young, so we have a labour force in the city which gives us an advantage. The city also has an international competence... people from Malmö know many languages and cultures and this could be something private businesses can benefit from. (interview M4)

The same narrative is used in policy documents: 'Migrants are a necessary resource in order to meet the labour shortages created by a strong economic development and in order to foster the creativity and entrepreneurship needed to support such a development' (Malmö Stad 1999b, 3).

Migrants constitute a significant resource for the city's well-being. In particular, the second generation is considered as having the advantage of being multilingual and multicultural:

> 45% of pupils in Malmö have their background in other countries.... A diverse population is a prerequisite for Malmö's successful development.... Children's knowledge and experiences should be valued even if they come from other religions and cultures. (Malmö Stad 1999a, 19, 25)

Migrants' international social network, and language and cultural skills position them as the ideal cosmopolitan – a clear asset in the contemporary globalized economy. Notably, in celebrating their diversity as a business resource, policy actors maintain the perception that differences between migrants and Swedes are natural and unchangeable (Scuzzarello 2008).

To implement the 'cosmopolitan migrant' narrative, the council has funded a number of initiatives to recognize the qualifications and skills gained outside of Sweden. Between 2001 and 2002 it funded a programme (*Akademikerintroduktionen*) to support highly educated, newly arrived migrants. Since 2003, it has also co-funded MINE, a not-for-profit organization that aims to increase ethnic diversity in Malmö's private businesses.

Bologna

Policy actors in Bologna construct 'integration' mainly according to three narratives. The first presents migrants with a valid permit of stay as economic resources for the city. The second stresses the importance of migrants' political participation on equal terms to Italians. The third positions migrants as a potential security threat. As in Malmö, these narratives present different plots that position migrants differently in relation to the recipient society.

'Migrants as economic resources' narrative

In the late 1990s, policy actors depicted migrants as a potential resource for the city, although it was not clear how migrants could contribute to Bologna's society.

CITIES, DIVERSITY AND ETHNICITY

The Municipality of Bologna believes that differences (individual, social, cultural, ethnic) are of great value and resource to society (Comune di Bologna 1998, in Pero' 2005, 839).

Ten years later, this narrative gained visibility. The 2008 yearly report from the Intercultural Integration Service states: 'The different linguistic, cultural, professional and relational qualifications of migrants and autochthonous are... something we should value' (Comune di Bologna 2008, 4). Migrants' cultural diversity is not the only valued aspect. Migrants are necessary for the city's socio-economic well-functioning. A union representative stresses their importance in the care sector: 'The municipality provides good elderly care, but it's not enough. That's why [migrant] carers are of fundamental importance' (interview Bo1).

A senior policy officer draws attention to migrants' role in the city's changing demographic and urban profile:

> Bologna's demographic development is clear: the autochthonous population is decreasing and the migrant population is rising. So it's clear that even if there is a demographic decline, this is contained by migratory flows. ... There has been some resistance obviously, but I think that [migration] brings significant advantages. For instance, family-run mini-markets have reappeared in the city centre... they disappeared for many years and the city centre was like a desert... they disappeared because the big supermarkets made them not profitable, which is true, but these economic parameters seem to be good enough for the families who arrive here and re-open these shops. From a service-perspective, this changes a lot for the city because to have a mini-market down the road and which is open till late – something that has never happened in Bologna before – and that can deliver groceries to the many elderly people living in the city centre... this changes the way one can live in the city. (interview Bo2)

Policy actors cast migrants in positive terms and see them as necessary for the demographic and economic development of Bologna. The local and regional authorities support this through initiatives providing, for example, training for migrant care workers. The local authorities also collaborate with the agricultural sector to simplify the employment of seasonal migrant workers, and they support migrant entrepreneurs to start their own business. This narrative does not only evaluate migrants' contributions to society positively. Migrants are generally employed in occupations that Italians no longer want. This has led some actors – mainly in the private sector, although not exclusively – to argue that migrants have better employment opportunities than Italians. The local representative of the Italian employers' federation *Confindustria* illustrates this:

> A businessman is in the weakest position. It seems strange but that's how it is because it's only migrants who would do some jobs and you find yourself in a position where the Italians are very disciplined and are kept under pressure by the factory owner and the migrant is given a lot of freedoms according to his necessities. So if he has to leave for two months and a half he can do that because no-one could substitute him and an Italian would never be able to leave for two months and a half. (interview Bo4)

The plot of the 'economic resource' narrative illustrated above shows that this story does not only have positive connotations. Migrants can be seen as taking over labour market sectors at the expense of Italians. Notwithstanding its connotations, the 'migrants as economic resources' narrative implies juxtaposed group construc- tions, Italians and migrants. 'Integrated' migrants are constructed as those who are taking on jobs that Italians are no longer willing to do, such as running mini- markets. They are portrayed as being satisfied with small economic returns. Italians, on the other hand, are described as either disciplined and allegedly unable to claim the same benefits as migrants, or as beneficiaries of the services provided by migrants, for example care or grocery delivery.

The 'participating migrant' narrative

Policy actors in Bologna have long adopted a narrative of integration emphasizing the importance of migrants' political and civic participation:

> The issue... is how to create the conditions which would enable migrants who live in our city to access citizenship rights... The way to have a city in which people of different backgrounds and cultures can live together as citizens is to fully engage the migrant community in the institutional processes and in giving them social, civil, and political rights. (Comune di Bologna 1995, 20)

To this end, the council supported the establishment of the *Forum Metropolitano* in 1995 to guarantee migrants a degree of political representation in the council. However, it was hardly ever consulted by the council. While migrants were formally positioned as important actors in defining integration policies, and their cultural diversity was seen as a resource for Bologna, they were excluded from the council's decision-making process (Pero' 2002).

As Bologna's foreign population settles down, migrants are increasingly positioned as potential members of the Bolognese society, as illustrated in the 2007 document establishing the neighbourhood-based consultative bodies for migrants:

> The concept of 'people'... has to include all residents, with or without [Italian] citizenship, including foreigners who are living in the municipality's territory and 'who then have the same right as [Italian] citizens to address to the public institutions their needs related to their life in the territory' (Cons. St., Sez. II, parere 28 luglio 2004, n. 8007/04). (Comune di Bologna 2007, 2)

The policy documents issued by the centre-left administrations in power between 1995– 99 and 2004–09 strongly endorsed this narrative. The introduction of consultative bodies for migrants in 2007 can be interpreted as the embodiment of this narrative. As put by a senior policy officer:

> The message here is of fundamental importance. If I establish a council for migrants it is not just a technical thing. It is a significant starting point. ... It suggests a shared horizon, that is to say that the Bolognese society is something we build together instead of saying that you have to enter into an existing context to which you have to adapt.... These are two very different messages. The practical actions differ, one's feeling of

CITIES, DIVERSITY AND ETHNICITY

identification differs and the feeling of being part of a broader process or not differs. (interview Bo5)

However, these bodies have limited power to influence integration policies. They have no independent budget and their initiatives have to be channelled through and approved by the council. Furthermore, their input to the council's political and decisional apparatus is limited to particular issues concerning migrants and integration, and their participation in the neighbourhood committees' meetings is conditional to the council's invitation. Considering these limitations, they are a highly unsatisfactory solution and do not compensate for the lack of voting rights and the exclusion of migrants from mainstream political organizations.

The 'migrants as security threats' narrative

Policy actors who position 'integrated' migrants as potential community members only include those who have valid permits of stay and who do not engage in criminality. The others are constructed as essentially deviant. The left- and right-wing administrations in power between 1997 and 2008 expressed this, as shown by their respective programmes of intent:

> The Council must break the perverse links between clandestine migration and criminality. This can be achieved by giving a permit of stay to those who can demonstrate that they are employed and by regulating seasonal employment. (Comune di Bologna 1995, 17)

> Bologna is traditionally a hospitable city... but hospitality cannot be confused with blind acceptance of criminality. ... It is a fact that among the migrant community living in our city there is a high crime-rate. This is mainly due to the state of deprivation in which many migrants live. [Criminality] has to be opposed and fought against in an efficient way. (Comune di Bologna 1999, 8)

> The Council must focus on protecting the weakest ones by guaranteeing them full citizenship.... At the same time it must be clear that those who behave unlawfully will not be included. (Comune di Bologna 2005, 1)

This narrative positions migrants who live in Bologna without a permit of stay as lawbreakers and therefore to be excluded from the community. Its continuity reflects national tendencies depicting migrants as security threats (Ambrosini 2013). Left and right in Bologna emphasize different aspects of this story. The right-wing coalition in power between 1999 and 2004 linked criminality and migration. The correlated policy solutions aimed at repressing criminality and included the establishment of a Security Office, the installation of CCTV cameras and the appointment more municipal police officers. The left-wing administrations in power before and after, tended either to position migrants as potential criminals whose behaviour was explained through essentialist notions of culture and difference (Pero' 2005), or to emphasize issues of legality rather than criminality. The administration in power in 2004–09 introduced measures for the prevention of criminality among the economically deprived (Scuzzarello 2010).

CITIES, DIVERSITY AND ETHNICITY

Analysis – the local and the national

This article highlights the importance of narratives adopted by policy actors in shaping policy-making. Through the study of narratives about integration in Malmö and Bologna, I want to draw attention to the normativity of integration policies, that is what is valued in a society and who is considered to be 'different'. Second, the study aims to show that narratives adopted by a local policy community are shaped not only by a local logic of policy-making, but also by national narratives and practices of integration that are incorporated in the logic of the nation state.

The local – Malmö as engine of growth and Bologna the hospitable city

During the 1960s, Malmö was considered a model of social democratic government as it brought together a flourishing industrial sector and an extensive welfare state. In the mid-1970s and 1980s, this changed partly because of the global restructuring of the industrial sector, and partly due to local demographic changes, as the middle class moved to nearby towns and the inflow of refugees increased. In the mid-1980s, Malmö found itself in the middle of a financial crisis that peaked ten years later. It created a window of opportunity for policy actors to introduce new visions and ideas about the city and the council (Dannestam 2009). From having been an industrial city, Malmö was to become the regional engine of growth and the council was going to be the key actor promoting it. Economic growth was presented as the precondition and generator of welfare.

These new narratives about Malmö shaped the council's stories about integration. As expressed in the 'employed migrant' narrative, the city can only grow if its residents are employed and secure tax revenues. The fact that parts of the city's population – migrants – are over-represented in the unemployment statistics is untenable. It is not only financially unfeasible, as expressed by policymakers who voice the 'employed migrant' narrative, it is also normatively impossible to maintain as the narrative of financial growth gains legitimacy among the public. The council's definition of integration in society as participation in the labour market became inseparable from the narrative of financial growth.

Bologna and the region Emilia Romagna are characterized by a high degree of social capital expressed in horizontal social structures and a high level of citizen involvement (Putnam 1993). The city is considered to embody the Italian left, having been run almost uninterruptedly by a left-wing majority since the end of the Second World War. This is expressed by the self-representation of Bologna as hospitable and inclusive, which has partly informed the positioning of migrants as having the right to take part in the city's civic life. The traditionally high level of civic involvement through the voluntary sector has also informed the establishment of bodies such as the *Forum* and the neighbourhood consultative bodies. In particular, the left-wing administrations have tried to promote multicultural integration policies that aim to foster the formation of migrants' organizations (Caponio 2005). Despite its legacy of social solidarity and political mobilization, reflected in the 'participating migrant' narrative, Bologna council has failed to include migrants in the local decision-making process. This is partly due to the limitations of national laws concerning migrants' political rights. It also suggests a lack of strong political will to translate a narrative of participation into practice. This and the positioning of some migrants as security threats indicate that migrants are generally positioned at the borders of the Bolognese society. They are only included if they can fill particular sectors of the labour market.

These examples show the strong normative component of stories in policy-making. As Stone (1989) argues, on the normative level, narratives position one group of people as the cause of a policy problem, for example lack of integration, financial burden or criminality. Unemployed migrants in Malmö and undocumented migrants in Bologna do not fulfil the most important conditions for participation and they are therefore narratively and normatively positioned at the margins of each community.

The national – political changes and national identity

Although the narratives presented here have a particular local dimension, they reflect political changes at the national level. There are variations in migrant integration policies at the local level that justify their study. However, these aspects cannot be decoupled from the national traditions of policy-making in which they are embedded. National integration policies are not just the result of cumulated local experiences; the two co-exist. The nation state remains the main frame of reference for migrants' claim-making (Koopmans 2004) and local integration policies are largely shaped by national repertoires of citizenship, model of steering and welfare regimes.

Following the financial crisis of the early 1990s, the Swedish government introduced structural changes in the organization and management of the economy and the welfare state. This resulted in the development of a business-friendly policy framework that stimulated entrepreneurship at the regional and local levels (Schierup 2010). Following the restructuring of financial politics, employment is no longer seen as the state's responsibility to guarantee revenues. It is redefined as full employability, and unemployment is framed as primarily tied to the individual's qualifications. In this perspective, individual work ethic and entrepreneurship function as instruments for community integration.

We can understand the support of the 'employed migrant' and the 'cosmopolitan entrepreneurial migrant' narratives in Malmö in the light of these changes. Full employment is the gateway to build solid relations between the majority society and migrants, but it also finds its legitimacy in the eyes of the public in the narratives of economic growth and change from industrialism. Hence, the primary threshold for inclusion that migrants have to overcome to become fully fledged members of Malmö is participation in the labour market.

Political changes in Italy have also affected Bologna. Since the early 1990s, the left has gone through a gradual ideological change that has brought it closer to centrist stands. This has led the left to emphasize issues of economic efficiency and rationality and also has implications for how issues of migrants' integration have been understood. Left-wing parties today tend to stress the economic benefits of migration, particularly in the care sector. The left in Bologna emphasizes entrepreneurship and economic efficiency, as illustrated by the 'migrants as economic resources' narrative. In addition, national left-wing parties have increasingly adopted a rhetoric that links issues of security with immigration. After being criticized for having been 'soft' on immigration, they are now framing their approach to immigration as being 'tough on crime' and advocating the implementation of preventive measures that position migrants, regardless of their status in the country, as a suspicious group (Pastore 2007).

Local integration policies in Bologna are also shaped by Italy's model of welfare. The Italian welfare state has a limited scope and it has traditionally relied on assumptions about the family and its gender and intergenerational responsibilities whereby women would care for elderly relatives and children (Saraceno 1994). Historically, the structural demand for care in Italy has been managed through national rural–urban migration. From the mid-1970s and onwards, the growing number of middle-class women entering the labour market as well as the rising standards in the quality of life, created a demand for carers that was supplied by international migration. In Bologna, located in a wealthy region that provided employment for women, this demand is particularly strong and it is therefore not surprising that the work of migrant carers is highly valued, as shown in this article.

Narratives about 'integration' also reflect national stories about the nation and its people. They create boundaries between the nation's people and migrants and define the thresholds for their inclusion in the institutions of the state (Wimmer 2006). The 'cosmopolitan entrepreneurial migrant' narrative in Malmö reflects stories about the Swedish people as socially progressive, tolerant of diversity and inclusive (Ringmar 1998). This representation of the Swedish people's collective identity depends upon its distinctiveness from other groups along relevant and valued dimensions. Migrants are positioned as bringing with them a cultural diversity that defines the cognitive boundaries of the host society. Their substantially different human-cultural capital can either contribute to their integration, if they embrace national values of democracy, tolerance and equality, or it can be detrimental to their participation in the Swedish mainstream society as they fail to participate in the labour market and end up between two cultures. A similar point can be made for the Italian case. The narrative about security in Bologna echoes narratives about the Italian national community that reject multiculturalism and present cultural differences as incommensurable. As Andall (2002, 400) argues: 'the very notion of the possibility of being both black and Italian remains a marginal concept within the broader framework of the contemporary immigration debate in Italy.' The question of national identity in Italy is not straightforward, however. There is a plurality of Italian self-representations, favouring the local over the national (Pratt 2002). The narratives discussed reflect this provincialism and relate to Bologna's hospitable character and strong sense of civic involvement rather than to stories about an Italian imagined community.

Conclusions

This article has shown how policy actors in two urban contexts construct migrants' integration and how, within this, they constructed the 'integrated' and the 'non-integrated' migrant. These understandings have been studied as narratives through which policy actors legitimize policy solutions and define the boundaries of a political community.

Through narratives, policy actors understand and express the meanings of the actions that take place within and around the organization in which they work. They provide the justifications and the arguments to implement policies by framing some events as problems to be addressed. These stories also reveal norms that are usually not called into play. Indeed, storytelling is made possible by the fact that people share a wider range of commonly accepted assumptions that seldom have to be questioned. Narratives about integration are particularly useful to identify these understandings because they demarcate the normative thresholds for migrants to become part of the recipient society. So for instance, in Bologna the 'integrated' migrant is expected to participate in civic life because of an assumption that the Bolognese are traditionally engaged in civic action. This also points to the relational character of narratives. Researchers can only understand the category of 'integrated' migrant by empirically examining its relations to narratives about 'non-integrated' migrants, as well as stories about the autochthonous local community (Malmö-er/Bolognese) and the collective national self (Italian/Swede).

By focusing on narratives in policy-making the article shows how the reasoning and justifications used by actors in the policy community are involved with relations of power. Depending on which narrative gains visibility and legitimacy in the public domain and which plot is emphasized, some groups' concerns are addressed while others' are excluded; responsibility for an issue is distributed; praise and blame are attributed. In the context of diverse societies, this has profound democratic implications. Migrants who are positioned as 'non-integrated' are more easily ignored – their needs not listened to or assessed, but rather interpreted by external experts. They are also easily blamed for wider societal problems such as unemployment and criminality and thus further positioned at the margins of society.

The narrative constructions of 'integration' are informed by specific local contexts as well as by national stories and practices about integration, the nation and its people. Hence, the article contributes to the debates advocating the continued importance of national narratives and political structures, while at the same time appreciating the importance of variations in the logic and strategies adopted locally to integrate migrants.

Future research could investigate how migrants and the majority society perceive and are affected by such constructions of integration as well as explore their understandings of integration. A comparison between policy actors' and citizens' narratives of integration would show the extent to which and how the former shape the space in which citizens (migrants and non-migrants) live. It would also tease out the different perceptions between the two groups. This would contribute to a more inclusive understanding of the perceptions and practices of integration.

Notes

1. I use 'narrative' and 'story' interchangeably.
2. This includes naturalized citizens.
3. It is estimated that additionally 10,000 migrants live in Bologna without regular permit of stay.
4. The interviews were conducted between 2007 and 2008 in Italian and Swedish by the author.
5. 'Welfare for all'.

CITIES, DIVERSITY AND ETHNICITY

References

Ambrosini, Maurizio. 2013. "'We Are Against a Multi-Ethnic Society': Policies of Exclusion at the Urban Level in Italy." *Ethnic and Racial Studies* 36 (1): 136–155. doi:10.1080/01419870.2011.644312.

Andall, Jacqueline. 2002. "Second-Generation Attitude? African-Italians in Milan." *Journal of Ethnic and Migration Studies* 28 (3): 389–407. doi:10.1080/13691830220146518.

Andrews, Molly. 2007. *Shaping History: Narratives of Political Change.* Cambridge: Cambridge University Press.

Boswell, Christina, Andrew Geddes, and Peter Scholten. 2011. "The Role of Narratives in Migration Policy-Making: A Research Framework." *The British Journal of Politics and International Relations* 13 (1): 1–11. doi:10.1111/j.1467-856X.2010.00435.x.

Caponio, Tiziana. 2005. "Policy Networks and Immigrants' Associations in Italy: The Cases of Milan, Bologna and Naples." *Journal of Ethnic and Migration Studies* (5): 931–950. doi:10.1080/13691830500177891.

Castels, Stephen, and Mark Miller. 2001. *The Age of Migration: International Population Movements in the Modern World.* Basingstoke: Palgrave.

Comune di Bologna. 1995. *Comunicazione dei componenti della giunta comunale. Indirizzi generali di governo per il mandato amministrativo 1995–1999.* Bologna: Comune di Bologna.

Comune di Bologna. 1999. *Comunicazione dei componenti della giunta comunale. Indirizzi generali di governo per il mandato amministrativo 1999–2004.* Bologna: Comune di Bologna.

Comune di Bologna. 2005. *Legalità e solidarietà per lo sviluppo economico, la coesione e la giustizia sociale.* Bologna: Comune di Bologna.

Comune di Bologna. 2007. *Approvazione del regolamento delle consulte di Quartiere dei Cittadini Stranieri.* Bologna: Comune di Bologna.

Comune di Bologna. 2008. *Attivita' del Servizio Integrazione Interculturale anno 2007.* Bologna: Comune di Bologna.

Dannestam, Tove. 2009. *Stadspolitik i Malmö. Politikens meningsskapande och materialitet.* Lund: Lund Political Studies.

Fischer, Frank. 2003. *Reframing Public Policy: Discursive Politics and Deliberative Democracy.* Oxford: Oxford University Press.

Fischer, Frank. 2009. *Democracy and Expertise: Reorienting Policy Inquiry.* Oxford: Oxford University Press.

Flick, Uwe. 2002. *An Introduction to Qualitative Research.* London: Sage.

Franzosi, Roberto. 1998. "Narrative Analysis – or Why (and How) Sociologists Should Be Interested in Narrative." *Annual Review of Sociology* 24: 517–554. doi:10.1146/annurev.soc.24.1.517.

Garbaye, Romain. 2005. *Getting into Local Power: The Politics of Ethnic Minorities in British and French Cities.* Oxford: Blackwell.

Kaplan, Thomas. 1986. "The Narrative Structure of Policy Analysis." *Journal of Policy Analysis and Management* 5 (4): 761–778.

Kaplan, Thomas. 1993. "Reading Policy Narratives: Beginnings, Middles, and Ends." In *The Argumentative Turn in Policy Analysis and Planning*, edited by Frank Fischer and John Forester, 167–185. Durham, NC: Duke University Press.

Koopmans, Ruud. 2004. "Migrant Mobilisation and Political Opportunities: Variation among German Cities and a Comparison with the United Kingdom and the Netherlands." *Journal of Ethnic and Migration Studies* 30 (3): 449–470. doi:10.1080/13691830410001682034.

CITIES, DIVERSITY AND ETHNICITY

Malmö Stad. 1999a. *Åtgärdsplan för att främja integration i Malmö stad.* Malmö: Malmö Stad.

Malmö Stad. 1999b. *Mål, inriktning och budget för arbetsmarknadspolitiska insatser i Malmö år 2000.*

Malmö Stad. 2004. *Välfärd för alla. Det dubbla åtagandet.*

Pastore, Ferruccio. 2007. "Se un delitto fa tremare l'Italia. Come si affronta una *security crisis.*" *Italianieuropei* 5: 1–9. http://www.cespi.it/PDF/delitto%20tremare%20Italia%20_Italianieuropei,%20novembre%2007_.pdf.

Penninx, Rinus, Karen Kraal, Marco Martiniello, and Steven Vertovec (eds) 2004 *Citizenship in European Cities: Immigrants, Local Politics and Integration Policies.* Aldershot: Ashgate.

Pero', Davide. 2002. "The Left and the Political Participation of Immigrants in Italy: The Case of the *Forum* in Bologna." In *The Politics of Recognizing Difference: Multiculturalism Italian-Style*, edited by Ralph Grillo and Jeff Pratt, 95–114. Aldershot: Ashgate.

Pero', Davide. 2005. "Left-Wing Politics, Civil Society and Immigration in Italy: The Case of Bologna." *Ethnic and Racial Studies* 28 (5): 832–858. doi:10.1080/01419870500158877.

Pratt, Jeff. 2002. "Italy: Political Unity and Cultural Diversity." In *The Politics of Recognizing Difference: Multiculturalism Italian-Style*, edited by Ralph Grillo and Jeff Pratt, 25–39. Aldershot: Ashgate.

Proposition. 1975. *Riktlinjer för invandrar- och minoritetspolitiken, Regeringens Proposition 1975:26.* Stockholm: Swedish Riksdag.

Putnam, Robert. 1993. *Making Democracy Work: Civic Traditions in Modern Italy.* Princeton, NJ: Princeton University Press.

Rein, Marin, and Donald Schön. 1996. "Frame-Critical Policy Analysis and Frame-Reflective Policy Practice." *Knowledge & Policy* 9 (1): 85–105. doi:10.1007/BF02832235.

Ringmar, Erik. 1998. "Re-Imagining Sweden: The Rhetorical Battle over EU Membership." *Scandinavian Journal of History* 23 (1–3): 46–63.

Roe, Emery. 1994. *Narrative Policy Analysis: Theory and Practice.* Durham, NC: Duke University Press.

Saraceno, Chiara. 1994. "The Ambivalent Familism of the Italian Welfare State." *Social Politics* 1 (1): 60–82.

Schierup, Carl-Ulrik. 2010. *'Diversity' and Social Exclusion in Third Way Sweden. The 'Swedish Model' in Transition, 1975–2005.* TheMES working paper 35. Linköping: Linköping University Electronic Press.

Schneider, Anne, and Helen Ingram. 1993. "Social Construction of Target Population: Implications for Politics and Policy." *The American Political Science Review* 87 (2): 334–347. doi:10.2307/2939044.

Schön, Donald, and Martin Rein. 1994. *Frame Reflection: Toward the Resolution of Intractable Policy Controversies.* New York: Basic Books.

Scuzzarello, Sarah. 2008. "National Security vs Moral Responsibility: An Analysis of Integration Programs in Malmö, Sweden." *Social Politics: International Studies in Gender, State & Society* 15 (1): 5–31. doi:10.1093/sp/jxn002.

Scuzzarello, Sarah. 2010. *Caring Multiculturalism: Local Immigrant Policies and Narratives of Integration in Malmö, Birmingham, and Bologna.* Lund: Lund University Press.

Spång, mikael. 2008. *Svensk invandringspolitik i demokratiskt perspektiv.* Malmö: Malmö University.

Stone, Deborah. 1989. "Casual Stories and the Formation of Policy Agendas." *Political Science Quarterly* 104 (2): 281–300. doi:10.2307/2151585.

Tajfel, Henry. 1982 (ed.). *Social Identity and Intergroup Relations.* Cambridge: Cambridge University Press.

CITIES, DIVERSITY AND ETHNICITY

Wimmer, Andreas. 2006. "Ethnic Exclusion in Nationalizing States." In *Handbook of Nations and Nationalism*, edited by Gerard Delanty and Krishan Kumar, 334–344. London: SAGE.

Social change and community cohesion: an ethnographic study of two Melbourne suburbs

Val Colic-Peisker and Shanthi Robertson

This paper looks comparatively at the process of social change and its impact on local community cohesion in two Melbourne suburbs, 'Northburb' and 'Greenburb'. The two localities are geographically close, part of the same local government area and both highly ethnically diverse, but considerably different in terms of their socio-economic and ethnic profiles. Based on ethnographic data collected through individual interviews, focus groups and participant observation in 2012–2013, the paper shows how the process of deindustrialization and the switch to service economy over the past decades took distinctly different turns in the two localities. Our data suggest that the processes of social change seem to have diminished local community cohesion in both localities. In Northburb, gentrification has contributed to socio-economic polarization, while Greenburb has lagged behind in socio-economic indicators and experienced ethnic fragmentation due to a considerable influx of new immigrant groups.

Introduction

In the social sciences much has been written about 'community', and more recently about 'social capital' – a shift in focus and terminology that is interesting in itself. Much of this writing has been focused on the issue of social connectedness and social harmony or conflict, often framed as 'community cohesion', and more recently conceptualized as a 'depletion of social capital' (see Putnam 2000, 2007), lamenting urban anonymity and social disconnect. High mobility, heterogeneous populations, socio-economic fragmentation and the pursuit of individual success overriding communal considerations in the context of modern urban living and global capitalism have all been cited as reasons for this attenuation.

A recent surge of interest in 'social cohesion' – a notion closely intersecting with community and social capital – comes mainly from ethnically diverse English-speaking 'immigrant societies' (Robinson 2005; Chan, To, and Chan 2006). Social cohesion usually becomes a matter of intense public interest after a flare-up in local conflict, such as incidences of 'urban riots'. For example, Robinson (2005) analysed renewed policy interest in community cohesion in England following street confrontations in three English cities in summer 2001. A renewed emphasis on social cohesion by the Australian government in the late 1990s to 2000s has been seen by many as moving away from the ideology of multiculturalism, which treats diversity as an intrinsic value, towards a new 'assimilationism', which sees social cohesion as being potentially threatened by ethnic diversity (see e.g. Parliament of Australia 1998).

In this article, we focus specifically on the issue of community cohesion, using a case study of two Melbourne suburbs. The two localities are geographically close, within the same local government area in the north of the city, but with considerably different socio-economic and ethnic profiles, and both in the process of dynamic social change.[1] Melbourne's cultural diversity and socio-demographic change were the key starting points of the study that this paper reports on. Over the past decade, Melbourne has become the main Australian immigration gateway city, receiving the highest numbers of overseas arrivals from increasingly diverse sources (ABS 2012). 'Greater Melbourne' now matches the 'super-diverse' London with 36.7% and 37% of foreign-born, respectively (ABS 2012b; BBC 2012). 'Greater Melbourne' contains 4 million people spread over 9990 km² (2011 Census) and is indeed a 'city of cities', composed of vastly different, but invariably ethnically diverse local areas and suburbs (Forrest, Poulsen, and Johnston 2003). We set out to explore what it is like to live in a Babylon-like city for the locally born, for long-term immigrants, and for those who have recently arrived.

Our conceptual focus, which we illustrate by empirical data, is the impact of social change on community cohesion in the context of suburban ethnic diversity. We identified different processes of social change in the two localities: in 'Northburb', they are best subsumed under the notion of gentrification; while in 'Greenburb', we framed the dominant process as 'ethnic fragmentation'. We initially approached our fieldwork with a simple and grounded definition of community cohesion in mind, asking our participants about their suburbs – whether they found them safe, friendly and good places to live in, whether they knew their neighbours and got along with them – and worked inductively towards an empirically informed definition that includes the feeling of safety, inclusiveness, friendliness and other features of a neighbourhood and a suburb. The result is presented in Table 2 in the concluding section of the paper.

Unpacking community cohesion and social change

The literature reveals that the concepts of social cohesion and community cohesion are neither clearly delineated nor uniformly defined. The concept of social cohesion is often applied to large 'imagined' communities such as nations (e.g. Markus 2012; Parliament of Australia 1998). On the other hand, Robinson (2005) refers to 'community cohesion' following the nomenclature of government policy documents in England after the 2001 urban riots. Kearns and Forrest (2000) use 'social cohesion' to refer to all levels, from national to neighbourhoods, while Amin (2002, 960) sees community cohesion as a concept tainted by its policy use in which quick fixes are sought in a quest for an unrealistic community consensus. Chan, To, and Chan (2006) define social cohesion as a societal attribute, placing emphasis on trust, sense of belonging and willingness to participate. The Australian Scanlon-Monash Index of Social Cohesion (SMI) posits 'five key indicators of social cohesion: belonging, worth, social justice, participation and acceptance', also pitched at the national level

(Markus 2012, 1). Policy interest in social cohesion tends to be explicitly or implicitly linked to cultural diversity as a potential threat to social connectedness and harmony. It focuses on the key questions: can ethnoculturally diverse communities be socially cohesive and under what circumstances? Relative to other English-speaking societies, Australia represents a 'high-diversity, low-conflict' case, arguably due to its continual economic prosperity and low unemployment, enabling new immigrants to integrate in a key structural economic sense. A bipartisan consensus positions a large, highly selective and skills-focused immigration programme as a necessary condition for this very prosperity. Unlike in the UK and many continental European countries where anti-immigration parties have a significant political presence, in Australia immigration is an accepted method of nation building, and diversity deemed its inevitable consequence. Policies are therefore focused on 'managing' the diversity. The key 'social cohesion' policy question is how ethnocultural practices that may seem alien, if not antagonistic, in the Western context, can be 'contained' and reconciled with the minority's engagement in the civic sphere (cf. Amin 2002; Ozyurt 2013)? The 'difference in values' and visible ethnic residential concentrations – in populist discourse often perceived as self-segregation – are seen as especially problematic, and policies are devised to counter it, such as 'social mixing' in dedicated housing (Robinson 2005), spatial dispersion and regional resettlement of immigrants, and various community development initiatives encouraging diverse residents to interact and learn about each others' 'culture'. Post-9/11, social cohesion as a policy issue is especially focused on Muslim beliefs and practices as incompatible with 'Western values'. Although 'marginalization' is habitually mentioned, what is usually missing in the prevailing public discourse on social cohesion is sufficient attention to the overlap of ethnicity and class, that is, linking cultural difference with structural disadvantage. We use the concept of 'community cohesion' throughout this paper, but in a way that detaches it from much of its political and policy usage. We reject the political usage of cohesion that consistently implies, yet explicitly denies, that diversity is a problem and assimilation the solution. We choose the term 'community' rather than 'social' cohesion because the scale of our research is at the level of the neighbourhood rather than the broader national space.

The second concept central to this paper is social change. We start from the assumption that urban social change (demographic, economic and changes to built environments) brings in unfamiliar people, practices, businesses and buildings, and that this has the potential to unsettle a local sense of community cohesion. These processes were intensely studied by the Chicago School of sociology at the time of the rapid growth of American cities early in the twentieth century. A concept 'invasion-succession' was introduced by McKenzie (1924) and used by Park and Burgess (1925) to describe local residential succession of one ethnic group by another. Precipitated by structural forces, a new ethnic group 'invades' a neighbour-hood – the verb implies a relatively rapid development – which prompts existing residents who find the co-location with the newcomers undesirable to 'flee' (e.g. 'white flight'), or they are gradually 'squeezed out' (e.g. if newcomers 'gentrify' the area leading to increased local housing cost) even if the co-location of diverse groups is not an irritant in itself. Hoover and Vernon (1959) proposed a related idea of a 'neighbourhood cycle', describing the stages of growth, decline and renewal of urban communities, in terms of residential density, local economic life, built environment and ethnic and socio-economic profile of residents. The key issue of policy relevance within this conceptual framework is to identify the tipping point when 'invasion' becomes 'succession', that is, when a neighbourhood cycle – typically occurring over a few decades, possibly faster today than in earlier times – is completed. Dynamic social change, including local invasion-succession processes, represents a time of relative social anomie: partial suspension and gradual transformation of erstwhile familiar norms. An influx of ethnoculturally 'different' newcomers requires practising genuine tolerance of difference and an acceptance of a degree of cultural relativism. The latter is in itself a form of anomie: rule-suspension and rule-vacuum as a discursive intercultural space where different and even opposed cultural narratives and practices can coexist. At the same time, this is a space of constant balancing, deliberating and tension. Social change increases the likelihood of tension arising in the power struggle between proponents of the status quo (in this context, long-term residents) and those who practise and/or advocate new norms and customs. These newcomers may be new immigrants, or new residents identified through class difference, for example 'gentrifiers' and 'yuppies'. The latter have more economic power and are therefore likely to 'take over' and establish new rules with little resistance, as is the case currently in Northburb. In Greenburb, with socio-economically horizontal and relatively marginal but ethnically diverse groups coexisting, there is more potential for anomie and interethnic tension. Portes (2010, 1542, 1556), chiefly analysing the US situation, argued that ethnically diverse immigration flows into developed societies had little 'change-inducing potential' on a broader trans-local plane especially in the 'deep' structures of values, class and power. He proposed that migration-induced social change tends to be more far-reaching in developing 'sending' societies than in stable developed 'receiving' societies. In contrast, Australian society has undoubtedly changed due to increasingly diverse and skilled immigration, from a remarkably homogeneous white-Anglo nation after the war, to an ethnically diverse one where a struggle for redistribution of power between the dominant (Protestant) Anglo-whites, non-Anglophone-background 'ethnics' and the indigenous population have intensified over the past several decades. For example, a 'multicultural middle class' has been created through skilled immigration post-1980, the social mobility of the second immigrant generation and the creation of a small core of urban indigenous middle class, with all these groups now visibly present in professions, business and public offices, alongside Anglo-Australians. This situation sharply contrasts with post-war decades when Anglo-Australians and British immigrants were separated from non-Anglophone immigrants in a segmented labour market (Colic-Peisker 2011; Collins 1991; Colic-Peisker and Hlavac 2014).

In the following sections, we situate these conceptual discussions of the intersections of class, ethnicity, community cohesion and social change within the local case studies of Northburb and Greenburb. We do not attempt to 'measure' community cohesion; rather, we examine it ethnographically in a specific context of diverse communities going through a 'neighbourhood cycle'. We first outline the methods and provide a statistical profile of the two areas using existing databases. We then draw on our primary data to present two different local patterns of the impact of social change on community cohesion: gentrification and socio-economic polarization

CITIES, DIVERSITY AND ETHNICITY

in Northburb and immigration and ethnic fragmentation, with elements of incipient gentrification, in Greenburb.

Method and case study profiles

Our analysis of social change and community cohesion is focused on the level of the 'state suburb', which, in Australia, is a precisely delineated area representing a unit of analysis in the national census. This enabled us to start our investigation by inspecting suburb profiles predominantly using 2011 Census data (Table 1). Unlike other smaller and larger census units of analysis, suburbs also have clear urban identity and a regular presence in everyday discourse.

Table 1 illustrates the difference in geography, transport connectedness and socio-economic profiles of the two suburbs. The geographic closeness of the two suburbs and belonging to the same local government area eliminated potentially significant local historic and policy differences. Our primary data collection included seven focus groups, twenty-eight individual interviews and four 'transect walks'. An introductory focus group that informed our subsequent data collection was conducted with local service providers, followed by two single-gender focus groups in Northburb and three single-gender focus groups in Greenburb. A focus group with long-term Anglo-Australian residents in Greenburb was held in response to their expressed interest. We sought to draw interview participants from a range of local resident groups along the variables of age, gender, socio-economic background, ethnocultural and linguistic backgrounds and the length of residence in the area. We spoke to local residents, business owners, service providers (e.g. local youth and settlement workers) and local officials (e.g. local councillors), and in several cases people who combined these roles. We also engaged in transect walks – participant observation guided by local residents (two in each locality). In total, over 110 participants from different walks of life and with different perspectives on local issues took part in our study. Interviews and focus groups were audio-recorded and transcribed, and the conversations conducted during transect walks were selectively transcribed. Photographic evidence was also collected during transect walks. In the following two sections of the paper, we explore the processes of gentrification and ethnic fragmentation in two localities *as processes of socio-demographic change*, using our narrative data.

Northburb: gentrification and socio-economic polarization

Over the past four decades, economic restructuring has shrunk the manufacturing sector and its blue-collar workforce in Australia, including in Melbourne, previously the manufacturing capital of Australia (Forrest, Poulsen, and Johnston 2003). Over the past two decades, Northburb has transitioned from a typical working-class immigrant suburb, where low-density housing coexisted with manufacturing employ-ment, into a medium-density middle-class 'multicultural precinct' that attracts new residents, especially young professionals, but also visitors and tourists. Until recently, Northburb's population was dominated by southern European immigrants (Italians, Greeks, Turks and Maltese), most of whom settled in the area in the 1950s and 1960s. During the late 1970s to early 1980s, a considerable number of Lebanese migrants

CITIES, DIVERSITY AND ETHNICITY

Table 1. Northburb and Greenburb, select comparative data from 2011 Census.

	Northburb	Greenburb
Area/Population size	6.9 km²/25,000	5.1 km²/12,600
Distance from Melbourne CBD	9 km	14 km
Public transport connection	1 metro train line; 3 tram lines; 6 bus lines	1 metro train line; 1 bus line
Individual median weekly income	AU$548	AU$362
Median weekly household income	AU$1,325	AU$865
Median house/unit price[a]	AU$604,000/AU$400,297	AU$393,700/AU$341,247
Unemployment	5.9%	7.7%
SEIFA[2] rank (Australia/Victoria)	6/6	2/1
Tertiary educated	29%	13%
Professionals (% of 15+)	30.8%	16.4%
Australia-born/English only spoken at home (% of population)	60.35%/53.4%	47.4%/32.5%
Main (languages other than English (LOTE) spoken at home	Italian 11%	Italian 18.4%
	Greek 7.3%	Arabic 10.6%
	Arabic 7.3%	Urdu 6.1%
	Turkish 2.4%	Greek 4.6%
	Mandarin 1.8%	Turkish 3.3%

[a] Calculated from the monthly sales information from September 2012 to August 2013.
Sourced: http://www.realestate.com.au

arrived. Since the late 1990s, new 'trendy people', we were told, started moving in, attracted by the then still relatively affordable housing and good transport connections with the job-rich central business district (CBD) and inner suburbs. Census data provide some reliable indicators of gentrification: the 2011 Census recorded 30.8% 'professionals' among Northburb residents, significantly higher than 12% in the 2001 Census and 27.5% in the 2006 Census (ABS 2002, 2007). Northburb has now surpassed the national rate of 21.3% and the Greater Melbourne rate of 24.1% of professionals among the population over fifteen years of age. Northburb has also reached average or above average values (with Greater Melbourne as the reference point) in key economic indicators such as income, employment, education and housing prices (Table 1). However, a closer look at the Socio-Economic Indexes for Areas (SEIFA) reveals that Northburb's population is atypically distributed and polarized, with an above-average proportion of both well-off (young professionals, the 'gentrifiers') and low-income residents (retired post-war migrants, students, casually and part-time employed people) (ABS 2013).[3]

The development of Northburb as a 'multicultural precinct', with its increasing variety of consumption options, has reflected changes in local demography. At the street level, the intense cultural diversity is often depicted, by residents and visitors alike, as a 'cosmopolitan feel'. Unsurprisingly, the most visceral type of cosmopolitan consumption – a variety of foods – seems to be the greatest multicultural connector. 'Consuming' other cultures in restaurants and shops may be a pleasant way of encountering 'cultural difference' and the 'Other', but this enjoyable and non-challenging aspect of diversity is reserved for those on a good income. Those on a modest income may find the close proximity of cultural difference more challenging: one respondent, for example, complained about having to put up with 'multicultural smells' from the neighbours' kitchen. In contrast to unreserved satisfaction of local politicians with the process of gentrification improving key economic indicators, local residents had mixed feelings towards social change in their suburb. Rising housing costs threaten to squeeze out long-term residents on lower incomes. In one focus group, a long-term Northburb resident described the impact:

> I've noticed the gentrification slowly. ... It's creeping into Northburb and I just feel like families and people of lower incomes... there're people that want to live in a house for a decent price and have a yard and a dog but it's getting less and less accessible I think. And people are getting pushed out to places like Craigieburn and Caroline Springs [outer suburbs] ... and that again I find isolating.

High residential mobility that has accompanied the rapid gentrification of Northburb has led to a break-up of relatively close-knit southern European working-class immigrant neighbourhoods, thus increasing urban anonymity and social isolation. This most keenly affects ageing post-war migrants. One middle-aged Anglo-Australian woman, a long-term resident of Northburb, deplored the loss of social transparency with new people moving in and the suburb going 'up-market':

> The businesses in the street, all the new ones, I don't really know... There used to be a shop there called Northburb Lighthouse... and the girl in there was just wonderful. I knew her and she knew the business of everybody in the street so if you wanted to know anything you just went in and asked her. She's moved. There's a hairdresser shop and he... and his partner live behind it upstairs and he's really nice but I don't really go in there much anymore because he's too expensive.

Another female respondent, a long-term resident, was concerned about densification and increasing anonymity:

> [T]here's going to be more high rises in the general precinct where I live because I'm right up near Sydney Road... Like, we're all trying to stop the one that's going to be built near me but I know that eventually it will be. ... It's just going to really change everything... the parking's going to be difficult, there's going to be more traffic in the laneways... really high density and really disconnected communities.

Gentrification is likely to gradually reinstate a level of socio-economic homogeneity at a higher level. At the moment, however, in the period of intense transition, Northburb seems to be a veritable 'social mix' – by default, rather than by a policy intervention – of older working-class immigrants, middle-income Anglo-Australians and incoming 'yuppies'. The lifestyles of these groups are quite different. We were told that in the past working-class immigrants knew their neighbours well and socialized in their homes, and provided mutual support through small-scale exchanges of goods and services, such as food from their gardens, childminding and transport. In contrast, incoming 'yuppies'

CITIES, DIVERSITY AND ETHNICITY

tend to socialize in public places, engaging in middle-class-style consumption. A man in his thirties explained:

> A lot of my friends live in the area and we do a lot of our living and just relaxing on Sydney Road... Sydney Road's reasonably priced with the Turkish restaurants too. Good food, good meal, belly dancer, and I think that whole area is known for things like that and I hope it doesn't change, but – you know

The middle-class gentrifiers tend to be devoted to professional pursuits that leave little room for spontaneous neighbourhood sociability; a reflection of what Gans (1962) termed the 'goal orientation' of the middle classes. Importantly, they do not need the everyday support of their neighbours. In contrast, working-class 'people-orientation' was marked by spontaneous local sociality based on mutual support as much as shared free time (Gans 1962). In the post-war decades, local factories, where neighbours worked side by side, were also loci of informal community development, as one middle-aged female service provider described:

> I remember when we used to have a manufacturing industry in this area. ... Just about everyone worked there, so it was, in a sense, probably a cohesion built around the workplace because... the work that was there and you probably didn't need to speak a lot of the [English] language to do some of those jobs.

Gentrification has brought in more individualistic people whose 'social capital' focus is normally not local. A middle-aged Anglo-Australian woman explained:

> In terms of neighbours... I don't have as great a sense of community as I did when I was younger in these areas. I find people a bit more individualistic. There's a few occasions where some of my neighbours are quite open and, you know, exchange lemons and this and that but it's kind of rare now whereas before it used to be the norm and the kids were on the street playing cricket and like.

A migrant 'gentrifier' in his thirties described high residential mobility and urban anonymity of a new high-density residential development where he had lived for 2.5 years and where he had 'really little contact' with neighbours who 'get home and they close doors and they don't talk to anyone'. Another migrant professional explained that several of his acquaintances moved to the same housing development but none of them liked it because of high turnover: 'The neighbourhood just did not work. ... They all moved out after a short time and one even sold at a loss in order to get out of there.' We were also told about positive aspects of gentrification: an increase in the availability of services and new 'trendy cafes'; traditional pubs frequented mainly by Anglophone locals becoming 'more civilized' places where 'one can take one's wife'; improvement in public transport connectedness; better public parks, where 'lots of used needles' used to be found before but now there are 'great children's playgrounds'. Overall, gentrification was endorsed by locals but not hailed as an unadulterated progress. The progress in economic indicators seems to have brought an increased socio-economic polarization and a diminishing sense of community cohesion. This was felt more acutely by less well-off long-term residents.

CITIES, DIVERSITY AND ETHNICITY

Greenburb: immigration and 'ethnic fragmentation'

Greenburb is a low-density suburb with key economic indicators considerably lower than Northburb's. The 2011 Census identified a high proportion of Greenburb residents outside the labour force, partly due to an above-average proportion of older people,[4] higher unemployment rate and much lower labour market participation of women compared to Greater Melbourne – 57% and 38% of women 'not in the labour force', respectively (ABS 2012b). After the war, manufacturing employment was available in nearby suburbs and hundreds of units of public housing were built in Greenburb to house workers and their families. Nowadays, this is an area with a residual amount of public housing and very few job opportunities. Like many other outer suburbs of Australian cities, Greenburb suffers from a relative lack of services and 'transport disadvantage' –locals told us about few public transport options and being dependent on cars. The main type of social change that we identified in Greenburb was a demographic transition– invasion-succession – caused by ageing and gradual attrition of long-term working-class residents who settled there after the war (Italians mostly, but also Greeks, Maltese and later also Lebanese) and the arrival of new immigrant groups, mainly of Muslim backgrounds (from Pakistan, India, Iraq and Lebanon) (ABS 2011, 2012b). A mosque and an Islamic college that opened in 1997 have attracted the latest intake, a considerable proportion of whom are secondary migrants. The recent arrivals are mainly skilled migrants, many with professional qualifications, but often facing barriers to successful professional transition and subsequently experiencing unemployment, underemployment and deskilling.

The most obvious process impacting on community cohesion in Greenburb was 'ethnic fragmentation'. We could identify four major resident groups: two older working-class groups of long-term residents – Anglo-Australians and southern European immigrants; and two younger and better qualified groups – a small group of 'gentrifiers' (professionals of various ethnic backgrounds attracted to Greenburb by affordable housing) and a larger recent Muslim intake attracted by lower housing costs and subsequently also by Islamic institutions, therefore arriving in a 'chain settlement' pattern. We noticed a relative separation of these groups during our fieldwork, an observation that was confirmed by a local councillor:

> [T]alking to one [Muslim] woman in Greenburb who had lived in other suburbs, she said to me that Greenburb was very divided… she said she felt it was very separate and segregated, like, there's the Italian shop… [and] the Muslim shopping centre… so there is a little bit of breaking down… There are various festivals the council puts on, then sometimes there're interfaith kind of activities… but it doesn't necessarily… it's not organic.

A long-term Greenburb resident (second-generation immigrant of Polish origin) who had recently moved back to the suburb was disappointed by the changes that she found, describing physical and social signs of community disconnect:

> It's also badly lit… Community shops, it looks rundown and dishevelled… At a café, at 3.30pm, the chairs are already up on the tables… The people who initially [in the 1950s–1960s] moved here were energetic young families, [they] had a consciousness…

CITIES, DIVERSITY AND ETHNICITY

a collective consciousness. They were all in the same boat about establishing a new house, moving a family. ...When I came back [to Greenburb] I started to say "hello" to people in the street... they would look at me horrified and some would just not acknowledge me.

An Australian-born Muslim man in his late twenties, a local service provider, offered his view on local community cohesion:

I think things right now are going fine but I do see a future where things can go wrong. Because, like I said, in Greenburb you do have quite a lot of Muslim people moving in because of the mosque and you do have a lot of Anglos moving out. ... They don't do anything, no one screams at each other, but there is still a bit of suspicion there. ... So the council tends to say "new migrants are just a bit shy, you know. Give them a generation or two and everyone will be getting along". Maybe that's true, but we can't wait a generation. And also, what happens if you end up like London where, you know, three generations down they are still not able to speak English properly and they are still living in... a ghetto. You can't risk that situation.

The flip side of Greenburb's ethnic fragmentation was seemingly strong intra-ethnic community cohesion. A group of older Anglo-Australians gathered around the local Anglican church told us that they were 'like an extended family and always helping each other'. Older southern European migrants told us that they tended to socialize mainly with their extended families and long-term neighbours, but their close-knit community was crumbling due to older residents dying or moving out of the suburb, while 'different' people replaced them in the neighbourhood. The new arrivals seemed to have formed close-knit communities of their own. A disconnect between southern European retirees and recent Muslim settlers was obvious during a men's focus group, where the two groups gathered at opposite sides of the room and told their respective stories without communicating with each other. Apart from the 'visibility' of many recent arrivals, which enables the established residents to identify them as the 'Other', older immigrants also tended to see the newcomers as people whose settlement in Australia is unduly supported by the government. This seemed to cause some animosity, particularly when these perceptions are contrasted with long-term migrants' own struggles. The following interview excerpt conveys a typical view, expressed by a retired Italian woman who had lived in Greenburb for forty-one years:

They [Muslims] are buying houses. They buy and even tear it down and build " palazzo" large houses. ... They must be bringing money from their own country. I don't know. Cars. They have everything. We are the poorest after sixty years in Australia. These seem already rich. ... I think the government helps them a lot. In the beginning they didn't help us. When my husband became unemployed [in the 1950s], St Vincent De Paul gave us $3 a week to buy food. (translated from Italian by a bilingual interviewer)

An older Anglo-Australian focus group participant believed that the government generously supported large families. He told us about a Muslim neighbour who 'only ever worked for months in the past eight years' and who 'doesn't even have to work because they have many children'. In contrast to these perceptions, many recent arrivals in Greenburb in fact lead precarious lives, experiencing unemployment, underemployment and occupational downgrading, and consequently also substandard and insecure housing and overcrowding. A Greenburb community worker explained:

> The new arrivals, the husbands probably, you know, they're professionals, they know how to go and find jobs, but they might not get them and they often end up taxi-driving. … The financial pressures are extreme because they're trying to establish themselves materially and have no income [and sometimes] they have no eligibility for [welfare] support.

Casual and low-skilled employment was an especially frustrating experience for professionals who were carefully filtered through immigration selection and consequently arrived with high expectations about their job prospects. During a focus group discussion, several professionally qualified Muslim men told us about their employment woes. One Pakistan-born man who held an Australian university degree told us about his work in low-skilled jobs – his current work as a courier was preceded by a factory job – and inability of employment services to assist him. In spite of his frustration, he was positive about the local community and nurtured good relations with his non-Muslim neighbours as well as with his Chinese Australian landlady. He strongly objected to the unjustified homogenizing of Muslims as 'one community' (cf. Parliament of Australia 2007) and emphasized ethnic, linguistic and religious differences between various Muslim groups. The Muslim men in the focus group were eager to discuss their difficulties in finding appropriate jobs and housing. One insisted that 'government should provide jobs once [they] brought us here [to Australia on a skilled visa]'.

The 2011 Census registered 24.4% of Muslims in Greenburb, compared to 9.3% in the local government area, 2.9% in Melbourne and 2.2% nationally. Catholics (42.6%) are a considerably larger religious group in Greenburb and Anglo-Australians still represent the largest single 'ethnic' (but not religious) group. Despite this, in a focus group discussion with long-term Anglo-Australian residents, we were told that they felt like a 'marginalized minority' and 'under pressure to sell their homes'. When asked about local issues they would like to discuss, their Muslim neighbours were the topic of the greatest interest. While the participants insisted that they were not only tolerant (e.g. putting up with parking congestion during Friday mosque attendance) but also welcoming neighbours, they complained about the suburb's shopping areas being of unacceptable standard, 'dirty' and not catering for non-Muslims ('they do not sell the usual things you can find in Australian shops') and Muslim men being disrespectful towards local non-Muslim women. The discussion focused particularly on alleged isolation and subordination of Muslim women, especially those who wear the niqab (facial veil). The retired Anglo-Australian residents argued that this practice seriously impeded interaction, which they were initially eager to establish with their Muslim neighbours in order to extend their welcome, and assistance if needed. Several elderly Anglo-Australian women reported having some interaction with Muslim neighbours, such as children dropping by after school to watch television, 'which they were not allowed at home'. The participants also reported instances of domestic violence in the neighbourhood and shared a view that Muslim husbands

CITIES, DIVERSITY AND ETHNICITY

were actively discouraging their wives and children from interacting with non-Muslim neighbours.

Local community workers told us a different story: about the widespread abuse of 'visible' Muslim women, especially those who cover their faces, by non-Muslims when the women venture beyond Greenburb. They therefore felt unsafe and were reluctant to leave their immediate neighbourhoods. In their recent Australian study, Salleh-Hoddin and Pedersen (2012) reported that 'visible' Muslims in Australia experienced more 'street discrimination' than any other group – being called names and being exposed to other types of disrespectful treatment in public places. In the face of such harassment, 'safety in numbers' is clearly one of the mechanisms contributing to ethnic residential concentration.

Discussion and conclusion

Juxtaposing our findings with previous research on the topic, an overview of elements of community cohesion is presented in Table 2.

It is not accidental that the terms 'perception' and 'feeling' have considerable presence in Table 2. Social reality is constructed, and people's perceptions, built through complex processes of social interaction and individual reflection, are key building blocks of the construct. In other words, in social life perception *is* reality; as Thomas and Thomas (1928, 571) famously stated, 'if men define situations as real, they are real in their consequences'. Therefore, a perception that a certain local group actively refuses to 'integrate' is as important as the 'real' motivation or reasons behind the inter-group disconnect; such perception can also become a self-fulfilling prophecy. The same applies to the perception reported above that recent migrants

Table 2. Local community cohesion: contributing and diminishing elements.

+ Contributing elements	−Diminishing elements
• Familiarity with the neighbourhood (many long-terms residents/low residential mobility)	• Unfamiliarity withthe neighbourhood (large numbers of recent arrivals; quick residential turnover)
• Feeling of local attachment and belonging; pride in the local community; 'ethnic pride'	• Dissatisfaction with the neighbourhood e.g. 'undesirable'neighbours
• Feeling safe, trusting other locals	• Feeling unsafe and threatened because of (perceptions of) delinquency and crime
• Perception of inclusiveness, mutual respect and fairness	• Feeling excluded; perception of unfairness, discrimination or socio-economic marginalization
• Neighbourly help: local, informal supportive networks	• Lack of local, informal supportive networks
• Local participation (commercial, community/informal, civic/political)	• Lack of local participation; feeling isolated
• (Perception of) equality and cultural homogeneity/cross-cultural awareness	• (Perception of) inequality and cultural diversity/lack of cross-cultural understanding
• Good local services (education, health, shopping, transport)	• Lack of local services

receive much assistance from the government, which does not correspond to reality but can nonetheless cause resentment and antagonism towards neighbours through a perception of unfairness.

Our study identified two different sets of factors potentially diminishing local community cohesion, one class-embedded and the other ethnicity-embedded. In some instances, both sets of factors seemed to be at work. Our data indicate that, overall, long-term residents of both Northburb and Greenburb perceived a degree of loss of familiar and supportive neighbourhood networks. It should be kept in mind that long-term residents may view the past of their suburbs through rose-tinted glasses. We are also aware that in contemporary urban settings communities are embedded in many different bases and formed through different media, and perhaps least of all on the basis of spatial propinquity. Yet, a degree of local community cohesion and 'local belonging' seems to remain important for the well-being of (sub)urban dwellers (Kelly et al. 2012, 21; Quinn 2013). The rapid social change with a strong element of demographic invasion-succession is currently a definite dampener of the local community cohesion in both localities. Rapid gentrification meant the increasing local domination of 'invading' middle classes, especially younger professionals, and an increasing prominence of consumption lifestyle in Northburb. Economic dynamism and spatial mobility, the key ingredients of gentrification in post-industrial cities, are generally seen as desirable. However, we learned that a rise in conventional economic indicators such as average income and dwelling size and price negatively affected lower-income locals, especially those on fixed incomes such as retirees and welfare recipients. This aligns with Zukin's (1998, 835) proposition that gentrification and its subsequent consumption patterns drive 'a wedge between urban social classes'. Typically, as exemplified by our case study locality, gentrification unfolds in the context of a latent, and occasionally also manifest, conflict of commercial and community, public and private interests. In gentrified areas, commercial service provision tends to replace self-help arrangements that previously connected neighbours. This leads to the marginalization of those unable to keep up with the rising cost of living and the pace of consumption.

The ethnic fragmentation in the second case study locality could be seen as a consequence of increased ethnic diversity (cf. Forrest, Poulsen, and Johnston 2003, 500) and co-location of ethnic groups who follow different religious customs. This process has become more noticeable after the recent 'invasion' of Muslim residents, but a degree of local ethnic fragmentation existed before between southern European post-war migrants and local Anglo-Australians. The economically precarious position of elderly residents on modest government pensions and new residents facing employment problems may exacerbate the tension created by the perception and practising of 'cultural difference'. In an environment of 'restricted consumption' such as Greenburb, a relative exclusion from the societal norm of consumption and competition may motivate locals to nurture informal community solidarity and networks of care, but, particularly in anonymous (sub)urban environments of large cities, it can also lead to social pathologies that make practising good neighbourliness a difficult task.

However, due to strong intra-ethnic bonds, Greenburb also resembled 'positive' cases of diversity, such as the relatively disadvantaged Manhattan Latino neighbourhood of Washington Heights, recently reported as having better health indicators than the general population despite low socio-economic indicators (Quinn 2013). This has been attributed to 'ethnic pride', local connectedness and a relative lack of the status anxiety that plagues mainstream America. The researchers argue, and we tend to agree, that 'there's increasing evidence that neighbourhoods do really matter in terms of health of residents' – and that an 'ethnic enclave' can be a good place to live (Quinn 2013). Portes (2010, 1546) argued that successful ethnic enclaves are temporary; they 'naturally' dissolve through mobility of the second- and third-generation immigrants. However, the social mobility of descendants seems to largely depend on the successful economic integration of immigrant parents. Due to the full employment and strong ethnic communities of working-class southern Europeans in post-war Australia, their children experienced social mobility; they profited from a 'protective ethnic enclave' effect. How this is going to turn out for recently arrived Muslims remains to be seen; its application in this particular case may be hampered by the fact that a 'Muslim enclave' has a special status in the post-9/11 Western public consciousness, causing considerable anxiety (Poynting et al. 2004). This anxiety, fuelled by the perception of unbridgeable cultural difference and a fear of Muslim radicalization, can develop into active prejudice and acts of hostility that may seriously impede immigrants' penetration into extra-ethnic employment markets and social networks. The economic and social marginalization increases the risk of radicalization (Hassan 2010), which then closes the vicious circle of social exclusion. Feeling threatened by the mainstream prejudice also means being precluded from developing 'bridging networks' in the wider society and therefore deprived of a crucial 'social capital' tool for social mobility. If immigrant residential concentrations do not gradually dissolve through 'spatial assimilation', primarily via social mobility of the second generation, a disconnect from the wider society may lead to gradual degeneration of residential concentrations into long-term disadvantaged enclaves. This phenomenon has been relatively unremarkable in the Australian cities where levels of spatial assimilation of immigrants have been higher than in the UK and the USA (Forrest, Poulsen, and Johnston 2003; Jupp 2002; Johnston, Poulsen, and Forrest 2007). For recently arrived Muslim immigrants, this process hinges on an immediate need for a 'protective enclave' and the seriousness of structural barriers in their path to integration, which requires further research.

Diminished community cohesion in both case study localities may be an unsurprising consequence of rapid social change, with invasion-succession creating 'transitional neighbourhoods', which by definition cannot be highly cohesive. The local processes of social change reflect broader structural processes and imperatives. The latter, embedded in a neo-liberal logic, may work against 'social cities' in general, giving undisputed primacy to 'hard' economic over 'soft' social indicators. However, there are signs that social indicators, including those of community cohesion, are gaining more prominence (see Stiglitz, Sen, and Fitoussi 2010, 51). In this context, we hope to have contributed to the understandings of community cohesion and social change at a local level, applicable to Australian and other Western immigrant-receiving cities of the early twenty-first century.

Acknowledgements

We are grateful to the City of Moreland for their in-kind support for the project. We also thank two anonymous reviewers for their useful comments on the earlier drafts of this paper.

Funding

The research project (Housing and employment for social cohesion in multicultural neighbourhoods 'in transition': building local best practice, 2012/2013) that this paper reports on was funded by the Scanlon Foundation, Melbourne.

Notes

1. We consider social change to be ubiquitous and constant in the modern urban contexts. The attribute 'dynamic' denotes the social change that affects the character of a local area within a span of a couple of decades and is therefore part of the lived experience of locals, featuring in everyday narratives of 'changed' local life.
2. First decile means the most disadvantaged (bottom 10% of the distribution, taking into account a range of socio-economic indicators) and 10th decile covers the most advantaged (top 10%).
3. SEIFA (ABS 2008) consists of several indexes that, when combined, provide a more nuanced profile of the area. For example, Northburb has a good score on the Index of Education and Occupation (8/8) and Index of Relative Socio-economic Advantage and Disadvantage (7/7) but a less favourable score on the Index of Relative Socio-economic Disadvantage (5/4). The combined reading of these scores indicates that Northburb may have a high number of well-educated people on low incomes (e.g. students, casually employed professionals) and a considerable number of older residents on low incomes, alongside well-off 'gentrifiers'.
4. The 2011 Census registered 1,239 people aged seventy to eighty (9.8%) and 969 people aged over eighty (7.7%) in Greenburb. Respective figures for the State of Victoria are 5.9% and 4.1%.

References

ABS (Australian Bureau of Statistics). 2002. *2001 Census Quickstats: Coburg (state suburb)*. Canberra: The Australian Bureau of Statistics.

ABS. 2007. *2006 Census Quickstats: Coburg (State Suburb)*. Canberra: The Australian Bureau of Statistics.

ABS. 2008. *City of Moreland, SEIFA index of relative socio-economic disadvantage, 2006*. Canberra: The Australian Bureau of Statistics. Cat no. 2033.0.55.001, SEIFA, data only, 2006.

ABS. 2011. *2011 Census of population and housing, Fawkner* (table B10). Canberra: The Australian Bureau of Statistics. Country of birth of persons by year of arrivals in Australia.

ABS. 2012. *Overseas arrivals and departures, Australia*. Canberra: The Australian Bureau of Statistics. Cat. 3401.0, Oct 2012.

ABS. 2012a. '*Cultural Diversity in Australia*', *Reflecting a Nation: Stories from the 2011 Census, 2012–2013*. Canberra: The Australian Bureau of Statistics. Cat. 2071.0, June 2012.

ABS. 2012b. *Basic Community Profiles*. Canberra: The Australian Bureau of Statistics. 2011 Census Quickstats.

ABS. 2013. *Census of population and housing, socio-economic indexes for areas (SEIFA).* State suburb indexes, Data Cube only, Cat. 2033.0.55.001, 2011.

Amin, Ash. 2002. "Ethnicity and the Multicultural City: Living with Diversity." *Environment and Planning A* 34: 959–980. doi:10.1068/a3537.

BBC. 2012. "Census Shows Rise in Foreign-born." *BBC News UK.*

Chan, Joseph, Ho-Po, To, and Elaine Chan. 2006. "Reconsidering Social Cohesion: Developing a Definition and Analytical Framework for Empirical Research." *Social Indicators Research* 75 (2): 273–302. doi:10.1007/s11205-005-2118-1.

Colic-Peisker, Val. 2011. "A New Era in Australian Multiculturalism? From Working-class 'Ethnics' to a 'Multicultural Middle-class.'" *International Migration Review* 45 (3): 561–586. doi:10.1111/j.1747-7379.2011.00858.x.

Colic-Peisker, Val, and Jim Hlavac. 2014. "Anglo-Australian and Non-Anglophone Middle Classes: 'Foreign Accent' and Social Inclusion." *Journal of Social Issues* 49 (3).

Collins, Jock. 1991. *Migrant Hands in a Distant Land: Australia's Post-war Immigration.* 2nd ed. Leichardt: Pluto Press.

Forrest, James, Michael Poulsen, and Ron Johnston. 2003. "Everywhere Different? Globalisation and the Impact of International Migration on Sydney and Melbourne." *Geoforum* 34 (4): 499–510. doi:10.1016/S0016-7185(03)00027-7.

Gans, Herbert. 1962. *The Urban Villagers.* New York: The Free Press.

Hassan, Riaz. 2010. "Socio-economic Marginalisation of Muslims in Contemporary Australia: Implications for Social Inclusion." *Journal of Muslim Minority Affairs* 30: 575–584. doi:10.1080/13602004.2010.533455.

Hoover, Edgar M., and Raymond Vernon. 1959. *Anatomy of a Metropolis.* Cambridge, MA: Harvard University Press.

Johnston, Ron, Michael Poulsen, and James Forrest. 2007. "The Geography of Ethnic Residential Segregation: A Comparative Study of Five Countries." *Annals of the Association of American Geographers* 97 (4): 713–738. doi:10.1111/j.1467-8306.2007.00579.x.

Jupp, James. 2002. *From White Australia to Woomera: The Story of Australian Immigration.* Melbourne: Cambridge University Press.

Kearns, Ade, and Ron Forrest. 2000. "Social Cohesion and Multilevel Urban Governance." *Urban Studies* 37 (5/6): 995–1017.

Kelly, Jane-Frances, P. Breadon, C. Davis, A. Hunter, P. Mares, D. Mullerworth, and B. Weidmann. 2012. *Social Cities: Grattan Institute Report No. 2012–4.* Melbourne: Grattan Institute.

McKenzie, Roderick D. 1924. "The Ecological Approach to the Study of the Human Community." *American Journal of Sociology* 30: 287–301. doi:10.1086/213698.

Markus, Andrew. 2012. *SMI: The Scanlon-Monash Index of Social Cohesion.* Fact Sheet 1. October 2012002E.

Ozyurt, Saba S. 2013. "The Selective Integration of Muslims Immigrant Women in the United States: Explaining Islam's Paradoxical Impact." *Journal of Ethnic and Migration Studies* 39 (10): 1617–1637. doi:10.1080/1369183X.2013.833691.

Park, Robert E., and Ernest W. Burgess. 1925. *The City.* Chicago: University of Chicago Press.

Parliament of Australia. 1998. *Immigration, Social Cohesion and National Identity.* Research Paper No. 1 1997–98, by Prof. Robert Holton. Canberra: Government of the Commonwealth of Australia.

Parliament of Australia. 2007. *Muslim Australians.* By Janet Phillips, Social Policy Section. Canberra: Government of the Commonwealth of Australia.

Portes, Alejandro. 2010. "Migration and Social Change: Some Conceptual Reflections." *Journal of Ethnic and Migration Studies* 36 (10): 1537–1563. doi:10.1080/1369183X.2010. 489370.

Poynting, Scott, Greg Noble, Paul Tabar, and Jock Collins. 2004. *Bin Laden in the Suburbs: Criminalising the Arab Other.* Sydney: Institute of Criminology.

Putnam, Robert D. 2000. *Bowling Alone: The Collapse and Revival of American Community.* New York: Simon and Schuster.

Putnam, Robert D. 2007. "'E pluribus unum: Diversity and Community in the 21st Century', The 2006 Johan Skytte Prize Lecture." *Scandinavian Political Studies* 30 (2): 137–174. doi:10.1111/j.1467-9477.2007.00176.x.

Quinn, Audrey. 2013. "'Latino Neighborhoods: Improving Health through Ethnic Pride?" *PRI's The World*, April 3. www.theworld.org/2013/04/latino-neighborhoods-improving-health-through-ethnic-pride.

Robinson, David. 2005. "The Search for Community Cohesion: Key Themes and Dominant Concepts of the Public Policy Agenda." *Urban Studies* 42: 1411–1427. doi:10.1080/00420980 500150755.

Salleh-Hoddin, Amiirah, and Anne Pedersen. 2012. "Experience of Discrimination by Muslim Australians and Protective Factors for Integration." *The Australian Community Psychologist* 24 (2): 43–58.

Stiglitz, Joseph E., Amartya Sen, and Jean-Paul Fitoussi. 2009. *Report by the Commission on the Measurement of Economic Performance and Social Progress.* A Report Commissioned by the French government. http://www.stiglitz-sen-fitoussi.fr/documents/rapport_anglais.pdf.

Thomas, William I., and Dorothy S. Thomas. 1928. *The Child in America: Behavior Problems and Programs.* New York: Knopf.

Zukin, Sharon. 1998. "Urban Lifestyles: Diversity and Standardisation in Spaces of Consumption." *Urban Studies* 35 (5–6): 825–839. doi:10.1080/0042098984574.

Narratives of ethnic identity among practitioners in community settings in the northeast of England

Judith Parks and Kye Askins

The increasing ethnic diversity of the UK has been mirrored by growing public awareness of multicultural issues, alongside developments in academic and government thinking. This paper explores the contested meanings around ethnic identity/ies in community settings, drawing on semi-structured interviews with staff from Children's Centres and allied agencies conducted for a research project that examined the relationship between identity and the participation of parents/carers in services in northeast England. The research found that respondents were unclear about, especially, white ethnic identities, and commonly referred to other social categorizations, such as age, nationality, and circumstances such as mobility, when discussing service users. While in some cases this may have reflected legitimate attempts to resist over-ethnicizing non-ethnic phenomena, such constructions coexisted with assumptions about ethnic difference and how it might translate into service needs. These findings raise important considerations for policy and practice.

Introduction

The context in which people experience local community in the UK is framed by ever-changing global dimensions of migration. While migration to and ethnic diversity in the UK is centuries old, the increasing complexity of contemporary migration trends and the ethnic make-up of communities in the local context require dynamic and open approaches to issues of identity and diversity. The term 'super-diversity' is used to emphasize that diversity cannot be seen 'solely or predominantly in terms of ethnicity or country of origin' and to recognize the 'dynamic interplay of variables' within country of origin (Vertovec 2007, 3), as well as the greater number of ethnicities and countries of origin of people living in the UK and concomitant complexities of needs, demographics and circumstances. Indeed, the range of legal statuses found in any single UK locality in a given ethnic or national group, from British citizens to undocumented migrants, 'underscores the point that simple ethnicity-focused approaches to understanding and engaging various minority "communities" in Britain... are inadequate and often inappropriate for dealing with individual immigrants' needs' (Vertovec 2007, 17).

However, government responses to this increasingly complex migration and diversity in the UK have largely remained focused around issues of ethnic identity, and have influenced increasing levels of public awareness, and concern, accordingly. Policies tied to multiculturalism in the 1980s and 1990s were intended to celebrate diversity and difference through public cultural events, with ethnic explicitness promoted. However, key events including 9/11, urban 'racial disturbances' in the northern English towns of Oldham, Bradford and Burnley, and the London bombings of 2005, saw widespread condemnation of multicultural policy as creating and maintaining a damaging version of identity politics that increased segregation rather than improved community understanding (Phillips 2008). Critiques of multicultural-ism argue that foregrounding difference further entrenches essentialism within a capitalistic project, wherein minority groups must compete for increasingly scarce resources (Kundnani 2007), and that a lack of clear conceptual definitions of racism and disadvantage has marginalized anti-racism, unnecessarily, within the multicultural project (Berman and Paradies 2008).

These events and critiques saw a major policy shift to 'community cohesion' in the UK, which attempted to build communities with a common vision and a sense of belonging for all and bring diverse communities together (CIC 2007). While this cohesion agenda acknowledges difference across gender, age, class and so on, ethnicity is heavily foregrounded: policy rests on the premise that the integration of visible (non-white) ethnic minority communities – their inclusion and incorporation into wider British society – is desirable (CRE 2007). Alongside moves to a specific kind of 'cohesion', there has also been a critical shift in debate from the politics of race and ethnicity to religion and Islamophobia. Global discourses around the 'war on terror' have informed the increasing use of 'Muslim' as a label by the wider public, and religion has become a significant marker of identity for Muslims in the UK. However, emphasis on religious difference remains embedded in dissimilarity, moving not towards community cohesion, but the 'racialization of Muslimness' (Ahmad and Evergeti 2010, 1698).

These developments have heightened sensitivity around how issues of ethnic identity are discussed across government and agency-led interventions as well as at the community level, particularly in the context of rising support for the extreme right among some white British communities (Bottero 2009). Mas Giralt (2011, 332) comments that '[i]n Britain, the race relations system underpinning multicultural and integration policies has created an immigrant incorporation context dominated by a visual regime of difference and sameness based on racial and ethno-cultural cues'– with stereotypical assumptions about minority ethnic groups prevalent in community settings. For example, Phillips (2007, 36) points to 'the continuing association between black and minority ethnic segregation and deprivation' in the community cohesion agenda, emphasizing the racialized discourse about residential segregation in the UK that ignores the role of social class and lifestyle.

This paper explores the contested meanings around ethnicity in community settings, specifically how service facilitators and practitioners may strive to be open to more than ethnicity, in line with 'super-diversity' above, but at the same time express ethnicity-based assumptions and expectations about service need and use. We begin with the relevant literature, drawing upon work that conceptualizes ethnic (and other) categorizations as socially constructed and contextually contingent. This demands that we explore the central role of representation and language/terminology within processes of boundary-making and 'othering', and critically consider the validity of various productions such as 'ethnic', 'minority' and 'black'. This review includes the ways in which 'whiteness' as a social construction remains largely hidden in political and popular discourse, given the multi-ethnic dimensions to migration evidenced in this research, including white minority ethnic groups. We also briefly examine the difficulties evidenced in speaking about ethnicity in everyday settings, embedded in concerns about being or not being 'politically correct'. We then outline the research methodology that this paper draws upon, before discussing the empirical findings. We argue that respondents were unclear about, especially, white ethnic identities, and commonly referred to other social categorizations, such as age, nationality, and circumstances such as mobility, when discussing service users. While in some cases this may have reflected legitimate attempts to resist over-ethnicizing non-ethnic phenomena, such constructions coexisted with assumptions about ethnic difference and how it might translate into service needs and delivery. In conclusion, we point to the implications of such issues for policy and practice, and offer suggestions for future research in this area.

Constructing ethnicity and identity

Contested representations of race and ethnicity

There is a well-established body of literature around race and ethnicity construction, grounded in theoretical understandings of identities as socially produced and contextually contingent. We focus here on the contested ways in which such productions are conceptualized and utilized, predominantly in the UK given our research context, in relation to issues of migration and community. For example, for Clarke and Speeden (2001, 17) the construction 'minority ethnic group' can 'encapsulate both similarities in and the increasing diversity of experience of migrants and their children and grandchildren', as well as 'needs and interest-based identities produced by group members themselves, rather than an externally-imposed focus on skin colour' (see also Blanc and Smith 1996). Agyeman (2002, 51) explains the similar term 'ethnic minority groups' as imperfect, but uses it 'to mean all people from African-Caribbean, Asian, Chinese and other communities... whose experience of discrimination is shared as a result of their race, colour, nationality or ethnic origin'. Key here is the claiming of (ethnic) identity to challenge exclusion/ marginalization based on social constructions of the 'ethnic other' as always already linked to difference in essentialized ways.

However, Samers (1998, 124) argues that the term 'ethnic' 'can be colonialist, victimizing and patronising', often excluding 'multiple identities shaped by age, gender, sexuality, class and divisions of labour', pointing out that 'we are *all* ethnic, otherwise we would be a-historical'. Indeed, the use of 'ethnic' alone as a descriptor is highly problematic, normatively singling out non-white people as having ethnicity and hiding the multiple ethnicities of the white population, and/or constructing white as non-ethnic versus non-white as ethnic (Ware and Back 2002). Indeed, work on whiteness across the social sciences attempts to deconstruct precisely such normative, totalizing discourses around some homogenous white ethnicity, pointing to multiple white identities in terms of intersecting identities of nationality, gender, age and so on that cut through all productions of ethnicity (cf. Samers' quotation above).

Certainly, the political use of signifiers is a complex and sensitive issue. Work on racism and ethnicity in the USA often uses the term 'people of colour' (Morello-Frosch et al. 2009), while in the UK, Alibhai-Brown (2001) discusses 'visible communities' in an attempt to avoid the homogenizing tendencies of the term 'black' and the power-laden term 'minority'. Similarly, Mas Giralt (2011, 341) emphasizes 'the visual regime of difference and sameness which underpins the integration framework of immigrants and their children'. The paradox here is that visible characteristics, within specific ideological perspectives, are the very basis for racialized exclusion; thus, foregrounding visible difference may also risk reiterating it and foreclose the anti-racist aim of ultimately moving 'beyond the colour line' (Gilroy 2001).

What we can be certain of is that struggles over the making and representation of identities are embedded in histories and geographies of exclusion, racism and lack of equality of opportunity (Askins and Pain 2011). Ang (2001) reminds us that boundary-making around identity is contested between hegemonic, (mostly but not always) majority groups and minority groups, with discursive categories shifting within and in relation to cultural systems. Beyond academic debate, these conceptual difficulties are clearly evident in policy-making and organizational praxis – for example, Morris (2003, 3) identifies 'many inconsistencies in the use of terminology within policy documents'. It is unsurprising, then, that there is uncertainty among communities and practitioners regarding ethnicity. Furthermore, as mentioned through some of the literature considered above, productions other than ethnicity-based are also part of social relations. It is to work that emphasizes the latter that we now turn.

More than ethnicity

Carter and Fenton (2010, 1) contest the use of ethnicity itself as a putative objective category of group formation, commenting that 'sociologists have come to see societies as structured around "ethnicity"', partly in response to 'the decline of class analysis'. They point to the methodological difficulties of considering ethnic populations as such, since these are determined by 'aggregating individuals defined by a single attribute (e.g. that each individual has ticked the same box in an offered array of ethnic identities)' (Carter and Fenton 2010, 3). They question the presumption of group-ness inherent in this classification, including assumptions of social interaction among members, while recognizing that some ' sense of shared-ness' can be drawn from an imagining of 'people like us' with whom we are not in regular contact, but who share many characteristics and circumstances. Much debate around migration and diasporic identities hinges on the latter, while often embedded in 'ethnic' terminology, and we can think here about Bhabha's (1994) notion of ambivalence.

Key is how we are to describe, understand and relate to each other in local communities, and, for practitioners, to enable more positive social relations between service users. Hacking (2002, 113) has argued that ' numerous kinds of human beings and human acts come into being hand in hand with our invention of the ways to name them', leading to the notion of ' making people up'. In some settings, 'communities of interest', 'new arrivals' or 'faith communities' replace 'black and minority ethnic'

(BME) as generic terms. With regards to migration, Elias and Scotson (1994) describe 'established-outsider' relations in a suburban community in England, where an established group 'closed ranks' against an 'outsider group', based on 'differences in power ratio', and argue that:

> What one calls "race relations"… are simply established-outsider relations of a particular type. The fact that members of the two groups differ in their physical appearance or that members of one group speak the language in which they communicate with a different accent and fluency merely serves as a reinforcing shibboleth which makes members of an outsider group more easily recognisable as such.

It is instructive here to take such conceptualization *together with* work on representation considered previously. We would suggest that such boundary-making processes are more than 'simply' established-outsider relations that draw on convenient, recognizable markers; rather, that in/outsider categorizations may simultaneously be *prompted by* visual (and audible) difference, as research regarding the social and spatial exclusion of *established* BME communities in Britain has shown (e.g. Nayak 2012). That is, neither 'outsiderness' nor 'visible difference' has ontological priority; rather, they are produced, reproduced and understood in complex and complicated social relations.

Further complicating approaches to move beyond ethnicity, Norton et al. (2006), in research in the USA, found that, while white individuals may desire to be unprejudiced, leading to efforts to appear 'colour-blind' in discourse, they often still acted on essentialized constructions of 'race'. Similarly, Moras (2010, 234), in a US study of white women who employ domestic workers, found that relationships with workers from minority ethnic backgrounds were often discussed in a non-racial manner, but drew on cultural and linguistic markers to construct 'alternative dimensions of racial privilege'. She argues that racialized ideologies were communicated by referring to difference in reductivist ways, for example always already attached to language, accents or immigration status. In addition, there were problematic constructions of the category 'white': one respondent struggled to classify a Portuguese employee as white because of her 'lack of US citizenship, her accented English and her country of origin' (Moras 2010, 244). While productions of race and ethnicity in the USA are somewhat different to those in the UK, there are common issues here regarding how people may (re)produce ethnic identities, even while attempting to construct otherness in non-ethnic ways, aware of the difficult and sensitive issues caught up in 'political correctness'.

At root are ideological and political perspectives, clearly also exemplified by recent research on the construction of religious identities in public discourse. Ahmad and Evergeti (2010, 1701) argue that what is crucial is when 'one aspect of personal or group identity becomes more salient through a web of social interactions in various social and historical contexts', and that 'war on terror' discourses have increasingly produced the 'Muslim other' as a predominant category, attached to visible signifiers (veils, hijabs, mosques) and essentialized. The research that this paper draws on found little mention of Muslim identities, perhaps because Islamic communities in the northeast of England are small, and discussions predominantly centred on other categories: religion was generally only mentioned in relation to specific customs being considered in service delivery. As such, while recognizing its contemporary relevance, we do not dwell on religion in detail.

While we discuss 'ethnic difference', then, we do not intend to reproduce this unproblematically as an ontological given. Our underlying understanding is that narratives of ethnic identity/ies are embedded in contested, plural and politicized social constructions of self, 'other', community, belonging and place, which have implications for how people engage with each other in everyday settings. Before discussing the findings of the research, we outline the methodology, which itself was caught up in locally produced narratives and politics.

Methodology

This paper draws on semi-structured interviews conducted by Author 1, exploring interethnic interactions in community settings in the northeast of England (2007–08), specifically how practitioners construct the identities of parents/carers and how such constructions may impact approaches to service delivery. This region of England (Figure 1) is not widely associated with ethnic diversity, given its relatively low BME population: 6% compared to 14% across England and Wales in the 2011 census (ONS 2012), and slightly lower during the time of research.

Children's Centres and related community settings were chosen as a sampling frame as spaces of potential interethnic and intercultural encounter with one common purpose across staff – the delivery of services to provide child and family support. Two urban areas were selected (unnamed to protect respondents' anonymity) to represent different communities in terms of ethnic make-up: one having established BME groups as well as newer arrivals, the other being a traditionally white area but a receiving community for refugee families. The two areas are broadly similar in socio-economic status, being predominantly working class, with some particularly deprived and some more affluent pockets. In one area, one Children's Centres operated from two separate purpose-built centres approximately 0.75 miles apart. In the other, two Children's Centres operated services from a variety of community venues. These Children's Centres were selected as they were actively seeking to increase the uptake of their services by minority ethnic groups.

The empirical data used in this research comes from interviews with staff engaging or seeking to engage parents/carers with Children's Centres services. Individual and small-group interviews were undertaken with a total of thirty-three members of staff based at the Children's Centres and allied local agencies. This included all core Children's Centres staff (managers and service facilitators), a representative of the administration team in each area, and a sample of health and community staff involved in delivering Children's Centres services, suggested by Children's Centres staff as offering useful perspectives on the issues central to the research. While this meant that Children's Centres staff acted as gatekeepers to staff from allied agencies, the latter covered a range of professions and broadened the respondent sample. Practitioners across agencies were diverse in terms of educational, vocational and socio-economic background. Twenty-eight interviewees (85%) were female, reflecting the gender ratio in employment in this sector – men make up only about 2% of the childcare workforce in England (DfES

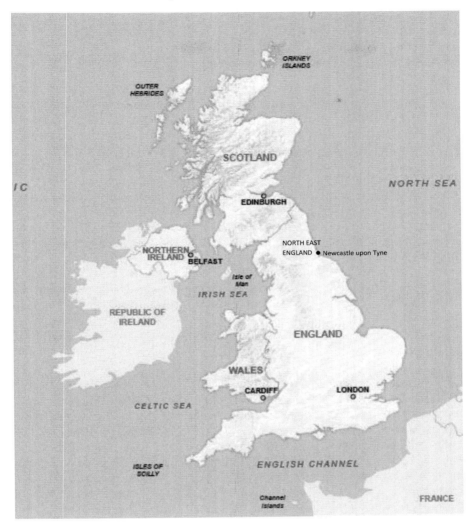

Figure 1. Map of the UK showing the northeast region and Newcastle upon Tyne. Reproduced from Ordnance Survey map data by permission of Ordnance Survey © Crown copyright 2013.

2005). Thirty-one respondents identified as white British and two as BME. The methods were approved by Northumbria University ethics committee; interviews were recorded and transcribed; and they were analysed using a 'grounded theory' approach (Glaser and Strauss 1967), identifying key themes and typologies.

Interviews were conducted based on a broad set of questions, which led to further questions and prompts where necessary. Author 1 explained the aims of the research and its focus on minority ethnic groups. Indicative questions included:

- What services do you facilitate?
- Who uses these services?

- Who would you define as 'hard' and 'easy to reach' in relation to the services you offer? Why?
- What do you think are barriers to accessibility?
- What are the links between these barriers and identity?

Given the ways in which it is contested (outlined previously), Author 1 did not use the term 'race' when interviewing, referring instead to 'ethnicity' and 'country of origin'. Respondents are identified in this paper by gender (M/F = male/female) and ethnicity: interviewees often shifted across identities for themselves, thus where relevant we adopt the category 'BME' in line with long-standing use of this term (in the UK) to indicate all, including white, ME groups/individuals, and 'white British' (WB) to describe the majority ethnic group in the population.

Author 1 was conscious of her own identity as white Northern Irish; how this was constructed through the interview setting, particularly through her accent; and how respondents' perceptions of her might affect what 'truths' and 'accounts' she was told (Neal and Walters 2006). Indeed, both authors reflected on their positionalities in writing this paper, mindful of feminist debates regarding the part that we, as individuals, play in our academic endeavours, the need to understand/foreground situated knowledges, and the need to recognize how our subjectivities are caught up with a politics of position. Author 2 identifies as a white Anglo-Irish woman, who, like Author 1, ticks 'British' on monitoring forms.

Findings and discussion

Ambivalence and ethnicity in identity construction

A central theme that emerged through the research was uncertainty around identity as relating to whiteness. Most respondents were unclear whether white Eastern European families could/should be categorized as BME, with the inclusion of the word 'black' causing confusion. Respondent 23 (M/WB) addressed this uncertainty by distinguishing between 'minority ethnic groups and BME groups', while Respondent 25 (M/WB) referred to 'the white community, in inverted commas'. As Bradby (1995, 408) argues in relation to the word 'race', using quotation marks around a word indicates ambiguity 'as it is not known which part of its meaning the author intends, and which part is being renounced'. In Respondent 25's case, this may indicate recognition of the lack of clarity in a term that crosses ethnic majority and minority lines, and reflects the lack of conceptual clarity in official categories detailed earlier in the paper.

Generally, however, the term 'white' was predominantly used to refer only to white British residents, often conflating being born in the area with whiteness. For example, Respondent 1 (F/WB) spoke of the 'predominant white[ness]' of services, and then referred to a Turkish mother who only occasionally accessed services and was clearly not considered part of this 'predominant white[ness]'. Likewise, Respondent 16 (F/WB) stated: 'I think it's important for them [ME groups] to not just come and see a white face', adding that she advertises 'multicultural' events 'to English people as well, and say they would be very welcome to come along, especially if you want to mix with other races'. These comments suggest normative constructions of whiteness that essentialize people migrating to the area as non-white, alongside the assumption that if you are not white you are 'not from here', while placing non-British white parent/carers in the ambiguous position of neither black nor white. Such productions exemplify the problematic nature of hegemonic whiteness (Ware and Back 2002).

However, some respondents described long-term residents without recourse to ethnicity. Respondent 22 (F/WB) discussed 'the people who have sort of like lived here and are proper... I don't know how to say it – proper – real... like lived [here] all their life and haven't experienced like moving'. Respondent 3 (F/WB), when outlining the crossover between ethnic and other demographic categories, stated: 'And when I say male parent, I don't necessarily just mean of the core – I think I mean, you know, male parents in some of the black and minority ethnic communities as well.' It was clear from the wider interview that this respondent used the term 'core' to refer to the white British ethnic majority, perhaps to resist using the word 'white' as this would have incorporated white minority ethnic groups new to the area. These responses could be understood in line with Elias and Scotson's (1994) conceptualization of 'established and outsiders' identities, considered earlier. Indeed, references were made to 'tribalism' (Respondent 19, M/WB) and 'intense... pockets of community spirit' (Respondent 23, M/WB) among white British residents, as potentially exclusionary to newcomers. Similarly, Respondent 25 (M/WB) stated:

> In an area like [X], being an outsider can be an issue; not being of [X] can be an issue. It depends how well you fit in. It depends how well you keep your head down. It depends on whether or not you stand out.

Here, difference is discussed in terms other than ethnicity, such as 'core', 'proper – real' and 'outsider', yet consistent across interviews where the term white was not drawn upon was a simultaneous return to visible markers of difference from a white majority. For example, while Respondent 3 (above) uses the term 'core', she also classifies non-core parents/carers as BME, and Respondent 25 emphasizes that standing out is an issue, implicitly from the majority, which is white British. This highlights, we argue, the ambivalent ways in which ethnic identities are constructed, with boundary drawing read/produced/represented as *both* not-ethnic (in line with Elias and Scotson's (1994) interpretation of identity construction) *and also* grounded in visible difference that is largely reducible to ethnicity (Nayak 2012). This evidence seems to support Morriss (2003) belief that there is widespread confusion in policy and public discourse, embedded in the conceptual complexities outlined here.

Ambivalence was further evidenced through the study when respondents discussed specific groups as easy/hard to reach. Certainly, respondents commonly mentioned factors other than ethnicity as central to parents'/carers' propensity to access services, such as life experience, personal attributes and age. Easy-to-reach groups included 'English speakers', 'the motivated, educated, got Internet access, read a lot, take the children to school, are interested in the children's upbringing' (Respondent 1, F/WB) and 'increasingly fathers – I just think with the government agenda, and dads are wanting to engage' (Respondent 4, F/WB). Meanwhile, Respondent 6 (F/WB) outlined hard-to-reach groups as 'those that haven't had the good parental role models, that have perhaps fallen – you know, dropped out of school – the teenagers... and those that are new to the area... the asylum-seekers, the refugees'. However, a close analysis reveals that the majority of respondents predominantly linked *other-than-ethnicity* factors to *white British parents/carers* – the latter tended to be categorized according to circumstances, past experiences, upbringing and so on, while *BME parents/carers* were more usually *categorized by ethnicity and/or nationality*, which was predominantly linked to length of residence across the interviews (as in the quotation above). For example, two respondents highlighted Eastern Europeans as easy to reach (Respondent 1, F/WB; Respondent 17, F/WB), with comments around greater motivation to access services attached to fixed ethnic and concomitant cultural attributes.

However, for Respondent 27 (M/BME) this motivation was connected to recent mobility rather than ethnicity. He described 'the white European ones' as having 'nothing local, so they're isolated', while 'BME families culturally have family support', referring to established second- and third-generation BME communities in the area. Respondent 28 (F/WB) made the same distinction between long-term Asian parents/carers and those from newly arrived families. This could arguably be understood as seeing beyond ethnicity to a non-ethnic phenomenon, namely migration and correlated existence or otherwise of local family support networks. However, local support networks among white British families were rarely mentioned, suggesting that the latter were *presumed* to not migrate. Such constructions resonate with calls to deconstruct hegemonic notions of 'whiteness' that work to hide diversity across the 'majority' group (Phillips 2008).

More nuanced identity construction was at times evidenced across the research. For example, Respondent 2 (F/WB) described BME fathers as 'a bit more assertive about what they want for their children... compared to young, white dads in the area', framing her comments in terms of age and confidence rather than essentializing cultural behaviours as linked to ethnicity. The study area has a high number of young white British fathers, and this respondent distinguished between their lack of assertiveness and BME fathers who tended to be older. Likewise, Respondent 4 (F/WB) emphasized personality rather than ethnicity or being part of an established community as key in building connections with clients:

> The newer families that are coming in don't necessarily see me as a local person, but just someone with a Geordie accent who's daft and who they can relate to. And I think... that it's that empathy and it's you as an individual I think that people relate to that more than the fact that you've got an accent or where you live.

Her manager, Respondent 7 (F/WB), supported the centrality of personality in such a role: '[S]he's very effective at what she does, because she is fun, she's very open and uses herself very much as humour.' She added that coming from a similar kind of background and experience helped to build relationships with parents/carers, more than being from the area itself, as 'you maybe empathise somewhat with the community... I would say was more important than the accent that goes with it'. Further, Respondent 25 (M/WB) outlined a potential danger of staff being 'genuine local people', arguing that 'it can bring with it local prejudices'. Respondent 4 may also have been seeking to remove herself from certain prejudices by foregrounding personality over local and ethnic identity.

Indeed, many respondents demonstrated a reluctance to ask BME parents/carers about their ethnic or national backgrounds. Respondent 28 (F/WB) is typical: 'I don't usually ask what nationality people are but I got the feeling she would have been perhaps Czech, Kosovan, something like that.' This response was given within a broader discussion around how asking people where they are from may be perceived to be openly acknowledging someone's difference, and therefore as having prejudiced undertones. At times, like Moras (2010), Author 1 felt as though she had crossed over some invisible line by asking respondents about ethnic and other identities, in relation to their interactions with parents/carers. While there was uncertainty throughout interviews regarding 'identity', in part due to lack of clarity around concepts and terms, then, we also analyse this as reflective of concerns around the sensitivity of 'race'.

In this section, we have highlighted the contradictory narratives that, we believe, reflect the lack of conceptual clarity in official categories outlined earlier in the paper, and may indicate respondents' awareness of how 'offialdom' is 'making people up' (Hacking 2002), in ways that both include and go beyond ethnic representation. How to name/represent users of services is inherently caught up in issues regarding equality of access, and what is critical to this study is that, alongside attempts to understand more than ethnicity in identity construction, respondents simultaneously revealed specific perceptions and expectations with regard to BME groups' needs as service users, which we move on to consider next.

Ethnicity-based assumptions about service needs

Essentialist constructions clearly shaped respondents' expectations of service use by particular groups, and thus their approaches to service delivery, in the main tied to ethnicity and/or nationality. For example, Respondent 32 (F/WB) described how she 'linked up' a Romanian mother with a mother of 'similar nationality', who was Albanian, making assumptions about who someone of a given nationality might prefer to socialize with, while Asian families were understood to all be impacted by working long hours in shops and takeaways. Indeed, there were mostly quite static understandings of different groups' approaches to childcare and interacting with their children. For example, Respondent 29 (F/WB) described 'Indian families' as having a culture of *caring for* their children among extended family, rather than *playing with* their children: 'They're very much not seen as individuals until they reach a certain age, so there's not a lot of toys in an Indian household ... Their children are very much routine-orientated.'

Conversely, although equally essentialist, Respondent 6 (F/WB) felt that African families do place a particular emphasis on playing with their children:

> [They] are very... up on play, they interact with their children a lot and so they don't always see the benefit of coming to a group because they don't necessarily see that socialising side of it as necessarily a benefit.

In both responses, reductivist productions of BME groups' cultural behaviours were given as reasons for not accessing services. Across the research, such fixed productions of groups' needs in relation to service delivery were notably contrasted with those of the white British community. Respondent 19 (M/WB) referred to differences in terms of the social value of attending services and participating in groups: '[W]hite British women will be happy, sitting, chewing the fat with a cup of coffee, whereas the BME women will be knitting, they will be making something, repairing something.' Respondent 16 (F/WB) echoed this, saying that the multicultural mother and baby group was 'not really working because they [BME families] aren't coming because there isn't a specific thing to do'. Similarly, Respondent 28 (F/WB) outlined African parents/carers as wanting a clear purpose to services: 'If it wasn't about getting them a job or a better lifestyle... I don't think they could really see the purpose of the group... and that was about trying to provide mutual support.' Rather than questioning whether their service was delivered in the right way or by the right person, most respondents made ethnic-based assumptions and implied that potential BME service recipients were not interested in receiving what they offered. This may reflect a professionally centred approach to understanding reasons for non-take-up of services, incorporating a lack of recognition that the service in question may not be meeting specific needs for practical help and activities, for example to address wider local discrimination in employment. It must be recognized that other factors, especially class, may contribute to staff perceptions of why some groups are absent from services; yet in our research, perceptions of absence were predominantly based on ethnicity, as these examples show.

However, one interviewee (Respondent 19, M/WB) suggested that established BME communities do use services for mutual support:

> Because of the way that a lot of the larger BME communities still work, because the Children's Centre provides a networking hub, they will use it because they still have that cultural norm of networking and supporting each other through good times and bad.

However, rather than understanding such access/behaviour as similar to established white communities, it was grounded in a discourse of BME communities strengthening (their) existing ethnic ties. Further, many respondents held ethnicity-based perceptions about approaches to 'integration' that shape expectations of service use. We acknowledge that notions of integration are deeply contested and conceptually blurred, and are wary of the political implications of different meanings embedded in differential power relations (Askins and Pain 2011). However, careful analysis suggests that, in this research, the term 'integration' was used across interviews to refer to instances of interaction between different communities or groups, rather than a broader process through which new and existing residents may 'adapt to one another' (CIC 2007, 9), and it is in the former (respondents') sense that we use it here.

For example, Respondent 29 (F/WB) commented that 'Indian people operate within their community' and that 'Indian women tend to stay within the family, there's always something for them to do at home'. Respondent 1 (F/WB) stated that the 'Asian community' is 'very involved with their own community and they don't seem to want to blend in', and Respondent 19 (M/WB) stated that Asian families were often regulated by elders or community leaders. In addition, Respondent 16 (F/WB) stated that BME men act as gatekeepers for their wives: 'I've had a dad come to my group before, to see what it was about for his wife – a Chinese man'; while

Respondent 27 (M/BME) described 'problems with certain Muslim families' whereby 'the woman is actually in a different room while I'm telling the fella'. Respondent 29 (F/WB) commented:

> When they do come in that they do not mix. They don't talk to the other women... because they see them as different as well... We've got Asian families, we've got Polish people, who all stay within their separate little communities.

Non-interaction in service use, then, was commonly linked to the construction of minority ethnic groups as living in distinct communities: key here is that this is the dominant narrative, whether factually correct or not, re-emphasizing the racialized discourse regarding residential segregation that Phillips (2007) warns of. Tellingly, Respondent 22 (F/WB) recognized that such a stereotypical association was prevalent among the white British residents with whom she worked: 'Like those flats... people will say "Ah, Kosovan Towers... don't go to them places, it's full of Kosovans."'

Issues regarding integration are complicated by language barriers, and many respondents highlighted lack of English as a major barrier to parents'/carers' participation in groups or services. For example, Respondent 5 (F/WB) commented: 'I suppose there's a big difference in language and whether those people that... come to baby social and other things have got a reasonable knowledge of English... The biggest barrier is language and it always will be.' Similarly, Respondent 17 (F/WB) stated: 'The main barrier to me is the fact that they can't speak English, nothing else. Everything else can be overcome, but if they can't speak English they're at such a disadvantage, and they just won't go out.' Further, Respondent 30 (F/WB) believed that a possible barrier to service use by local Muslim women stemmed from a lack of understanding of the services by a Muslim gatekeeper who provides some services jointly with the Children's Centres: 'I suspect there's more of a language barrier there than she is perhaps letting me know. I think she thinks the Children's Centre is something different to what it is – I think she sees it as being childcare.'

Critically, recognizing lack of (confidence in) English as a barrier to service use was never explicitly connected to other barriers or issues discussed above. In this, respondents' constructions were more in line with Elias and Scotson's (1994) conceptualization of established/outsider.

Two respondents, while framing integration and service use in terms of migration (i.e. factors other than ethnicity), simultaneously returned to ethnic essentialism by constructing all 'new settlers' as coming from BME backgrounds: Respondent 33 (F/BME) felt that BME groups were more likely to integrate and use services especially if they were 'new settlers', while Respondent 22 (F/WB) commented:

> [BME families are] more likely to want to integrate because they're new to the area, so they might want to come in and use the services for that purpose. There's a lot of the new people who've moved to the area that are accessing things.

Meanwhile, long-term white British residents, despite being the main users of services, were sometimes also perceived as disengaged, with a more inward approach due to non-migration, paradoxically leading to a weaker propensity to use services.

Respondent 1 (F/WB) felt that white British parents/carers 'don't think that there's a wider community out there that they could integrate and learn from... I think the ones that have lived here all their life... perhaps aren't as motivated for different reasons'. Similarly, Respondent 19 (M/WB) referred to a 'tribalism' that prevented some white British residents from accessing services at certain venues, a perceptual boundary grounded in local historical issues, which he felt was not likely to affect BME families. In both cases, non-mobility is the factor in not accessing services, yet to some extent this is simultaneously linked to ethnic background.

These empirical findings suggest contesting accounts of how identities and backgrounds are constructed among respondents, at times supporting conceptual work on Self/Other as complex, moving across social categorizations and individual circumstances and characteristics; at others reduced to visible markers of difference, especially ethnic identity, connected often to notions of insider/outsiderness. We conclude the paper by thinking about what this may mean for policy, praxis and future research in this area.

Conclusions

One interpretation of interview responses is that respondents attributed difference in service needs/use to non-ethnic factors such as age, confidence, mobility, gender and class. Indeed, many respondents were skilled in distinguishing a range of factors contributing to parents'/carers' approaches to service use, and we stress here that all clearly outlined their motivation to support all parents/carers in the local community as grounding their professional work. However, essentialist assumptions about how ethnic difference might translate into service needs, particularly in relation to cultural practices around approaches to childcare and playing with children, coexisted with attempts to resist ethnic descriptors. In most cases, the apparent confidence with which respondents made ethnic-based assumptions of service needs contrasted with the uncertainty that they displayed in how to talk about ethnic difference, echoing Norton et al.' s (2006) findings discussed earlier. Certainly, the framing of the interview questions with reference to 'ethnicity' must be recognized as contingent in responses, and was intended to enable participants to consider this factor in particular (given the research aim). The extent to which other factors are caught up in the complex and simultaneous resistance to and production of ethnicity needs further in-depth research, especially to further the policy recommendations we outline here.

Such disparities within discourse, and between discourse and practice, certainly reflect wider policy and conceptual confusion, and have implications for policy and praxis across the public sector. In order to achieve equality of opportunity, policymakers need to carefully reconsider representation and terms used – not least working to ensure better consistency at the conceptual level – in line with the complex and fluid societies of a super-diverse contemporary Britain. This in turn, we argue, requires new approaches to the ways in which practitioners are trained, in relation to how they direct and deliver services and organize service settings. For example, if specific services come to be associated with particular ethnic groups, there will be implications for the community cohesion agenda; and if (potential) service users are presumed different in terms of behaviour or needs, due to ethnic or cultural markers, this may mean that they are treated differently in essentialist ways.

Difference will remain a critical issue, of course, as a diverse society has divergent needs. And while 'targeting' can be seen as a problematic leftover from multiculturalism, focusing only on difference, action is nevertheless required to redress imbalances in access to local services and support (Berman and Paradies 2008), in more nuanced ways open to *more than ethnicity* and *more than difference*. In the research here, there was little conceptualization of similarity by respondents, despite the fact that all parents/carers with whom staff worked had at least two important factors in common: they all had young children and lived in the localities in question. Such similarities can and should be recognized and built upon in the organization of service settings, since, as Lamphere (1992, 2) points out, 'interrelations are not just a matter of race, ethnicity, or immigrant status but can be influenced by the organization of a workplace, apartment complex or school'.

This paper does not consider interactions between people in service settings, which are critical in improving our understanding of social relations and a key avenue for future research. Moreover, such work should pay close attention to the cross-cutting positions such as age, gender, language ability, as well as religion, and how these identities intersect with one another, as part of social relations in service delivery. Further, the relative strength of the northeast identity (Parks and Elcock 2000) was a factor in this study (but beyond the capacity of this paper), and future research could explicitly explore how local and regional identities and narratives also interplay with national, ethnic and cultural backgrounds.

Acknowledgements

We would like to thank the editor and two anonymous referees for extremely helpful and thoughtful feedback, and Ian Fitzgerald for his comments on an earlier draft.

Funding

This paper stems from a project conducted by Author 1 and funded by the Economic and Social Research Council [RES-000-22-2172].

References

Agyeman, J. 2002. "Constructing Environmental (In)Justice: Transatlantic Tales." *Environmental Politics* 11 (3): 31–53. doi:10.1080/714000627.

Ahmad, W. I. U., and V. Evergeti. 2010. "The Making and Representation of Muslim Identity in Britain: Conversations with British Muslim "Elites"." *Ethnic and Racial Studies* 33 (10): 1697–1717. doi:10.1080/01419871003768055.

Alibhai-Brown, Y. 2001. *Who Do We Think We Are? Imagining the New Britain*. London: Penguin.

Ang, I. 2001. *On not Speaking Chinese: Living between Asia and the West*. London: Routledge.

Askins, K., and R. Pain. 2011. "Contact Zones: Participation, Materiality, and the Messiness of Interaction." *Environment and Planning D: Society and Space* 29 (5): 803–821. doi:10.1068/d11109.

Berman, G., and Y. Paradies. 2008. "Racism, Disadvantage and Multiculturalism: Towards Effective Anti-Racist Praxis." *Ethnic and Racial Studies* 33 (2): 214–232. doi:10.1080/01419870802302272.

Bhabha, H. 1994. *The Location of Culture*. New York: Routledge.

Blanc, M., and D. Smith. 1996. "Citizenship and Ethnicity in Germany, France and the UK." In *Immigrants in Europe: The Citizen Challenge* (translated from French), edited by M. Blanc, G. Didier, and A. Flye Sainte Marie. Paris: Editions l'Harmattan.

Bottero, W. 2009. "Class in the 21st Century." In *Who Cares about the White Working Class?*, edited by K. P. Sveinsson, 7–15. London: The Runnymede Trust.

Bradby, H. 1995. "Ethnicity: Not a Black and White Issue: A Research Note." *Sociology of Health and Illness* 17 (3): 405–417. doi:10.1111/1467-9566.ep10933332.

Carter, B., and S. Fenton. 2010. "Not Thinking Ethnicity: A Critique of the Ethnicity Paradigm in an Over-Ethnicised Sociology." *Journal for the Theory of Social Behaviour* 40 (1): 1–18. doi:10.1111/j.1468-5914.2009.00420.x.

CIC (Commission on Integration and Cohesion). 2007. *Our Shared Future*. Wetherby: CIC.

Clarke, J., and S. Speeden. 2001. *Then and Now: Change for the Better?* London: Commission for Racial Equality.

CRE (Commission for Racial Equality). 2007. *Promoting Interaction between People from Different Ethnic Backgrounds*. London: CRE.

DfES (Department for Education and Skills). 2005. *Every Child Matters: Children's Workforce Strategy*. Nottingham: DfES. http://www.education.gov.uk/consultations/downloadableDocs/5958-DfES-ECM.pdf

Elias, N., and J. L. Scotson. 1994. *The Established and the Outsiders*. London: SAGE.

Gilroy, P. 2001. *Against Race: Imagining Political Culture beyond the Color Line*. Cambridge, MA: Harvard University Press.

Glaser, B. G., and A. L. Strauss. 1967. *The Discovery of Grounded Theory: Strategies for Qualitative Research*. New York: Aldine de Gruyter.

Hacking, I. 2002. *Historical Ontology*. Cambridge, MA: Harvard University Press.

Kundnani, A. 2007. *The End of Tolerance: Racism in 21st Century Britain*. London: Pluto Press.

Lamphere, L., ed. 1992. *Structuring Diversity*. Chicago, IL: University of Chicago Press.

Mas Giralt, R. 2011. "In/Visibility Strategies and Enacted Diversity: Sameness and Belonging among Young People of Latin American Descent Living in the North of England (UK)." *Children's Geographies* 9 (3–4): 331–345. doi:10.1080/14733285.2011.590712.

Moras, A. 2010. "Colour-Blind Discourses in Paid Domestic Work: Foreignness and the Delineation of Alternative Racial Markers." *Ethnic and Racial Studies* 33 (2): 233–252. doi:10.1080/01419870802604008.

Morello-Frosch, R., M. Pastor, J. Sadd, and S. Shonkoff. 2009. *The Climate Gap: Inequalities in How Climate Change Hurts Americans and How to Close the Gap*. http://dornsife.usc.edu/pere/documents/The_Climate_Gap_Full_Report_FINAL.pdf

Morris, N. 2003. *Black and Minority Ethnic Groups and Public Open Space: Literature Review*. Edinburgh: OPENspace Research Centre, Edinburgh College of Art/Heriot Watt University.

Nayak, A. 2012. "Race, Religion and British Multiculturalism: The Political Responses of Black and Minority Ethnic Voluntary Organisations to Multicultural Cohesion." *Political Geography* 31 (7): 454–463. doi:10.1016/j.polgeo.2012.08.005.

Neal, S., and S. Walters. 2006. "Strangers Asking Strange Questions? A Methodological Narrative of Researching Belonging and Identity in English Rural Communities." *Journal of Rural Studies* 22 (2): 177–189. doi:10.1016/j.jrurstud.2005.08.009.

Norton, M. I., S. R. Sommers, E. P. Apfelbaum, N. Pura, and D. Ariely. 2006. "Color Blindness and Interracial Interaction: Playing the Political Correctness Game." *Psychological Science* 17 (11): 949–953. doi:10.1111/j.1467-9280.2006.01810.x.

ONS (Office of National Statistics). 2012. *Ethnicity and National Identity in England and Wales 2011*. http://www.ons.gov.uk/ons/rel/census/2011-census/key-statistics-for-local-authorities-in-england-and-wales/rpt-ethnicity.html http://www.ons.gov.uk/ons/rel/mro/news-release/census-2-1——north-east/census-gives-insights-into-characteristics-of-the-north-east-s-population.html

Parks, J., and H. Elcock. 2000. "Why Do Regions Demand Autonomy?" *Regional and Federal Studies* 10 (3): 87–106. doi:10.1080/13597560008421133.

Phillips, D. 2007. "Experiences and Interpretations of Segregation, Community and Neighbourhood." In *The Power of Belonging: Identity, Citizenship and Community Cohesion*, edited by B. Rogers and R. Muir, 36–49. London: Institute for Public Policy Research.

Phillips, D. 2008. "The Problem with Segregation: Exploring the Racialisation of Space in Northern Pennine Towns." In *New Geographies of Race and Racism*, edited by C. Dwyer and C. Bressey, 187–192. Aldershot, Hants: Ashgate.

Samers, M. 1998. "Immigration, "Ethnic Minorities", and "Social Exclusion" in the European Union: A Critical Perspective." *Geoforum* 29 (2): 123–144. doi:10.1016/S0016-7185(98)00003-7.

Vertovec, S. 2007. *New Complexities of Cohesion in Britain: Super-Diversity, Transnationalism and Civil-Integration*. Wetherby: Commission on Integration and Cohesion.

Ware, V., and L. Back. 2002. *Out of Whiteness*. London: University of Chicago Press.

Little of Italy? Assumed ethnicity in a New York City neighbourhood

Elisabeth Becker

Utilizing the case study of Albanian Kosovars employed in the restaurant business in Little Italy, New York, this paper introduces the concept of *assumed ethnicity*. This concept describes one ethnic group strategically presenting itself as another ethnic group, neither assimilating into mainstream society ethnicity nor validating place of origin ethnicity. Such assumed ethnicity is outwardly expressed (assumed) by the ethnic group in question, as well as accepted (assumed to be true) in both mainstream encounters and understandings of self. Applying and building on Goffman's theory of the front stage and back stage elucidates this phenomenon, where migrants instrumentally assume an ethnicity different from their own, in order to facilitate front-stage (mainstream) encounters. On the backstage, they expose their 'true' ethnicity, in the process drawing connections between Kosovo, Albania and Italy: ironically, authenticating assumed ethnicity by linking their front- and back-stage performances of everyday life.

The waiters are old school Italian. What else to expect in Little Italy[1]

Street signs marking the 'Historic District of Little Italy' pair with open-air restaurants decorated in chalkboards claiming 'authenticity'. Men in three-piece suits and swanky jackets call *'ciao bella'* to women walking by, attempting to attract business into the line of eateries that remain side by side, now studded with tourist shops between them. Tourists abound on Mulberry Street, decked out in identity-laden outfits: 'Wisconsin Badgers' T-shirts stretched across the chests of a dozen laughing men. This is the Little Italy of our stereotyped imaginations: Gambino brothers and supposed mob shoot-outs; cheap-eats, quintessential *cannolis* and the annual San Gennaro Festival. But what lies beyond the fac(ad)es of Little Italy witnessed in its bustling streets?

Classic sociological *migration* debates have tended to use objective indicators to understand assimilation and integration processes (e.g. Alba and Nee 1997). Scholarship referencing the communities formed from post-1970 migration flows focuses specifically on the diffusion of migrants into broader society over multiple generations, or on ethnic enclaves that develop 'parallel' to mainstream society (Model 1985; Light, Sabagh, and Bozorgmehr 1994). Recent work on integration has come to highlight social and symbolic boundaries separating minority groups from mainstream society, specifically noting the varied permeability of said boundaries depending upon group characteristics (Alba and Nee 1997; Zolberg and Woon 1999;

Alba 2005; Wimmer 2008; Lamont 2012). While important to understanding societal change, these strands of migration theory fail to fully account for migrant agency and processes of engagement with mainstream society that neither preserve nor dissolve ethnic identity.

Studies of *ethnicity* have responded to the lack of agency assigned to migrants in mainstream migration theories. Overwhelmingly qualitative in nature, they portray meanings and practices as situational. Numerous scholars point towards the instrumental employment of ethnicity in presenting identity, emphasized or de-emphasized dependent on the social situation. According to these scholars, migrants either accentuate place of origin ethnicity or the host country's mainstream ethnicity (aiming for a generic, assimilated identity) (e.g. Nagata 1974; Calgar 1997; Al-Haj 2002; Sanders 2002). Case studies have been employed to demonstrate this theoretical positing. Al-Haj (2002), for example, deconstructs the perceived dialectic between assimilation and ethnic preservation, finding that most migrants from the former Soviet Union in Israel express multifaceted identities, where origin ethnicity remains key only *in tandem with* Jewish and Israeli-based components of identity. Zevallos (2003) similarly explores concurrent alignment with Latin American culture and adoption of Australian gender ideals among women of South and Central American origin in Australia. Specifically, Zevallos (2003, 81) illuminates having both an 'Australian side' and a 'Latin American side' of identity, with selective characteristics adopted for a multifaceted identity as 'the paradox of ethnic identity'. Further underscoring agentive manoeuvring as central to the presentation of migrant identity in a society of resettlement, Valenta (2009, 360) demonstrates how Bosnian, Croatian and Iraqi immigrants in Norway employ passing and covering to 'downplay' 'ethnic markers'.

While successfully deconstructing the perceived dialectic between assimilation and ethnic identity retention, scholars of ethnicity have not yet homed in on the way of managing everyday life in a new society suggested by this analysis. This paper pioneers in showing how some groups of migrants neither circumstantially emphasize place of origin ethnicity nor host country, mainstream ethnicity, but rather assume an *alternative* ethnicity in an open and expressive way. As suggested by the work of Nagel (1994), this analysis focuses not only on ethnicity options but also the meanings underlying specific ethnic identification. It thus brings Goffman's (1959) ethnographic theory on the presentation of self (including the concepts of passing, authenticity and the front/back stage) to bear on migration discourse in the development of a new concept: *assumed ethnicity*. This concept describes one ethnic group strategically presenting itself as another ethnic group, neither assimilating into mainstream society ethnicity nor validating place of origin ethnicity. Such assumed ethnicity is both outwardly expressed by the ethnic group in question, as well as accepted in mainstream encounters, drawing on the dual definition of 'assume': (1) to pretend to have or be (feign); and (2) to take as granted or true (suppose).[2] In this process, individuals remain 'other', bounded by an identity distinct from the mainstream 'melting pot' where ethnicity dissolves.

In *The Presentation of Self in Everyday Life*, Goffman (1959) explains that individuals present themselves to others in accordance with the structure of relations (as stranger, as friend, as kin). According to Goffman (1959, 2), an individual

CITIES, DIVERSITY AND ETHNICITY

purposively performs in order to somehow 'impress' upon the other. Goffman (1959) emphasizes the role of 'passing' among the stigmatized: a performance that creates the pretence of belonging to a non-stigmatized group. This requires the managed concealment of actual identity and its markers. He cites differences between 'front stage' (i.e. mainstream) performances and 'back stage' (i.e. authentic) presentation of self. Goffman (1959) further emphasizes the importance of authenticity in identity presentation, also explored by Turner and Schutte (1981), and expanded by Erickson (1995), who focuses on the lack of authenticity in the workplace. The interplay between authenticity and inauthenticity in the workplace is important to the following analysis, where an inauthentic presentation of self is utilized to provide an authentic experience of Little Italy for visitors. Furthermore, the front stage and backstage are imperative, as Albanian Kosovars present differing ethnic identities in accordance with mainstream (front stage) and co-ethnic (backstage) interactions. In my analysis, I additionally link and thereby enhance the concepts of authenticity and front/back stage, arguing that front-stage identity is justified in back-stage encounters, in an attempt to claim to oneself the authenticity of these everyday performances.

Albanian Kosovars capitalize on the dual economic and social opportunity to take the place of (by passing as) Italians in the restaurant market, creating a front stage characterized by Italian physical and linguistic markers. In back-stage encounters, moreover, they expose and express an Albanian ethnicity, justifying their front-stage performances by establishing linkages between Kosovo and Albania with Italy. In this process, they at once ascend the dichotomous options of mainstream assimilation or ethnic preservation, and break down the barriers between the front and back stages: playing the part of the Italian on the little left of Little Italy.

Overview

This ethnographic study was undertaken in Little Italy on Mulberry Street, located in southern Manhattan, at the crossroads of Soho, Chinatown, the Lower East Side and the West Village, between October 2011 and April 2013. To better understand the dynamics of Albanian Kosovar identification, I employed a combination of field methods, including: participant observation in restaurants, cafes, Italian stores and the Italian American Museum; semi-structured interviews; life histories; and informal interviews, conducted with Albanian Kosovars, Italians, other restaurant workers and restaurant patrons. In particular, I targeted managers, waiters, hosts and busboys in six restaurants on Mulberry Street for interviews, and spent half of my time at a single site (here referred to as Vinny's Restaurant).[3]

Limited academic work has been undertaken on Little Italy on Mulberry Street (Alba, Logan, and Crowder 1997). According to news sources, however, an influx of Italian migrants into the USA at the turn of the twentieth century resulted in a population of over two million Italians, with the largest concentration in New York City (370,000 individuals in 1914) (Corsi 1942; Baily 1999). According to an article in *New York Times* on October 15, 1904, Little Italy on Mulberry Street was at this time one of 'six colonies' of Italians, and the banking centre for Italians in New York. Since the middle of the twentieth century, Little Italy has been a centre for tourists and others seeking an 'Italian experience' (Wells 2005). Interest in the neighbourhood

CITIES, DIVERSITY AND ETHNICITY

was also fed by public fascination with 'La Cosa Nostra' , spiking with the 1972 assassination of mobster Joey Gallo at Umberto's Clam House, located in the heart of Little Italy (*The New York Times*, January 9, 2005). The neighbourhood has retained 'an ethnic character' and its attractiveness for ethnic tourism 'even after the relevant ethnic population has left' (Alba, Logan, and Crowder 1997, 909).[4]

Although Albanian Kosovars do not live in Little Italy on Mulberry Street, many work in restaurants on this historic avenue. An estimated 20,000 ethnic Albanians from Kosovo were resettled in the USA between 1999 and 2000, following the Wars of Succession in Bosnia, Croatia and Kosovo (Duffy 1999). With the large number who accepted US residency, as well as the continued influx of thousands of asylum seekers, this population has grown significantly over the past fourteen years. Initially relocated in Fort Dix, New Jersey, a large Albanian community has formed in Pelham Parkway, the Bronx, which is credited with revitalizing the local economy (*CNN Focus on Kosovo*, May 21, 1999; Gorman and Richman 2001). While this research focuses on Mulberry Street in Manhattan, New York's other formerly Italian enclave, Arthur Avenue in Pelham Parkway, is also predominantly staffed by Albanians (many of whom actually *reside* in the vicinity of this avenue) (*The New York Times*, June 6, 2004). Multiple interview subjects previously worked on Arthur Avenue and/or had family members employed in its industry at the time of my fieldwork.

The question of the contemporary identification of Albanian Kosovars emerges from this crucible of political migration and urban resettlement and, in its footsteps, the concept of assumed ethnicity. In this case study, assumed ethnicity draws on three opportunities: (1) structural opportunity to take the place of Italians in Little Italy's restaurants; (2) performative opportunity for front-stage expressions of assumed Italian ethnicity; and (3) cultural opportunity to complicate back-stage Albanian ethnic identity.

1. Structural opportunity

Albanian Kosovars working in Little Italy's restaurants capitalize on both the out-migration of Italians and co-ethnic networks, in order to find jobs in the neighbourhood. They further assume the front-of-the-house (host, waiter, manager) jobs of the Italians, rather than back-of-the-house (cook, dishwasher) jobs mainly filled by Latin American migrants.

According to restaurant workers of all backgrounds, the 'Italians have left', 'they are gone', 'now it's Albanians'. A young restaurant host from Eastern Europe, posted on a Mulberry Street corner to draw in patrons, similarly described the current restaurant staff as almost entirely 'Albanian! [pointing across the street, next door etc.] He is Albanian, he is Albanian.' Futosh, a recent migrant from Kosovo and waiter in Vinny's Restaurant, discussed his daily commute from Pelham Parkway, the Bronx to Little Italy on Mulberry Street: 'When I look up, I see Albanians everywhere, also coming to work here... I feel like I am there [in Kosovo].' An Italian American butcher on the corner of Mulberry Street cited the out-migration of Italians, a group 'too rich to work in this neighborhood, and too poor to live here', as contributing to the structural opportunity for the employment of other ethnic groups. He has owned an Italian supermarket in Little Italy for thirty years, witnessing the movement of the Italians to 'the suburbs' of Connecticut, New Jersey, Long Island and Staten Island over the past decade. Joseph, an Italian American and former long-term resident of the area noted: 'It's changed a lot because people [living in Little Italy] have a lot of money. And us who don't, who didn't, we left a long time ago.' Lack of contemporary Italian migration to New York City further facilitates what Joseph referenced as the 'takeover' of this 'ethnic market'.

In addition to job openings, co-ethnic networks encourage the movement of Albanian Kosovars into Little Italy: 'You will learn that everybody from Kosovo knows each other.' The longest-standing Albanian Kosovar restaurant workers gained employment in the late 1990s, after fleeing regional conflict, and facilitate job attainment for those more recently migrated from Kosovo. Dardan, an Albanian Kosovar restaurant manager, explained:

> I just came in here and asked for a job and got one. Now people also get jobs from their cousins... That is why so many Albanians work here. Either they are family or they are friends, they know each other from Kosovo, Albania, or they just know Albanians work here.

Other restaurant staff echoed this network-based process, including Max, the son of a Jewish American restaurant owner, who explained the role of 'fictive kin' (close friends, family-like relationships) (Ebaugh and Curry 2000, 189) in the ethnic dominance of the market: 'The Albanians sometimes bring their "cousins"... if they work in different restaurants and are looking for a change.' As highlighted in interviews with restaurant staff of all backgrounds, co-ethnic networks have led to a proliferation of Albanian Kosovars not only in Little Italy, but within the Italian restaurant market in New York; individuals gain experience, know-how and language that allows them to move up within this specific industry. This is most apparent in the saliency between workers of the Little Italy of Arthur Avenue in the Bronx and Mulberry Street in Manhattan. Additionally, ethnic Albanians own or co-own three of the Italian restaurants on Mulberry Street. While a small population (est. 194,000 in 2010), and thus unlikely to dominate Italian American restaurants across the USA, ethnic Albanians increasingly assume leadership roles in New York's Italian restaurant industry (USCB 2010).

Carving out a 'space' or 'place' within the Italian restaurant economy, and within a specific restaurant, entails not only economic opportunity and co-ethnic networks, but also associating with a successful ethnic group that has 'made it' in American society and thus made it out of the unrecognized, or even stigmatized, role of the 'other'. This undoubtedly relates to racialized understandings of society that cannot be ignored in discussions of ethnicity in America, with Italians designated to the 'white' category only in the contemporary (Waters 1990; Steinberg 2001). It is imperative to keep in mind that in passing as Italians, Albanian Kosovars also pass as white (Gans 1992). Mobility and opportunity thus draw on racial classifications at the heart of uniquely American understandings of belonging, where assimilation from non-white into white racial classifications (like the Italians, Jews and Irish in the past) simultaneously signals mobility, and concurrent ascendance of the hierarchies of economy and society (Gordon 1964; Nagel 1994; Jacobson 1997; Nagel and Staeheli 2005).

CITIES, DIVERSITY AND ETHNICITY

Dynamics within the restaurant are themselves most certainly hierarchical, with Italian (and occasionally Jewish or Albanian) owners; Albanian hosts, waiters and managers; and Mexican and Ecuadorian busboys, kitchen staff and bathroom attendants. Working front-of-the-house primarily relates to three phenomena: physical characteristics similar to the Italians; language ability; and legal status. Ordinarily equipped with similar racial markers, working papers and English proficiency, Albanian Kosovars in Little Italy adamantly reject back-of-the-house positions. They strongly emphasized that 'we Albanians run the floor'; 'it's Albanians who keep these restaurants going'; 'we are the face of the restaurant'. The first step in passing as Italian is therefore accomplished by Albanian Kosovars through the opportunity to take the place of Italians, formerly front-of-house workers in the restaurants and no longer residents in the area. Thus, structural opportunity, established through out-migration of Italians and co-ethnic networks of Albanian Kosovars, allows for the creation of a front stage, where Albanian Kosovars can become the literal face(s) (albeit facades) of the Italian restaurant.

2. Performative opportunity

The structure outlined above creates both the opportunity and desire to perform.[5] Upon arrival at the site of Little Italy, markers and demarcations of Italian-ness abound. Red, white and green flags fly high above storefront windows; signs for gelato, *cannolis* and brick oven pizza act as permanent decor. On weekends, tourists stand everywhere, snapping photographs, sidling up to historic establishments such as the Ferrara Café and Umberto's Clamhouse. This material area is thus concurrently a symbolic arena. And the available repertoires of Italian stereotypes/signs prevalent in American society – replicas of famous artworks, imaginings of mobsters, familiar foods – facilitates this opportunity in a unique way. Common knowledge of the supposedly Italian provides a vast array of iconic, recognizable symbols signalling the Italian presence (something that is not necessarily true for many other ethnic groups in the USA). Both as a whole, and within individual Italian restaurants, this stage facilitates the assumed ethnicity of Albanian Kosovars – clearly marked and marketed – as Italian. This is not accomplished through explicit deceit but rather through subtle, performative cues: the creation and maintenance of both Italian space and self. Italian *space* is forged through what Goffman (1959) calls 'props': background music, wording on signs, as well as drawings and watercolour paintings of Italy. The presentation of the Italian *self* emerges with the adoption of Italian 'nicknames' (i.e. Frankie or Joe), displacing Albanian names in everyday utterances on the front stage of the restaurant, and the colloquial Italian learned, most often to draw in customers. Coupled with the agency of Albanian Kosovar workers in the assumed ethnicity, the expectations of tourists and the economic motivations of store owners serve to further fortify performative opportunity.

On the sidewalks of Mulberry Street, signs mark the 'Historic District of Little Italy'. Italian flags, alongside American, fly high outside the restaurants. Italian paraphernalia decorates the tables and walls of the restaurants, cafes and stores. This includes miniature statues of Italian saints, full-wall paintings of gondolas, Italian architecture and wooden signs carved with words in the language of the 'mother country'. Chalkboards display Italian specials, printed gracefully in the Italian language. iPods repetitively blast familiar Italian and Italian American songs. This backdrop thus provides a fully fledged front stage appealing to all senses (taste, sight, sound, scent and touch) for Italian ethnicity to be assumed by Albanian Kosovars.

Turning towards the self, one must note that restaurant workers on Mulberry Street identify each other by language rather than country of origin. On all accounts, when asked about the demography of the neighbourhood, they explain that the majority of those employed in Little Italy are 'Italians, Albanians and Spanish'. No one differentiates between Italians and Italian Americans; Albanians from Kosovo, Albania (and beyond); nor Mexicans and Ecuadorians. Thus, language allows for identification within the micro-world of Little Italy, as a whole. The specific presentation of the Italian self by Albanian Kosovars through language is evidenced in the names of managers, hosts and waiters: 'Joey' , 'Mario' and 'Luigi' are only a few of the Italian names used in place of given Albanian names. According to one of the few remaining Italian waiters, 'There are so many Frankies from Kosovo around here.'

Language utilized to engage (potential) customers provides another clear expression of the assumed Italian ethnicity. '*Bonjiorno bella!*' call the Albanian Kosovar hosts lined up on Mulberry Street; '*grazie!*' proclaim Albanian Kosovar waiters, as their patrons tuck in chairs before exiting restaurants. 'I know a few people from around here say "*mangia bene!*" or "*mangia, bella!*" to get people into the restaurant,' explained Max (the aforementioned Jewish American restaurant owner's son) one evening, as he helped clear outdoor tables. While Albanian Kosovars often use Italian in interaction with patrons, Italian owners or fellow (non-Albanian) workers, at times they even call each other *paesano* (ironically, 'countryman'). This language further infiltrates their expressive, individual colloquialisms. On multiple occasions, the Albanian Kosovar manager of Vinny's, Cima, shouted '*mama mia!*' when the phone rang incessantly or when a busboy knocked down a shelf of glasses. 'Something I love about New York,' he sighed one late autumn afternoon, as the cool breeze of early winter whistled at the door, 'are the *quattro stagioni* [four seasons].'

It is difficult to make sweeping claims regarding the experience of this performance, as individual expressions range from the playful (e.g. chatting up female passersby) to the problematized (e.g. in relation to religion). As most Albanian Kosovars are Muslim, one might surmise difficulties arising from the Christian atmosphere, including wooden saint statues and crosses dotting the interior of the restaurants as well as the prevalence of pork and alcohol on the menu. It is also explicitly forbidden in Islam to hide evidence of religious beliefs, unless under extreme threat (Virani 2007). This could conflict with portraying onself as Italian. Cima alluded specficially to the limitations that working in Little Italy has on his religious practice, specifically during Ramadan, suggesting underlying tensions between (en)acted and origin identities: 'I can't fast here. How could I fast, standing here eleven, twelve hours on my feet all day?'

It is imperative to note both by and to whom enacted identities are directed. 'It's tourists, all tourists' who visit the restaurants in the contemporary. The accompanying expectations of tourists both encourage and facilitate the assumption of Italian ethnicity. A long-term Italian resident, Silvestro, explained this dynamic: 'There are Italian-looking waiters, which is all the tourists care about.' Dardan (Albanian Kosovar host) observed that most tourists think he is 'Southern Italian. They can't tell the difference.' Seli, a Greek waiter, emphatically noted that tourists assume Albanians (from Kosovo

CITIES, DIVERSITY AND ETHNICITY

and beyond) to be Italian: 'They just don't know much. Me, they know I can't be Italian but these Albanians they look the same as Italians from South Italy.' Moreover, many Albanian Kosovar restaurant workers explained that 'tourists come here for a little bit of Italy', highlighting their responsibility to provide this specific experience.

Such expectations, and thus facilitation of passing, are reflected by tourists in both interviews and online restaurant reviews of Little Italy restaurants run by Albanian staff. Tourists in Little Italy expressed a desire for 'an authentic Italian experience'. In the words of a young woman visiting from southern Florida: 'We wanted to experience a new culture, something different, not like Olive Garden [a nationwide chain of standardized Italian restaurants], traditional Italian.' In restaurant reviews, tourists cite Italian names (Tony, Giovanni etc.), when describing interactions with waiting staff, with positive experiences marked by perceived authenticity: 'Our waiter's name was Giovanni... compete with the old country accent and all. He had the look of someone who would just as soon sprinkle parmesan on your pasta as cut your throat'; 'Our waiter was "old" school Italian'; 'Every server there is from Italy and you get the sense they started working here 30 years ago when they first arrived in the US and have remained ever since'.[6]

Most of the actual remaining ethnic Italians in Little Italy own restaurants and thus strive for economic success in their enterprises. This includes Albanian Kosovars plausibly passing as Italians to draw in clientele. At no time throughout the study did I witness restaurant owners react against the implicit presentation of Italian identities. Allowing Albanian Kosovars to present themselves as the Italian 'face' of the restaurant (they 'look Southern Italian') can only serve to solidify the perceived Italian authenticity of their establishments, which indisputably declined following Italian out-migration from the area at the turn of the century. Owners thus participate in attempts to preserve the old world in the new, Italy in Little Italy, as authenticity remains difficult to achieve even for Italians in the 'melting pot' society of the USA. Efforts made to establish authenticity are evidenced in restaurant websites claiming historical precedence, Italian roots and the ability to 'bring the warmth, class, and charm of Italy to your doorstep'.[7]Despite the triangle (of Albanian Kosovars, tourists and restaurant owners) bounding the opportunity to pass and therefore assume ethnicity, others elucidate the inauthenticity of this performance. Italians/Italian Americans working in or visiting the neighbourhood who do not own restaurants – as both less naive than the tourists visiting the area in relation to Italian ethnicity, and less invested in the Italian experience than restaurant owners – portray critical views of this population. According to Janice, a young Italian American store clerk who has worked in the area for over a year:

> One hundred per cent they pretend they are Italian! They act Italian in dress, talk, imitating. They don't represent their own. They try to assimilate into the Italian culture … The Albanians even had a section in the Columbus Day Parade and I mean, no one's being racists here, but what the fuck are they doing here?

Italian American former resident of the area, Joseph, critiqued the motivations of the Albanian Kosovars even further: 'We have a lot of Albanians. They make believe they are Italian... you should stay away from them. They are like the Big Bad Wolves... stay away from the Big Bad Wolf! They're big phonies.'

Regardless of such scathing critiques, none of the Italian Americans who were aware of this assumed ethnicity expressed the desire to undermine it. I believe this arises from their own fragile 'Italian' identities. Of the 3rd generation and beyond, multiple Italian Americans with whom I spoke explained that they do not speak Italian, many never having been to Italy. Thus, attempting to 'call uncle' on ethnic Albanians could force them to reflect on their own tethered ties to the Italian ethnicity beyond history – present claims they, themselves, can make on being 'authentically' Italian. This has been demonstrated in the work of Crispino (1980), Alba (1985, 1990), Gans (1992) and McDermott and Samson (2005), who cite decreased identification as Italian in the third and fourth generations; a movement from classification as Italian to white in broader American society; and decreased involvement in 'Italian' activities (e.g. the San Gennaro Festival on Mulberry Street) by Italian Americans.

3. Cultural opportunity

Assumed ethnicity is not an assimilative process, as these migrants concurrently present their Albanian Kosovar identities to 'insiders' on the back stage. Hidden in cabinets, next to cash registers and on key rings, Albanian and Kosovar flags hold an undeniable presence within the restaurant world of Little Italy. In Goffmanian (1959) terms, the back stage is conceptualized as entirely separate from the front stage. However, in the case of Albanian Kosovars in Little Italy, the front and back stages are not independent. Assumed ethnicity is, in fact, justified through authenticating linkages between Kosovo and Italy. The importance of multiple allegiances is physically evident in the four flags taped to the cash register of Vinny's: a small American flag pasted next to a slightly bigger Italian flag, an even larger Kosovar flag to the right and the biggest of all, the Albanian flag on the far right. Cultural opportunity in the restaurant, where the front and back stages become linked, thus draws on Weber's (2002) conception of elective affinity, here referencing the deep affiliation or unconscious coherence between Albanian and Italian ethnicities (Howe 1978).

While the front stage is clearly presented, the back stage reveals the complexities of assumed ethnicity. Long-term workers in Little Italy, in contrast to recent recruits, discuss connections to Italy. This suggests the relationship of such ties to both time and hierarchy in the world of the restaurant. It additionally elicits a reversal of Benedict Anderson's (1993) conception of the imagined community, which emphasizes that while most members of society are not in direct contact, they imagine themselves as a collective entity and define their understanding of civil society on the basis of such. In contrast, the environment of Little Italy on Mulberry Street – the structural and performative opportunities of this space – forge a cultural opportunity to imagine ties to Italy, through which individuals can justify switching between ethnicities to themselves.[8]

Elective affinity here requires two stages: (1) breaking down boundaries between Albanians from Kosovo and Albanians from Albania; and (2) connecting Albania (and ethnic Albanians, as a whole) to Italy. First, elective affinity is forged through

CITIES, DIVERSITY AND ETHNICITY

claims of close relationships – thereby collapsing the boundaries – between Albanians from Kosovo and Albanians from Albania. Despite a conflicted history, almost all of the Albanian Kosovars interviewed noted the singularity of these groups. This draws from markedly improved country relations since Kosovo gained independence in 2008. More importantly, living together in the Bronx and Brooklyn has led to social solidarity among Albanian migrants from Kosovo and those from Albania, a re-fusing of these split nations – even prior to the recently improved relationship between their two states. 'We are not different.' 'All Albanians are the same.' As Cima noted in his discussion of this relationship: 'Here it's our language; here we all live together, the older Albanians in Pelham Parkway and the Albanians from Kosovo who came during the war.' This entails 'recasting the material of the past [and present] in innovative ways', in which distinctions between Albanians from Albania and Albanian Kosovars become less important than in other discussions (e.g. whether Kosovo should be absorbed into a greater Albania) (Nagel 1994, 167).

The second step in elective affinity is that drawn between Albania and Italy, as the vast majority of ethnically Albanian (whether from Kosovo or Albania) individuals interviewed espouse Italian selves. 'Albania is right on the border of Italy too, so that connection is there, there are Albanians who live in Italy. And the Albanians from Albania, 80% of those actually speak Italian.' 'There was a place in Albania called *Toskaria* and that is where the word *Toscana* or Tuscany comes from.' The *idea* of a shared history (whether distorted or even false as in the case of 'Toscana'[9])– in particular that 'so many Albanians' lived in Italy 'for hundreds of years' prior to the 'splitting' of Albania and Kosovo– serves to further fuse these two migrant groups in the Albanian Kosovars' understandings of Italian linkages. As summarized by Dardan:

> Yes, there is an old community from hundreds of years ago of Albanians in southern Italy and they speak old Albanian. We used to call this the "capital of Albanians". The Albanians from Italy actually went there 600 years ago and live mostly in Calabria – the old Albanians and many of them are now in Boston too. Also, before 1913 Italy was the biggest supporter of Albania – before it was divided, Kosovo given away as a province. There was even once an Albanian prime minister of Italy! (Francesco Crispi). Once, someone asked him "are you a republican or a monarchist?" and he said, "no, no I am an Albanian!"

Thus, drawing on (at times imagined) history, in combination with contemporary national and migrant community narratives, long-term Albanian Kosovars working in Little Italy express elective affinity with Italy. These may consist of macro-level instances, as noted above. They may also consist of emphasizing micro-level experiences of visiting or actual migration to Italy prior to migration to the USA, where some lived for years or even decades. Albanian Kosovar, Naim, elucidating concurrent Italian and Albanian identities, said: 'I could pass for both easily. I am bicultural…I lived in Italy. I am Albanian. I am both.'

The cultural justifications of assumed ethnicity draw in the ability to facilitate historical connections to Italy, often through the idea of a single Albanian identity, thus far only actualized in the ethnic enclave of Pelham Parkway, the Bronx.

Paradoxically, unifying Albanian Kosovar and Albanian identities in turn facilitates elective affinity between Albanian and Italian ethnicities. This further facilitates the internal psychological justifications of the performance or technique of the self in assumed ethnicity. Rather than falsifying Italian identities, these migrants internalize Italian-ness, perceived *as part of* their complex identities. Conditioned by, and conditional upon, the specific (hi)stories of Kosovo, Albania, Italy and Little Italy on Mulberry Street, migrants are not only economic but also identity entrepreneurs. Here Roots (to Italy) grow down, out of this experience, rather than this experience out of 'real' roots in Italy.

4. Discussion

Classic migration theories have pointed towards a tendency of ethnic groups to seek assimilation into the mainstream in order to accomplish economic saliency and avoid stigma; and more recent theory highlights attempts to permeate boundaries between the mainstream and the ethnic other (Brubaker 2001; Alba 2005; Wimmer 2008; Lamont 2012). This analysis suggests another phenomenon of interest, which reveals additional micro dynamics involved in ethnic identification. The multicultural of today's societies means more than recognizing or even prizing diversity. It also means the instrumentality of multiple identities – being able to draw not only on various *facets of* identity (ethnicity, race, religion, nationality), but entirely *alternative* identities in the everyday presentation of self.

This analysis has elucidated how and why ethnic Albanians from Kosovo assume Italian ethnicity in Little Italy on Mulberry Street, on the front stage, while maintaining back-stage Albanian ethnicity. It has further drawn attention to the ties between the front and back stages, developed over time and ascendency in the occupational hierarchy of Little Italy. Strategy – performative opportunity – is thus informed by structural opportunity. Cultural opportunities (i.e. to build bridges to Italy in identity, back rather than forwards in time) are then born in the arms of this strategy-structure union.

Drawing broader strokes on the sociological landscape, this study has responded to the need for on-the-ground research aimed at understanding everyday de-stigmatiza-tion strategies of specific ethnic or racial groups (e.g. Light, Sabagh, and Bozorgmehr 1994; Lamont 2012). Options and opportunities in the presentation of self are informed by societal boundaries (e.g. black and white racial conceptions in the USA), understandings of authenticity and stigmatized identities. While negative connotations of Albanian ethnicity and Islam proliferate, the ability to put forth Italian face(t)s of identity interacts both with a reality of European origin and perceived physical ethno-racial markers (as in the case of Bosnian migrants in Norway, see Valenta 2009). Moving beyond this specific case, one may ask: Why would Pakistani restaurant owners on Brick Lane, London title their restaurants 'Indian' establishments? Why would Americans in Europe sew Canadian flags onto their backpacks during the Iraqi war? Why would Shi'ite Muslims officially allow for passing (*taqiyyah*) as Sunni Muslims?[10] All beg the question of why specific ethnic, national or religious groups seek to 'pass' as other ethnic, national or religious groups – rather than simply attempt assimilation into the mainstream or reify existing ethnic/national/religious identities? Such diverse forms of identity entrepreneurship suggest the presence of multiple boundaries in determining acceptance, if not success, in everyday encounters.

5. Conclusion

> He would say untruths and be ever double, both in his words and meaning (Shakespeare 1999, 180)

Moving beyond visions of situational switching between ethnicity and assimilation as the two options for minority populations, this study suggests a third option: assuming an alternative ethnic identity, employed instrumentally in mainstream encounters. Confronted with transnational reality, the migrants in this story create transmutable selves through a combination of structural, performative and cultural opportunities, aimed at succeeding in a new society.

In this first case of exploration, engaged to develop a new concept, assumed Italian ethnicity by Albanian Kosovars is shown to facilitate everyday encounters on the front stage of Little Italy on Mulberry Street. Both economic opportunity and avoidance of social exclusion play roles in encouraging this process of constructing (a place in the market) and concurrent deconstruction (of stigma). For Albanian Kosovars in Little Italy, structural circumstances (an available identity through which a specific group can 'pass') allow for successful place-making, followed by the creation of a front stage on which to perform the skilful assumption of an alternative identity. Finally, unlike Goffman (1959), I suggest that the back stage is not entirely distinct from the front. In fact, justifications of assumed ethnicity to oneself are made through back-stage identity, by drawing micro- and macro-historical connections between Kosovo, Albania and Italy. In this Italian-marketed market, Albanian Kosovars are identity entrepreneurs who facilitate everyday encounters with the mainstream by switching to assumed, 'real deal' Italian ethnicity.

This study reaches not only to expand on conceptions of ethnicities and boundaries in the discipline of sociology, but concurrently across disciplines in illuminating the nuances of deception. In the philosophical tradition of Nietzsche (1873), it suggests *untruths* or *unlies* rather than lies: 'white' lies on two counts as they are both racialized and innocuous. The idea suggested by this analysis, a level of deception implicitly assumed rather than explicitly stated, is further in dialogue with studies in law (Yoshino 2007) and social psychology (Hopper and Bell 1984). Specifically, Hopper and Bell (1984) propose a broadened concept for deceptive acts, assumptions and interactions. They emphasize that deception is not always verbal or explicit. What they term *unlies – deception through implication –* captures the sphere of social life explicated in this analysis. The concept of assumed ethnicity thus falls into a tradition developed in the literary, the philosophical, the legal and the psychological: an implication not of distinction, but rather the disintegration of boundaries– between disciplines, selves and here ethnicities.

And so we return to the lively streets of Little Italy: red, white and green signage marketing a district supposedly 'dying' and yet still filled with verve, with venues serving 'authentic Italian cuisine' in 'godfather-esque' environs. Only time will tell whether the tactic of assumed ethnicity will lead to ethnic transformation of the area, or instead continue to project–and paradoxically thereby protect – the little of Italy left on Mulberry Street. In conceiving of future implications, we must keep in mind that the environment of cultural possibility shifts in accordance with structural and performative opportunities. For instance, one might consider the example of actors utilizing black face paint to portray the black man – once aspired to for roles like Othello, today considered a racialized caricature. To 'black face' now connotes not only inauthenticity, but much worse, bigotry (Strausbaugh 2006). One must ask whether this play on ethnicity is entirely different in that the ethnic performers are not merely putting on a show, but (have come to) believe that they possess partial Italian identities. And as more individuals become aware of the Albanian presence, one must also ask whether this tactic will remain socially viable and virtually innocuous. Will it challenge the comfort zone of these performers when they have to justify their assumed ethnicity, not only on the back stage to compatriots and selves by developing imagined ties, but also on the front stage for patrons?

Or will patrons simply participate in Little Italy as the child participates in the pretence of Disneyland – imagining mobsters, whispering *ciao* to the waiters – and relish it all the same? In the words of Nietzsche (1873), 'men do not flee from being deceived, as much as from being damaged by deception.' Many tourists in search of a pseudo-Italian fantasyland may in fact gain from the assumed ethnicity of Albanian Kosovars. They may simply continue to take part and play parts in staging, maintaining and mystifying Mulberry Street.

Acknowledgements

Many thanks to Julia Adams, Jeffrey Alexander, Sara Bastomski, Ellen Becker, Jonathan Endelman, Thorn Kray, Elizabeth Roberto, Philip Smith and Elisabeth Wood for their detailed feedback and close reading of this paper.

Notes

1.   Yelp restaurant review http://www.yelp.com/biz/da-nico-ristorante-new-york?start=40.
2.   Merriam Webster online dictionary: http://www.merriam-webster.com/dictionary/assume?show=0&t=1389181366.
3.   This research was evaluated and approved by the Human Subjects Committee. All informants have been kept anonymous, including replacing all names and identifying markers with pseudonyms.
4.   Little Italy on Mulberry Street is almost entirely a single long avenue at the southern tip of Manhattan. It is bounded on the north by Broome Street, south by Canal Street, west by Baxter Street and east by Mott Street and is thus six square blocks.
5.   Assuming Italian ethnicity provides the opportunity for both economic and social mobility. Macro-level economic success interacts with the micro-level desire to de-stigmatize individual experience, suggesting linkages between the structural and performative aspects of assumed ethnicity. While many Americans remain unaware of Albanian identity and politics, as 'the forgotten part of Europe', mass media accounts and academic studies focus on stigmatized aspects of this ethnicity (Hysen Demiraj, cited in *The New York Times* on June 16,

CITIES, DIVERSITY AND ETHNICITY

2009). A history of the worst kind of communism (King and Mai 2009), participation in illegal activities (most notably the mob) (reported in *The New York Times* on March 18, 1991 and June 16, 2009), and the religion of Islam (Jenkins 2006; *The New York Times*, May 10, 2007) have coloured these representations since the late twentieth century. Albanian community representatives have expressed fear of negative impacts on the image of Albanians in the USA. In 2013, an Albanian migrant filed a New York Federal District Court suit (Kajoshaj v. City of New York), claiming that his son failed to progress in school because of discrimination on the bases of Islam and Albanian ethnicity (USDCM 2013).

6. Yelp: http://www.yelp.com/biz/il-cortile-new-york#query:Best%20Places%20To%20Eat%20 Little%20Italy; http://www.yelp.com/biz/angelo-of-mulberry-st-new-york?start=40; http://www. yelp.com/biz/il-cortile-new-york?start=40; http://www.yelp.com/biz/angelo-of-mulberry-st-new-yo rk?start=80.

7. Angelo's of Mulberry Street website: http://www.angelosofmulberryst.com/location.htm.

8. This does not mean that no real ties exist, rather that they are referenced regardless of whether individuals migrated to Italy or visited Italy, themselves.

9. In fact, the word *Toscana* was a term coined in the Middle Ages to describe the early Etruscan civilization of *Tuskia* (Liebeb 1851).

10. Due to a history of persecution, the Shi'ia denomination of Muslims is allowed to dissimulate (conceal their religious identity), in order to avoid discrimination or threat (see Virani 2007).

References

Alba, Richard. 1985. *Italian-Americans: Into the Twilight of Ethnicity*. Englewood Cliffs, NJ: Prentice Press.

Alba, Richard. 1990. *Ethnic Identity Transformation of White America*. New Haven, CT: Yale University Press.

Alba, Richard. 2005. "Bright vs. Blurred Boundaries: Second-Generation Assimilation and Exclusion in France, Germany and the United States." *Ethnic and Racial Studies* 28 (1): 20–49. doi:10.1080/0141987042000280003

Alba, Richard, John Logan, and Kyle Crowder. 1997. "White Ethnic Neighborhoods and Assimilation: The Greater New York Region, 1980–1990." *Social Forces* 75 (3): 883–912.

Alba, Richard, and Victor Nee. 1997. "Rethinking Assimilation: Theory for a New Era of Immigration." *International Migration Review* 31 (4): 826–874. doi:10.2307/2547416

Al-Haj, Majid. 2002. "Identity Patterns among Immigrants from the Former Soviet Union in Israel: Assimilation vs. Ethnic Formation." *International Migration* 40 (2): 49–70. doi:10. 1111/1468-2435.00190

Anderson, Benedict. 1993. *Imagined Communities: Reflections on the Origin and Spread of Nationalism*. New York: Verso Press.

Baily, Samuel. 1999. *Immigrants in the Lands of Promise: Italians in Buenos Aires and New York City, 1870–1914*. Ithaca, NY: Cornell University Press.

Brubaker, Rogers. 2001. "The Return of Assimilation? Changing Perspectives on Immigration and its Sequels in France, Germany, and the United States." *Ethnic and Racial Studies* 24 (4): 531–548. doi:10.1080/01419870120049770

Calgar, Ayse. 1997. "Hyphenated Identities and the Limits of Culture." In *The Politics of Multiculturalism in the New Europe: Racism, Identity and Community*, edited by Tariq Modood and Pnina Werbner, 69–185. London: ZED Books.

Corsi, Edward. 1942. "Italian Immigrants and their Children." *Annals of the American Academy of Political and Social Science* 223: 100–106. doi:10.1177/000271624222300116

Crispino, James. 1980. *The Assimilation of Ethnic Groups: The Italian Case*. Charlottesville, VI: Center for Migration Studies.

Duffy, Michael. 1999. "Clinton: Making Peace with War." *Time Magazine* 153 (13): 37.

Ebaugh, Helen, and Mary Curry. 2000. "Fictive Kin as Social Capital in New Immigrant Communities." *Sociological Perspective* 43 (2): 189–209. doi:10.2307/1389793

Erickson, Rebecca 1995. "The Importance of Authenticity for Self and Society." *Symbolic Interaction* 18 (2): 121–144.

Gans, Herbert. 1992. "Ethnic Invention and Acculturation, a Bumpy-Line Approach." *Journal of American Ethnic History* 12 (1): 42–52.

Goffman, Erving. 1959. *The Presentation of Self in Everyday Life*. New York: Doubleday.

Gordon, Milton. 1964. *Assimilation in American Life: The Role of Race, Religion and National Origins*. New York: Oxford University Press.

Gorman, Eric, and Stacey Richman. 2001. "The Albanian-American Community in New York City." Voices of New York. New York: New York University. Accessed 11 March, http://www.nyuvoicesofnewyork.com/Communities/2001/albania.html.

Hopper, Robert, and Robert Bell. 1984. "Broadening the Deception Concept." *Quarterly Journal of Speech* 70 (3): 288–302. doi:10.1080/00335638409383698

Howe, Richard. 1978. "Max Weber's Elective Affinities: Sociology within the Bounds of Pure Reason." *American Journal of Sociology* 84 (2): 366–385. doi:10.1086/226788

Jacobson, Jessica. 1997. "Religion and Ethnicity as Alternative Sources of Identity among Young British Pakistanis." *Ethnic and Racial Studies* 20 (2): 238–256. doi:10.1080/0141 9870.1997.9993960

Jenkins, Brian Michael. 2006. *Would be Warriors: Incidents of Jihadist Terrorist Radicalization in the United States since September 11, 2001*. Santa Monica, CA: Rand Corporation.

King, Russell, and Nicola Mai. 2009. "Italophilia Meets Albanophobia: Paradoxes of Asymmetric Assimilation and Identity Processes among Albanian Immigrants in Italy." *Ethnic and Racial Studies* 32 (1): 117–138. doi:10.1080/01419870802245034

Lamont, Michel. 2012. "Ordinary People Doing Extraordinary Things: Responses to Stigmatization in Comparative Perspective." *Racial and Ethnic Studies* 35 (3): 365–381. doi:10.1080/01419870.2011.589528

Liebeb, Francis, ed. 1851. *Encyclopedia Americana*. Philadelpha, PA: T.K. & P.G. Collins.

Light, Ivan, George Sabagh, and Mehdi Bozorgmehr. 1994. "Beyond the Ethnic Enclave Economy." *Social Problems* 41 (1): 65–80. doi:10.2307/3096842

McDermott, Monica, and Frank Samson. 2005. "White Racial and Ethnic Identity in the United States." *Annual Review of Sociology* 31: 245–261. doi:10.1146/annurev.soc.31.0413 04.122322

Model, Suzanne. 1985. "A Comparative Perspective on the Ethnic Enclave: Blacks, Italians, and Jews in New York City." *International Migration Review* 19 (1): 64–81. doi:10.2307/2545656

Nagata, Judith. 1974. "What is a Malay? Situation Selection of Ethnic Identity in Plural Society." *American Ethonologist* 1 (2): 331–350. doi:10.1525/ae.1974.1.2.02a00080

Nagel, Joanne. 1994. "Constructing Ethnicity: Creating and Recreating Ethnic Identity and Culture." *Social Problems* 41 (1): 152–176. doi:10.2307/3096847

Nagel, Joanne, and Lynn Staeheli. 2005. "'We're just like the Irish': Narratives of Assimilation, Belonging and Citizenship amongst Arab-American Activists." *Citizenship Studies* 9 (5): 485–498. doi:10.1080/13621020500301262

Nietzsche, Frederich. 1873. "On Truth and Lie in an Extra-Moral Sense." Accessed November 29. http://oregonstate.edu/instruct/phl201/modules/Philosophers/Nietzsche/Truth_and_Lie_in_an_Extra-Moral_Sense.htm

Sanders, Jimy. 2002. "Ethnic Boundaries and Identity in Plural Societies." *Annual Review of Sociology* 28: 327–357. doi:10.1146/annurev.soc.28.110601.140741

Shakespeare, William. 1999. *King Henry III*. New York: Oxford University Press.

Steinberg, Stephen. 2001. *The Ethnic Myth: Race, Ethnicity, and Class in America*. Boston, MA: Beacon Press.

Strausbaugh, John. 2006. *Black* like *You: Blackface, Whiteface, Insult and Imitation in American Population Culture*. New York: Penguin Press.

Turner, Ralph, and Jerald Schutte. 1981. "The True Self Method for Studying the Self-Conception." *Symbolic Interaction* 4 (1): 1–20.

USCB (United States Census Bureau). 2010. "American Community Survey." Accessed November 29. http://factfinder2.census.gov/faces/tableservices/jsf/pages/productview.xhtml?pid=ACS_10_1YR_B04003&prodType=table

USDCM (United States District Court Memorandum). 2013. Kajoshaj v. City of New York. Accessed November 29. http://docs.justia.com/cases/federal/district-courts/new-york/nyedce/1:2011cv04780/322601/20/0.pdf?ts=1359038361

Valenta, Marko. 2009. "'Immigrants' Identity Negotiations and Coping with Stigma in Different Relational Frames." *Symbolic Interaction* 32 (4): 351–371. doi:10.1525/si.2009.32.4.351

Virani, Shafique. 2007. *The Ismailis in the Middle Ages: A History of Survival, a Search for Salvation*. Oxford: Oxford University Press.

Waters, Mary. 1990. *Ethnic Options: Choosing Ethnic Identities in America*. Berkeley, CA: University of California Press.

Weber, Max. 2002. *The Protestant Ethic and the Spirit of Capitalism*. New York: Penguin Books [first published in German in 1905].

Wells, Matt. 2005. "'People's Pope' Moves New Yorkers." BBC News, April 3.

Wimmer, Andreas. 2008. "The Making and Unmaking of Ethnic Boundaries: A Multilevel Process Theory." *American Journal of Sociology* 113 (4): 970–1022. doi:10.1086/522803

Yoshino, Kenji. 2007. *Covering: The Hidden Assault on our Civil Rights*. New York: Random House.

Zevallos, Zuleyka. 2003. "'That is my Australian side.' The Ethnicity and Sexuality of Young Australian Women of South and Central American Origin." *Journal of Sociology* 39 (1): 81–98. doi:10.1177/0004869003039001321

Zolberg, Aristide, and Litt Woon. 1999. "Why Islam is like Spanish: Cultural Incorporation in Europe and the United States?" *Politics and Society* 27 (1): 5–38. doi:10.1177/0032329299027001002

Levelling the playing field: patterns of ethnic philanthropy among Los Angeles' middle- and upper-class Latino entrepreneurs

Jody Agius Vallejo

This paper examines whether middle- and upper-class Latino entrepreneurs retain a sense of ethnic solidarity expressed through community giving that is aimed at promoting the mobility of co-ethnics. I find that middle-class Latino entrepreneurs engage in more unstructured philanthropic activities, such as volunteering their time at Latino-centric organizations or mentoring low-income Latinos. In contrast, elite Latino entrepreneurs are creating ethnic social structures that focus on education and Latino business development.

Latinos' increasing presence in the middle and upper classes in the USA (Agius Vallejo 2012; Jimenez 2010; Vasquez 2011) and the fact that some are accumulating high levels of wealth through business ownership (Valdez 2011), might be a harbinger of Latino philanthropy directed at ethnic communities as some affluent Latinos retain an ethos of giving back to family and community (Agius Vallejo 2012). However, whether successful Latino business owners give back to low-income Latino communities has not been carefully examined and documented.

The central question of this research is do Latino entrepreneurs cut ties to ethnic communities once they attain middle- or upper-class status or do they maintain a sense of ethnic solidarity expressed through community giving that is aimed at promoting the mobility of co-ethnics? Three questions guide this analysis. First, do successful Latino business owners retain ties to ethnic communities? Second, to what extent do successful Latino business owners give back to the community? Finally, what are Latino business owners' motivations for giving back?

Examining successful Latino business owners' patterns of giving back is important for several reasons. First, the number of Latino businesses increased 44% between 2002 and 2007– more than double the 18% increase in the total number of small businesses nationwide (US Survey of Business Owners 2007). This increase outpaced the growth rate of the Hispanic population, which grew 36% in almost the same time period (US Census). We know little about successful Latino entrepreneurs because scholars primarily examine low-class Latino entrepreneurs who are touted as owning small subsistence-only businesses in ethnic enclaves (Farlie and Robb 2008). Second, Latino communities are generally portrayed as lacking social capital (Baca Zinn and Wells

2000; Portes and Zhou 1993) – the ability to mobilize resources and networks based on group membership (Coleman 1988; Portes and Sensenbrenner 1993) – resulting in a dearth of networks and ethnic social structures that can guard against downward or stagnated assimilation and advance the mobility of co-ethnics. In this vein, research on ethnic enterprise has been most concerned with what makes specific immigrant groups succeed or fail in day-to-day business operations rather than non-business activities and its effects on the social processes and mechanisms that foster community building, social capital and group mobility.

This has resulted in a substantial conceptual gap regarding how entrepreneurs' philanthropic activities affect ethnic communities (Zhou 2004). This research is important because successful Latino entrepreneurs may make an impact at the community level by infusing the community with financial and social capital that promotes upward mobility. Finally, low-income Latino communities are severely underfunded. A 2011 report by the Foundation Center finds that between 1999 and 2009, Latino communities received just one cent from every dollar distributed by funders (i.e. independent, corporate and community foundations). Thus, if they do give back, middle- and upper-class Latino entrepreneurs – the Latino elite – may help to close social and economic capital gaps in Latino communities and help to accelerate Latino mobility into the middle class.

This study draws on forty-five in-depth interviews with Latino entrepreneurs in Los Angeles, California and ten interviews with people active in Los Angeles' Latino business community (i.e. politicians, non-profit directors, corporate executives). Los Angeles is a natural social laboratory for studying Latino enterprise because Latinos comprise nearly half of Los Angeles' population; California is home to a quarter of all Latino-owned firms in the nation, the largest concentration of any state; and Latinos own 20% of all firms (359,885) in the Los Angeles region, more than any other minority group (US Survey of Business Owners 2007).

Previous research

One traditional mobility ladder for immigrants and their descendants is entrepreneurship. However, Latinos have historically lagged behind whites and other immigrant groups, especially Asians, in rates of entrepreneurship, leading scholars to express pessimism about the extent to which Latino communities can benefit from ethnic enterprise[1] (Lofstrom and Wang 2006; Portes and Zhou 1992).

The majority of research on Latino entrepreneurs in Los Angeles, and the USA more generally, makes noteworthy contributions but it is concentrated on unauthorized or low-wage immigrant business owners whose businesses require low levels of education and start-up capital (Lopez and Trevizo 2009; Ramirez and Hondagneu-Sotelo 2009). Observers note that Latino immigrants, especially Mexicans, are less likely than other immigrant groups to engage in enterprise because Latino migration is generally a low-wage labour migration, which means that Latino immigrants, especially Mexicans, have low levels of family capital (Sanders and Nee 1996, 245, 246) and human and social capital resources that are critical to business start-up and long-term success (Farlie and Robb 2008). Relatively low levels of education and personal wealth constrains the ability of Latino immigrants and their descendants to start and grow businesses (Lofstrom and Wang 2006; Farlie and Robb 2008), which potentially hinders their ability to give back to the community. Scholars also argue that Latino communities are generally lacking in 'high-quality' class and social capital resources that can facilitate upward mobility (Baca Zinn and Wells 2000, 256), such as those generated by business (Raijman and Tienda 2003), an assertion that contributes to the notion that Latinos are at risk to follow a downward or stagnated incorporation trajectory over the generations (Portes and Zhou 1993).

In sharp contrast, Asian entrepreneurs, especially Chinese and Koreans, are lauded as exemplars in business. Their high levels of education, wealth and ethnic solidarity – which is an ability to draw on class and social capital resources, such as group trust, financial and social reciprocity exchanges, and co-ethnic embeddedness in niches – facilitates not only business success but also the creation of ethnic social structures that benefit the larger community (Light and Bonacich 1991; Raijman and Tienda 2003). Ethnic social structures in minority communities are important because they assist in incorporating immigrants and their children, which advances a more linear assimilation path into the middle class for succeeding generations (Zhou and Kim 2006). Ethnic business elites have proven important for the advancement of non-Latino immigrant groups as they provide social and financial capital and introduce resources that generate community capital and the advancement of successive generations. For example, Chinese and Korean communities are known for their strong business and trade associations and financial institutions, which buttress Asian businesses (Min 2008; Zhou and Kim 2006). Elite Asian entrepreneurs have also been instrumental in creating community resources and non-business ethnic social structures – such as scholarship funds and supplementary educational institutions that help prepare the second generation for selective colleges – that generate resources for second-generation mobility and incorporation (Zhou and Kim 2006; Min 2008). As Zhou and Kim (2006, 6) argue, 'intangible community forces and social capital must be supported by tangible ethnic social structures in order to generate resources for upward social mobility beyond mere survival.'

Wedded to the idea that Latino ethnic communities, especially those primarily comprised of Mexicans, are lacking middle-class resources and tangible ethnic social structures that advance mobility, scholars have generally overlooked successful Latino business owners and they have not sufficiently examined whether they channel resources into Latino communities that facilitate incorporation. Traditional assimilation theory posits that economically assimilated immigrants and their descendants will cut ties to ethnic communities as they leave immigrant enclaves and continue to incorporate into the host society's social and economic institutions (Gordon 1964). In this vein, some have argued that minorities abandon inner cities and ethnic communities as they achieve mobility, resulting in a dearth of institutions and social resources in urban communities (Wilson 1987). Valdez (2011, 152) argues that Latino entrepreneurs 'characterize themselves as rugged individualists striving for the American dream... Latino/a entrepreneurs reproduce the ideology of individualism and meritocracy, even as they experience structural inequality.' We might hypothesize then that elite Latino entrepreneurs will exhibit an individualistic orientation to mobility where they do not funnel time and resources into Latino communities with the goal of advancing Latinos as a group. While traditional assimilation theory suggests that economically integrated immigrants and their descendants will cut ties to the ethnic community and not retain a collective identity, and others argue that Latino entrepreneurs are rugged individualists, recent research examining the transnational philanthropic activities of ethnic organizations (Portes, Escobar, and Radford 2007), and the civic engagement of immigrants and their descendants (Terriquez 2012), suggests that ethnic philanthropic activity increases with time in the USA, demonstrating that these activities are not incompatible with assimilation. Thus, today's successful Latino entrepreneurs might retain a collectivist orientation to mobility and engage in ethnic philanthropy that advances mobility.

Like Asian immigrants, Latinos in the USA have their own unique history of ethnic philanthropy that is born out of negotiating their social mobility within a negative economic and social context. Latino communities have long been home to community organizations where the focus initially concentrated on settling newcomers and providing help to immigrant workers and slowly shifted to tackling issues of discrimination and exploitation. For example, in the mid-nineteenth century, Mexican Americans imported *mutualista* organizations from Mexico that were focused on Mexican nationalism and providing social and material support to co-ethnics (Hernandez 1983). And during the civil rights movement a number of organizations emerged aimed at redressing discrimination and inequality, such as United Farm Workers and the National Council of La Raza (Marquez and Jennings 2000). While researchers have richly detailed the rise of national Latino advocacy organizations, we know little about what is occurring on the ground in local communities and whether successful Latino entrepreneurs channel their financial and social capital into tangible ethnic social structures in an attempt to advance Latino mobility and incorporation.

Data and methods

Latinos own 20% of all firms (where a Latino owns at least 51% of the firm) in Los Angeles, more than any other minority group. They are concentrated in transportation and warehousing (45%), administrative support (42%) and waste management (42%), and under-represented in others, such as real estate (13%) finance and insurance (9%). People of Mexican origin own nearly two-thirds of all firms, followed by Cubans at 3%, Puerto Ricans at 2% and 'other' Latino at 25%. Mexican Americans dominate in nearly all sectors (US Survey of Business Owners 2007). The majority are sole proprietorships; however, 8% of firms in 2007 had paid employees and employed more than 155,000 people (US Survey of Business Owners 2007).

This research is based on fifty-five in-depth structured interviews. Forty-five interviews were conducted with Latino entrepreneurs. Respondents are defined as middle class if they have an annual household income over the national median of $51,413, and the majority have a household income above Los Angeles' median income, which is $55,700 (Current Population Survey 2008). Upper-class business owners are defined as having an income above $159,000, which is the top 5% of income earners in the USA based on the Internal Revenue Service's 2010 database. Just under 40% of the respondents are upper-class business owners. Fifteen per cent of the sample is first generation (foreign-born and migrated to the USA as an adult); 30% are 1.5 generation (migrated to the USA before the age of twelve); 38% are second generation (the native-born children of immigrants); and 13% are third generation or higher (the grandchildren of immigrants). Only one of the respondents did not graduate high school and the majority hold bachelor's or graduate degrees. The respondents own businesses in sectors where Latinos have high representation, such as construction, and in sectors where they are under-represented, such as finance. The majority of the respondents own firms outside the ethnic community and do not specifically target Latino customers. However, five enterprises revolve around the Latino population, such as Hispanic marketing and advertising firms.

The respondents' ages range from twenty-nine to sixty-nine, with a median of forty-three. Forty-two per cent of the respondents are female. Years in business range from one to thirty-one, with the median being ten years. The majority of the respondents are of Mexican origin. Two of the respondents are Cuban, one is Nicaraguan, one is Peruvian, one is Puerto Rican, one is Guatemalan and three are Salvadoran.

Lasting between two to three hours, the interviews were conducted by the author and two Latino graduate students, either at the subject's office or in public, between October 2010 and July 2012. The interviews were open-ended, tape-recorded and then transcribed verbatim. The interviewer took an inductive approach and asked respondents questions about their educational, work and entrepreneurial trajectories, class background, access to capital, networks, and patterns of financial and social support. The transcribed interviews were read line by line and coded using Dedoose, a qualitative software program. The interviews were coded for the following themes: giving back through business, community, service to the Latino community and to the non-Latino community; reasons for giving back; reasons for not giving back.

Respondents were sampled in several ways in order to obtain a varied sample of middle-class and high-income Latino entrepreneurs. Latino-owned banks in Los Angeles referred us to their customers. We were also referred to middle-class and high-income business owners through certified public accountants and financial planners whose clientele include Latino-owned businesses. We then used a snowball-sampling technique to recruit additional participants, resulting in the inclusion of Latino entrepreneurs who do not conduct business at the banks and who were not referred by the accountants and financial planners, in order to achieve maximum variation of results. Snowball sampling is often the best way to locate participants with particular attributes, such as middle and upper-class status and the ownership of professional firms (Berg 2007). I purposefully did not sample respondents through Latino professional or business organizations (although many of the respondents were involved in these organizations) in order to avoid bias towards those who are already active in the Latino community. The data are by no means representative of or generalizable to all middle- and upper-class Latino entrepreneurs in Los Angeles, but the respondents are diverse in terms of business sector, immigrant generation and length of time in business.

Finally, interviews were undertaken with four executive officers of two Latino-owned banks in Los Angeles and six people active in Los Angeles' business community (i.e. politicians, non-profit directors) who work with Latino business owners, giving a total of fifty-five interviews.

Results

Middle-class Latino entrepreneurs: agents of social capital

The majority of Latino entrepreneurs interviewed for this study retain a sense of ethnic solidarity with co-ethnics, which is expressed by giving back financially or socially to the Latino community. When Los Angeles' Latino entrepreneurs refer to the 'community', they are generally not alluding to a specific neighbourhood or enclave economy, such as East Los Angeles. They are referring to a larger sense of identity and set of social relations bound by pan-ethnicity that is scattered among many different Latino-concentrated urban areas of the region that suffer from concentrated poverty, crime and subpar schools.

While the majority of both middle- and upper-class Latino entrepreneurs retain a sense of ethnic solidarity and give back to the community, they do so in ways that differ depending on their current class status, which is indicative of the types of social and financial resources they have access too. I detail these differences in two separate sections, focusing first on the giving patterns of middle-class Latino entrepreneurs. Only a small fraction, less than 15% of middle-class Latino entrepreneurs, does not engage in ethnic philanthropy. The majority of those who do not give back are less established and have been in business less than four years and they indicated that they do not give back because they must direct their social and financial resources back into their businesses.

While the majority of middle-class Latino entrepreneurs give back to the community, they do so in different ways. Nearly three-quarters are engaged in activities at the community level. For example, they write cheques to or are board members of Latino organizations, sponsor community events, or work *pro bono*. Others sit on task forces working towards issues affecting the Latino community such as comprehensive immigration reform. About a quarter of middle-class Latino business owners spend a considerable amount of time sharing their upward mobility narratives with low-income Latino youth who attend urban schools. For example, Miguel, a first-generation Mexican American who owns a company that produces promotional materials, relayed that he gives back by inviting groups of low-income students to visit his plush, glass-fronted building, or by speaking at urban elementary and high schools, where hundreds of students hear his success story:

> I hope to inspire people. And so anytime I have an opportunity to touch someone, I think that's sort of the way to give back and to give people the understanding that they can make it happen. Yesterday, we had a group of students here – high school students. And they wanted me to explain to them what I thought was so important about getting a college education and a little bit about my story, about how I got in how I made it happen. That type of stuff, I love. Most of them come from a poor background. Most of them have families who have never attended college. So this is sort of the first opportunity for their career, for their families, to further their education. And I probably do this a couple times a year.

A number of Latino entrepreneurs are involved in activities focusing on Latinos as individuals. For example, Larry, a second-generation Mexican American and financial planner, explained that his workforce is '100% Latino'. Larry needs bilingual employees because a segment of his business targets monolingual Latino immigrants. However, Larry also explained that his passion is in long-term personal mentoring of at-risk Latino youth so that they can achieve upward mobility through higher education and business ownership. Growing up in a poor Latino community, Larry knew few business owners engaged in professional enterprise whom he could look up to or turn to for advice. Thus, he feels that it is his responsibility to give back to the ethnic community by helping others from poor backgrounds to succeed. As he explained:

> I have two gentlemen who are certified financial planners who are working with me who came from the barrio as well. One of them when I met him as a student came to me through one of those mentorship programs at Los Angeles High School. He had five F's and one D when I met him, and the kid was brilliant, and I talked to his counselor in high school to figure out a way to get him to graduate. Got him into junior college and then he got accepted into UCLA and graduated from UCLA. He's a certified financial planner and grew up in the barrio very, very poor. So they have the same heart that I have to try and help out the community. So, now going forward, it's just hiring the best person for the job but I think originally I was intentionally trying to hire within the community to give people an opportunity.

As these results indicate, Los Angeles' middle-class Latino entrepreneurs are engaged in various types of activities that benefit Latino communities and individuals. Middle-class Latino business owners are not creating large-scale ethnic social structures aimed at promoting the mobility of co-ethnics, but their philanthropic activities are extremely important for two reasons. First, they are making an impact at the community level by infusing the ethnic community with financial and social capital. Latino business owners donate their money and time to Latino-focused organizations and political causes. Moreover, when a successful Latino entrepreneur, like Miguel, recounts his mobility narrative to students at a low-income high school, he is showing a traditionally marginalized population what it is possible to achieve. Second, as Larry's case illustrates, Latino entrepreneurs are helping to promote the mobility of low-income co-ethnics individually by acting as long-term mentors to Latino youth. This is important because Latino communities have been lacking in professional mentors that can help low-income Latinos bridge human and social capital gaps in families and community (Matute-Bianchi 1986). Research shows that professional mentors are critical to low-income Latinos' educational success and advancement into the middle-class as they provide information about higher education and access to networks that result in occupational mobility (Agius Vallejo 2012; Portes, Fernández-Kelly, and Haller 2009; Smith 2005).

In all, middle-class Latino entrepreneurs are not rugged individualists. Contrary to traditional assimilation theory, they do not cut ties to ethnic communities once they achieve success; however, their ethnic-centric philanthropic activities are not antithetical to traditional assimilation theory as the ultimate goal is to foster mobility into the mainstream.

The Latino elite: building ethnic social structures

The most successful Latino business owners in this study (those who own firms that generate annual revenues ranging from $1,000,000 to nearly $100,000,000) are creating large-scale ethnic social structures that revolve around education and Latino business and that aim to 'provide opportunities' to Latinos and 'grow the middle class'. One ethnic social structure that promotes educational attainment, with the long-term goal of building the Latino middle class, is Latino-centric charter schools in inner-city communities. Harry and Nancy Rivera are 1.5-generation immigrants from Mexico and both were raised in a low-income Latino community. The Riveras met in college, pursued careers in advertising, and eventually opened a Latino advertising agency. They have counted major global brands as clients for over twenty-five years and bill more than $80,000,000 a year in revenues. The Riveras are extremely active in the Latino community and have been instrumental in starting a number of charter schools in low-income Latino areas that focus on academic achievement and college preparation. As Harry explained:

> Part of our mission is to help the [Latino] community improve its life... For example, we've gotten involved in the charter school movement and have helped start a whole bunch of charter schools. Because these are great kids and they just need tools. When you look at the appalling dropout rate in our schools – you know we did a lot of focus groups with young people and we see their plight. The fact that they were in school until their father or mother told them okay, we need for you to bring income into the house... Yeah, and so it was like the tremendous dropout rates, nobody advancing, lots of problems in the *barrio* and we wanted to do something. And it's kind of cool because the schools that we've done before are all very successful and they're all now working.

Working with a well-known educational philanthropist, the Riveras are involved in various aspects of building and sustaining charter schools in urban Latino communities. They decide in which communities the schools should be located, they help to create the schools' educational philosophies, and they fundraise relentlessly. These alternative educational institutions are particularly important in a school district where three-quarters of the students are Latino and the majority attends urban schools with low graduation rates.

Latino elites are also creating ethnic social structures that advance educational attainment and incorporation by fashioning Latino alumni associations at their alma maters that provide millions of dollars in scholarships to low-income and first-generation Latino college students who often cannot afford college tuition, especially at elite private colleges. For example, Julia Cruz is a second-generation Mexican American woman and well-known educational philanthropist. She graduated college with a degree in accounting and founded her own accounting company, billing nearly $1,000,000 a year in revenues, after a successful career in the city's most prominent firms. As the first person in her family to attend college, she found it difficult to navigate the milieu of higher education. As a result, Julia, along with a group of other successful Latinos with whom she graduated, founded the Latino Alumni Association at their alma mater, a small private college located in an urban area of Los Angeles. They worked diligently to establish a scholarship endowment to fund low-income Latino students. As she elaborated:

> We worked really hard to establish an endowment there so that we have some sustainability with our scholarship program. My husband was the President of that for a time and I was on the Board and that was huge and we got that done. We worked a lot with [a well-known Latino philanthropist], he mentored us in those early years to really help us. They consider us as part of the founders. Well, now the Latino Alumni Association is now is like a $4 million endowment... and these are scholarships that go to students that can't afford to go to there. I mean some of these students, I'm sure you still see it today, they have to work like two or three jobs just to get through college, so how are they going to compete if they're working and working for someone else... our Latino students are not wealthy and can't afford to go to these universities. So we've done a lot in education.

Latino alumni associations also work to improve retention and college graduation rates, they help to professionalize students by holding workshops and mock job interviews, they hold corporate job fairs, and they are social spaces in which socially mobile Latino students who often feel out of place in elite educational institutions (Agius Vallejo 2012; Tovar and Feliciano 2009) can connect with successful Latinos who identify with their mobility struggles and who help them to navigate the labyrinth of higher education.

Elite Latino entrepreneurs are also creating more general ethnic scholarship funds that provide financial support to low-income Latino college students. George Romero, a 1.5-generation Mexican American who owns a law firm, is also a first-generation college student. He relayed that his parents' dream was for him to attend college: 'It was a dream for them, even though, again, they weren't able to help me because they didn't know how.' George has since spearheaded the Latino Education Fund as a way to give back to Latinos who cannot afford college and who lack access to Latino role models:

> Unfortunately, there's not enough role models to get kids to where we are. One of the things that we did about 13 to 15 years ago was we started a thing called Latino Education Fund. It's scholarships. The idea was, let's raise $100,000 for the community... because there were very few scholarships. At that time I'd gone through school and I was very fortunate. I had a lot of great opportunities for scholarships and during the Reagan years they started going away for economic reasons or whatever. We've grown that to over $3,000,000 now.

As my interviews demonstrate, elite Latino entrepreneurs are not rugged individualists. They are engaging in ethnic philanthropy by creating tangible social structures that promote academic achievement and educational attainment within ethnic environments. These ethnic educational structures are community resources that have the potential to make a major impact on Latino mobility and incorporation into the middle class because Latinos have a high high-school dropout rate and the lowest rate of college completion of all racial/ethnic groups (Fry 2002, 2011). Charter schools in urban Latino communities prepare low-income Latino youth academically for college and Latino alumni associations and scholarship funds support them financially and socially once they arrive, improving retention and graduation rates. Latino alumni associations also help to professionalize Latino college students and they increase their social capital by providing access to successful Latino alumni. Together, these ethnic educational structures help to advance Latino educational attainment and they may be critical in helping to narrow education gaps.

Los Angeles' elite Latino entrepreneurs are also focused on building ethnic structures that cultivate business development. Some have founded a Latino-owned bank, Americo, which provides Latino business owners with access to capital to start and grow their businesses. The bank's founders also hope that a Latino-owned bank will help to 'build wealth' in Latino communities, 'expand the middle-class' and increase 'Latino philanthropy'. Maggie Quintero is a 1.5-generation Mexican American whose mother worked as a housekeeper. Maggie is now a successful businesswoman and philanthropist who founded Americo Bank, Los Angeles' first Latino-owned bank in over a quarter of a century. Maggie relayed that Americo's approach is a sharp contrast from general market banks that typically turn down applicants that are missing critical pieces of their application, such as a business plan, or applicants who have not accumulated assets to use as collateral. Americo builds long-term relationships with Latino business owners and grooms them on business and financial practices so that they can qualify for large business loans. Although their stated goal is to support Latino business owners, the founders view their bank as also helping to create a larger social and economic movement within the Latino community. When I asked Maggie why she decided to establish a Latino-owned bank, she replied:

> The bank is a critical component of a successful community. Leveraging capital is a powerful tool. We have a role to reinvest in the community. When you think about it, the role of banks can play a vital role for communities and groups. It is not just about the bottom line for us, not just a business imperative but more about how do we build a sound and total community. How do I mind that community and be responsive? I mean, when we took a look at the community and if you map out the disparities you see that there is a lack of community banks and so we had to start our own bank.

Maggie is the brains behind the bank, but she did not build the bank alone. The 'we' that she speaks of are 400 of Los Angeles' 'top Latino families' whom she rallied to invest in the bank. As she relayed:

> The founders looked around at each other and said, "How do we get to replicate our story for others?" The top 400 families, the elite, they want to provide resources to the community, not just the capital but also the information.

When I suggested that the top 400 families are community role models, she replied in a serious tone:

> Oh no! They are more than role models. They go beyond. They get involved. That's the kind of thing they are going to get here; a much deeper and caring relationship. We connect them in ways they can't connect. We are also politically connected and can help smooth the way. It is really amazing what we do here.

Although the bank clearly has a for-profit focus, it fulfils an important function because the larger goal is to buttress financial and social capital in the Latino community by 'leveraging capital' and investing in Latino business owners who will help to create a financially sound community and grow the middle class.

Not surprisingly, Harry and Nancy Rivera, and Julia Cruz, are two of the 400 families who invested in Americo Bank. The following exchange details the Riveras' rationalization for their involvement:

> Harry: We helped start a bank. Right here in Los Angeles because Latinos have no access to credit so you have to start your own bank. This idea of Bank of America was started by a bunch of Italians who couldn't get credit so we thought we would do the same thing and maybe Americo in 20 years will be the biggest bank in the United States.
> Interviewer: So why was starting Americo Bank important to you?
> Norma: First, there hadn't been a Latino bank chartered in California for over 30 years and this is in a place where half the population is Latino and there's no bank that understands them... And this has really been helpful in being able to teach individual business owners about how to go about for requesting credit and doing the business plan and doing all of this kind of stuff, instead of just denying the loan and sending them on their way, even if we deny the loan we will tell them what it is they need to be able to get the loan. So there is an educational process.

The Riveras understand that Latino business owners have difficulty qualifying for loans. Like other immigrant entrepreneurs before them who have created ethnic financial institutions in immigrant communities, a Latino-owned bank provides an alternative to attain capital for those who are shut out of traditional lending institutions. Julia Cruz echoed this reasoning when she elucidated why the bank is important to the Latino community:

> I've seen enough examples of where we have made a difference by sort of going – I'm not saying we're going outside of our credit standards, but going the extra mile to help a business achieve the right reporting, or the right metrics, that are needed to then be able to come into the bank as a client. It's an investment of time and not all banks are willing to do that. But I also think that for us it's important that we're there for our Hispanic-owned businesses who want to expand and grow and need a good banking relationship with somebody that understands them... I'm very proud of the bank and of being affiliated with the bank because I do see that it serves a role and I think we need more of them.

Latino-owned banks are a tangible ethnic social structure that is critically important in providing financial capital to Latino business owners who lack access to traditional bank loans because of their low levels of wealth and assets (Robles and Cordero-Guzmán 2007). Latino-owned banks are also important because minority entrepreneurs often feel that discrimination based on their race or ethnicity prevents them from obtaining loans from large general market banks (Valdez 2011) – a belief that is well documented in empirical research that demonstrates that minority-owned businesses experience higher loan denial probabilities compared to white-owned businesses, even after controlling for creditworthiness (Cavalluzzo and Wolken 2005).

CITIES, DIVERSITY AND ETHNICITY

It is important to note that while middle-class entrepreneurs do volunteering, mentoring and smaller cheque-writing to Latino-centric organizations, the Latino elite favour private solutions to 'level the playing field'. Private Latino-centric social structures, such as charter schools, scholarship funds and Latino banks, are a break from the post-Second World War pattern of minorities using government policies and affirmative action to remedy social inequalities. The Latino elites' reliance on private solutions is reflective of the ways in which philanthropy is being incorporated into a larger neoliberal project (Raddon 2008). While the Latino elite themselves likely benefited from civil rights legislation and affirmative action, private solutions are viewed as the only possible way to remedy social inequalities in an era of declining tax bases and in a society that is often touted as post-racial. Thus, ethnic social structures are poised to help level the playing field, but the rise of private ethnic philanthropy also legitimizes the dismantling of the welfare state and growing inequality.

Motivations for giving back

Why do middle- and upper-class Latino entrepreneurs give back to the Latino community? Time and again successful Latino entrepreneurs, especially those raised in poor households, invoked memories of struggle and sacrifice that are embedded in the immigrant narrative. Research has shown that socially mobile Latinos retain an immigrant narrative that propels them to give back financially and socially to less advantaged family members (Agius Vallejo 2012; Smith 2005). This research demonstrates that the immigrant narrative also extends to the larger Latino community. Successful Latinos were often raised in urban neighbourhoods with subpar schools and a dearth of professional role models. At the same time, they watched their immigrant parents toil in low-wage jobs so that they could achieve upward mobility. Because they have experienced it first hand, they understand that the educational system is subpar and that Latinos face discrimination and social exclusion within it (Ochoa 2013). Although they are economically assimilated, successful Latino entrepreneurs recognize that Latinos more generally are not fully integrated into the mainstream, thus they engage in ethnic philanthropy by mentoring and creating ethnic social structures within which Latinos can succeed by obtaining financial resources, access to high-quality networks, information on higher education and business ownership, and access to financial capital. Their sense of ethnic solidarity with poorer co-ethnics is rooted in their own personal struggle for upward mobility and because they understand that Latinos face barriers within educational and financial institutions.

Illustrative of the immigrant narrative, Julia Cruz invoked an immigrant narrative of struggle and sacrifice when explaining her high level of support to the community. She also notes that although she has made it, she understands that Latinos face limited opportunities and structural barriers to mobility, leading her to feel a sense of responsibility for her 'people':

> I think when you come from parents like Pablo and I come from, our parents who worked
> so hard and really sweat it out… that you almost feel like a sense of responsibility for the

pride that your parents feel for you. I think we both feel a tremendous sense of responsibility where we are then fortunate to have recognized that education was important... If we as a people can move into more middle-class status then the road there starts with education and our people I think are still struggling with that. I think it goes back to that sense of responsibility. I don't know why I keep drawing on that, but I figure if my parents came here and worked as hard as they did, and I know that it wasn't easy with language barriers but they were out to accomplish something. They were out to seek a better world for their kids and it can be a good world and so I think that responsibility of wanting to be able to show that we can give back and do good things and do the right thing.

Overall, Latino entrepreneurs were reluctant to rely on discrimination as an explanation for why they engage in ethnic philanthropy; nevertheless, they understand that Latinos face discrimination in addition to structural barriers. For example, Maggie, who founded Americo bank, exclaimed:

I want to level the playing field! Honestly, even if I weren't Latina I would be fighting for the Latino community because I just feel that they are getting the short end of the stick. The media and larger society portrays us all as criminals or illegal, on welfare. Even my 'liberal' friends talk like this. It affects the ability of our community to move ahead.

As Maggie stated, the Latino elite are creating institutions and engaging in activities that will 'replicate our story for others'. Although they are economically assimilated, they have faced social exclusion in their professional lives and they understand that Latinos face significant structural barriers and discrimination. As a result, they evince a shared vision of advancing the mobility of co-ethnics through education and business development, and they seek to circumvent structural barriers through individual and collective behaviours that infuse ethnic communities with social and financial capital (Coleman 1988). Finally, they invoke an immigrant narrative born out of their struggle for upward mobility to explain why they retain a sense of ethnic solidarity and an ethos of giving to the Latino community. In all, race/ethnicity and class background intersect to shape the Latino elites' motivations for engaging in ethnic philanthropy.

Discussion and conclusions

The central question of this research is do middle- and upper-class Latino entrepreneurs cut ties to ethnic communities once they become middle or upper class, or do they retain a sense of ethnic solidarity expressed through community giving that is aimed at promoting the mobility of co-ethnics? Traditional assimilation theory posits that immigrants and their descendants will cut ties to co-ethnics and ethnic communities once they become economically assimilated. In this vein, some have argued that Latino entrepreneurs cling to the ideology of individualism and meritocracy even as they experience structural inequalities (Valdez 2011). This research demonstrates that elite Latino entrepreneurs do not turn their backs on ethnic communities once they achieve social and economic success. Hence, this research adds to the literature by demonstrating that, contrary to traditional immigration theory, an ethos of giving back to co-ethnics does not disappear once Latino immigrants and their descendants move into the middle and upper classes. This does not mean that the Latino elite are not assimilating. In fact, while their philanthropic activities are ethnic-centric, such as giving to Latino organizations, and starting Latino-owned banks and Latino-themed charter schools, the primary goal of these ethnic social structures is to promote mobility into the mainstream, an objective that is in line with traditional assimilation theory. That this type of philanthropy occurs among the most economically assimilated segment of Latinos demonstrates that ethnic philanthropy is compatible with assimilation (Portes, Escobar, and Radford 2007). Moreover, successful Latino entrepreneurs retain a sense of ethnic solidarity and an ethos of giving back to the community that is born out of the immigrant mobility struggle and in navigating through educational, social and financial institutions that have marginalized Latinos.

The majority of Latino business owners interviewed for this study engage in ethnic philanthropy and give back to the community, but they do so in different ways. Middle-class Latino entrepreneurs make financial contributions to Latino-centric organizations and they are also engaged in more informal exchanges of social capital when they mentor up-and-coming business owners or low-income Latino students. These non-economic activities aimed at advancing Latino mobility are extremely important because they infuse low-income ethnic communities with social and economic capital. The Latino elites' activities are more deliberate and centred on the goal of creating ethnic structures that foster long-term mobility. This difference is not surprising because upper-class Latino entrepreneurs have higher revenues; therefore they have more money, wealth and time to invest in large-scale philanthropic endeavours that aim to advance the Latino community in a broader sense. However, Latino elites' reliance on private solutions to 'level the playing field' reflects an ideology of neo-liberalism and the dismantling of the welfare state.

Overall, studies have neglected the ways in which the Latino elite have built institutions in ethnic communities. The various forms of philanthropy in which Latino entrepreneurs are involved – from volunteering, to financial and political support of Latino causes, mentoring and the creation of schools and Latino-owned banks – fill a vital need in a minority community that continues to experience extreme gaps in education and economic and social capital. While all Latino entrepreneurs bring economic and social capital to ethnic communities, elite Latino entrepreneurs are key factors in broad Latino community development. Thus, this research is important as it demonstrates that Latino elites are trying to move Latino communities towards a model of social and economic empowerment through privatization and the creation of ethnic social structures that promote educational attainment and Latino business development. The ultimate goal of these institutions is to foster incorporation into the mainstream and grow the Latino middle class.

This research is not generalizable and future studies should examine whether Latino entrepreneurs create institutions with a focus beyond education and business development. Future research should also try to measure the impact that ethnic philanthropy exerts on Latino mobility.

Acknowledgements

The author wishes to thank Pierrette Hondagneu-Sotelo for insightful comments and suggestions and Jazmin Muro and Stephanie Canizales for research assistance. This research

CITIES, DIVERSITY AND ETHNICITY

was funded by the American Sociological Association's Fund for the Advancement of the Discipline and USC Provost's Advancing Scholarship in the Humanities and Social Sciences Research Grant.

Note

1. Cubans are an exception because they are a refugee group who have been directly affected by governmental policies and programmes aimed to facilitate their successful resettlement and business growth. Moreover, the 'golden wave' of Cuban migrants were generally high skilled with high levels of human and social capital, which hastened the development of a Cuban ethnic enclave and Cuban business success (Portes 1987).

References

Agius Vallejo. 2012. *Barrios to Burbs*. Palo Alto, CA: Stanford University Press.
Baca Zinn, Maxine, and Barbara Wells. 2000. "Diversity within Latino Families." In *Handbook of Family Diversity*, edited by David H. Demo, Katherine R. Allen, and Mark A. Fine, 252–273. New York: Oxford University Press.
Berg, Bruce. 2007. *Qualitative Research Methods for the Social Sciences*. New York: Bacon.
Cavalluzzo, Ken, and John Wolken. 2005. "Small Business Loan Turndowns, Personal Wealth, and Discrimination." *The Journal of Business* 78 (6): 2153–2178. doi:10.1086/497045.
Coleman, James. 1988. "Social Capital in the Creation of Human Capital." *The American Journal of Sociology* 94: 95–120. doi:10.1086/228943.
Current Population Survey. 2008. *Annual Social and Economic Supplement*. Washington, DC: Bureau of the Census.
Farlie, Robert, and Alicia M. Robb. 2008. *Race and Entrepreneurial Success*. Cambridge, MA: MIT Press.
Fry, Richard. 2002. *Latinos in Higher Education: Many Enroll, Too Few Graduate*. Washington, DC: Pew Hispanic Center.
Fry, Richard. 2011. *Hispanic College Enrollment Spikes, Narrowing Gaps with Other Groups*. Washington, DC: Pew Hispanic Center.
Gordon, Milton. 1964. *Assimilation in American Life*. New York: Oxford University Press.
Hernandez, Jose Amaro. 1983. *Mutual Aid for Survival*. Florida, CA: Robert E. Krieger Publishing Co.
Jimenez, Tomas. 2010. *Replenished Ethnicity*. Berkeley, CA: University of California Press.
Light, Ivan, and Edna Bonacich. 1991. *Immigrant Entrepreneurs*. Berkeley, CA: University of California Press.
Lofstrom, Magnus, and Chunbei Wang. 2006. "Hispanic Self-Employment." Working Paper. University of Texas at Dallas.
Lopez, Mary, and Dolores Trevizo. 2009. "Mexican Immigrant Entrepreneurship in Los Angeles." In *An American Story*, edited by John Sibly Butler, Alfonso Morales, and David Torres, 127–150. Indiana: Purdue University Press.
Marquez, Benjamin, and James Jennings. 2000. "Mexican American and Puerto Rican Social Movement Organizations." *P.S. Political Science and Politics* 33 (3): 541–546.
Matute-Bianchi, Maria E. 1986. "Ethnic Identities and Patterns of School Success and Failure among Mexican-Descent and Japanese-American Students in a California High School." *American Journal of Education* 95 (1): 223–225. doi:10.1086/444298.
Min, Pyong Gap. 2008. *Ethnic Solidarity for Economic Survival*. New York: Russell Sage Foundation.

Ochoa, Gilda. 2013. *Academic Profiling*. Minneapolis, MN: University of Minnesota Press.

Portes, Alejandro. 1997. "The Social Origins of the Cuban Enclave Economy of Miami." *Sociological Perspectives* 30 (4): 340–372. doi:10.2307/1389209.

Portes, Alejandro, Christina Escobar, and Alexandria Radford. 2007. "Immigrant Transnational Organizations and Development." *International Migration Review* 47 (1): 242–281. doi:10.1111/j.1747-7379.2007.00063.x.

Portes, Alejandro, Patricia Fernández-Kelly, and William Haller. 2009. "The Adaptation of the Immigrant Second Generation in America." *Journal of Ethnic and Migration Studies* 35 (7): 1077–1104. doi:10.1080/13691830903006127.

Portes, Alejandro, and Julia Sensenbrenner. 1993. "Embeddedness and Immigration." *American Journal of Sociology* 93 (6): 1320–1350. doi:10.1086/230191.

Portes, Alejandro, and Min Zhou. 1992. "Economic Mobility and Domestic Minorities." *Ethnic and Racial Studies* 15 (4): 491–522. doi:10.1080/01419870.1992.9993761.

Portes, Alejandro, and Min Zhou. 1993. "Segmented Assimilation and its Variants." *The Annals of the American Academy of Political and Social Science* 530: 74–96. doi:10.1177/0002716293530001006.

Raddon, Mary-Beth. 2008. "Planned Giving and the New Ethnic Philanthropy." *Studies in Political Economy* 81: 27–48.

Raijman, Rebecca, and Martha Tienda. 2003. "Ethnic Foundations of Economic Transactions." *Ethnic and Racial Studies* 26 (5): 783–801. doi:10.1080/0141987032000109032.

Ramirez, Hernan, and Pierrette Hondagneu-Sotelo. 2009. "Mexican Immigrant Gardeners: Entrepreneurs or Exploited Workers?" *Social Problems* 56 (1): 70–88. doi:10.1525/sp.2009.56.1.70.

Robles, Bárbara, and Héctor Cordero-Guzmán. 2007. "Latino Self-Employment and Entrepreneurship in the United States." *The Annals of the American Academy of Political and Social Science* 613: 18–31. doi:10.1177/0002716207303541.

Sanders, Jimy, and Victor Nee. 1996. "Immigrant Self-Employment: The Family as Social Capital and the Value of Human Capital." *American Sociological Review* 61 (2): 231–249. doi:10.2307/2096333.

Smith, Robert. 2005. *Mexican New York*. Berkeley, CA: University of California Press.

Terriquez, Veronica. 2012. "Civic Inequalities?" *Sociological Perspectives* 55 (4): 663–682. doi:10.1525/sop.2012.55.4.663.

Tovar, Jessica, and Cynthia Feliciano. 2009. "Not Mexican-American, but Mexican." *Latino Studies* 7 (2): 197–221. doi:10.1057/lst.2009.18.

US Survey of Business Owners. 2007. Washington, DC: U.S. Bureau of the Census.

Valdez, Zulema. 2011. *The New Entrepreneurs*. Stanford, CA: Stanford University Press.

Vasquez, Jessica. 2011. *Mexican Americans across Generations*. New York: New York University Press.

Wilson, William Julius. 1987. *The Truly Disadvantaged*. Chicago, IL: University of Chicago Press.

Zhou, Min. 2004. "Revisiting Ethnic Entrepreneurship." *International Migration Review* 38 (3): 1040–1074. doi:10.1111/j.1747-7379.2004.tb00228.x.

Zhou, Min, and Susan Kim. 2006. "Community Forces, Social Capital, and Educational Achievement." *Harvard Educational Review* 76 (1): 1–29.

The bi-national road to immigrant rights mobilization: states, social movements and Chicago's Mexican hometown associations

Rebecca Vonderlack-Navarro and William Sites

Although immigrant hometown associations (HTAs) are most often recognized as important for sustaining transnational ties to sending societies, Chicago HTAs took a leadership role in the 2006 marches for US immigrant rights. Employing a binational historical framework focused on the influence of political opportunities and threats on social movement activism, we argue that the involvement of Chicago HTAs in US-oriented mobilization resulted from an evolving series of organizational responses to state actors in both Mexico and the USA. We find that these interactions conferred growing levels of organizational capacity and political legitimacy upon CONFEMEX, the Chicago-based HTA confederation, and played a key role in its embrace of US-centred strategies of popular mobilization in 2006. These findings suggest the utility of a long-term, binational focus on multiple state actors in order to understand the complex political evolution of HTAs and the emergence of the US immigrant rights movement.

On 10 March 2006, a 'sea of humanity' estimated at upward of 100,000 people marched from Chicago's Near West Side to the city's Loop in support of immigrant rights, as noted in *Chicago Tribune* the following day. Although the protest would be followed in the coming weeks by even larger rallies in Chicago and many US cities, this 10 March demonstration – and not the widely recognized rallies of 1 May – marked the first mass outpouring of opposition to the punitive provisions of the Border Protection, Antiterrorism and Illegal Immigration Control Act of 2005. Also known as the Sensenbrenner Bill (HR 4437), this piece of legislation passed by the US House of Representatives would have criminalized the status of undocumented immigrants as well as actions by citizens to assist them, as noted in *Chicago Tribune*, March 12, 2006. If participants and observers alike registered astonishment at the massive turnout on 10 March, no less surprising (at least for analysts attempting to reconstruct the genesis of this movement) was the coalition of lead sponsors who organized this pivotal early protest. This leadership committee included not only the usual collection of Chicago's immigrant rights organizations but also, most strikingly, a city-based confederation of Mexican hometown associations (HTAs) called *Confederacion de Federaciones Mexicanos*

(CONFEMEX), which ended up playing a crucial role in planning and mobilizing participants for the 10 March event.

Scholars have traditionally assumed that the political activities of migrant HTAs focus primarily on non-contentious projects in their countries of origin. How did such organizations in Chicago – having scant experience with contentious mobilization and containing many undocumented migrants vulnerable to deportation – come to play an important leadership role in an emerging US-centred social movement?

Scholarly approaches that employ a transnationalist lens, though focusing appropriately on the cross-border political ties between HTAs and their sending societies, fail to explain why the Mexican HTAs in Chicago became increasingly involved in US-focused activities and why government officials in Mexico as well as the USA might actively support such activities (Goldring 2002; Orozco and Lapointe 2004; Portes, Escobar, and Radford 2007). Recent analyses of the US immigrant rights marches, while recognizing migrant associations as important participants in the organizational networks behind the mobilizations of 2006, also neglect the potential role of states – both sending and receiving – in facilitating HTA participation and leadership in the marches (Cordero-Guzman et al. 2008; Fox and Bada 2009). What remains unexplained, therefore, is how associational groups with little history of contentious action and with a political agenda traditionally focused on Mexico might become mobilizing vehicles for an incipient US immigrant rights movement.

Social movement theory in certain respects provides a more fruitful explanatory framework for explaining HTA involvement in the immigrant rights movement. The concept of *political opportunity structure*, which focuses on how governmental institutions and actors shape the political terrain for mobilization, offers a potentially useful way to understand the shifting political constraints and incentives that confront movement groups. In particular, government actors may pursue certain strategic courses of action that confer political legitimacy on certain groups, thereby strengthening the latter's political capacities as well as their willingness to engage in contention (Walton 1993; Kriesi 2004). Recent scholarship has begun to give greater attention to *political threat* as a possible stimulus to movement activity (Reese 2005; Voss and Bloemraad 2011). Yet many government threats towards vulnerable social groups succeed in discouraging contentious behaviour, and the conditions under which political threats instead may mobilize remain poorly understood. In our case, why did a vulnerable and traditionally non-contentious Mexican migrant organization in Chicago respond to the dramatic threat posed by the Sensenbrenner Bill by taking on a leadership role in mobilization in the USA – rather than, say, by retreating or refocusing its energies on Mexico? To investigate this question, we examine how shifts over time in a transnational political opportunity structure – one in which various state actors on both sides of the border extend opportunities and pose threats – may influence the political activities of a particular set of migrant HTAs.

This paper examines the long-term political evolution of Chicago's Mexican HTAs in order to explain their leading role in the 10 March 2006 protest march. Drawing from social movement theory's approach to political opportunity and threat, we examine how state actors in both Mexico and the USA worked over several decades to build the organizational and political capacities of Chicago HTAs, encouraging the groups to gradually embrace US-focused activities while also maintaining their traditional ties to Mexico. We contend that a long-term pattern of state support for the HTAs served to confer upon the associations (not always intentionally) a growing sense of their own legitimacy, capacity and political purpose – qualities that encouraged the groups to respond to the potentially chilling threat posed by the Sensenbrenner Bill with a confident embrace of US-centred protest. By examining the long-term development of the Mexican HTAs since the 1990s, then, one can recognize how the 'political capital' (Smith 2007) accrued by HTAs through their interactions with Mexican governmental officials as well as with US officials in Illinois came to be an important resource that would fuel the groups' engagement in social movement activity in 2006.

Our case study retraces the evolving political trajectory of Chicago's Mexican HTAs through a combination of archival, interview and ethnographic data. These data, when examined through a historical lens, enable us to shed light on how the efforts by various government leaders to develop migrant associations as vehicles for their own purposes tended, over time, to enhance these organizations' efforts to become a unified – and eventually contentious – political actor. This process is important to understand, in part because Chicago HTAs came to be recognized as pioneers within the US immigrant rights movement. Yet the case also generates insight into a significant topic of general interest to scholars of contemporary immigrant politics: how migrant organizations operating within transnational political opportunity structures may draw unanticipated strength from certain state actors when they respond to powerful political threats launched by other state actors.

State strategies, immigrant mobilization

Mexican HTAs in US cities are widely recognized as important forms of first-generation Mexican immigrant civic and political participation at the grass-roots level. Much of the research on HTAs has focused on their ability to sustain transnational ties through participation in cultural, infrastructural and political activities in Mexico while fostering important *paisano* network and kinship connections in the USA (Goldring 2002; Orozco and Lapointe 2004; Portes, Escobar, and Radford 2007; Smith and Bakker 2008). In Chicago, HTAs have grown dramatically in number (from a mere thirty-five in 1995 to over 340 in 2008) and in organizational scale, combining to form nine state-level federations as well as, beginning in 2003, the Midwest confederation CON-FEMEX (Chicago Mexican Consular Materials on Midwest Region HTAs, acquired February 25, 2009). Researchers have generally failed, however, to observe how this dramatic growth has also been accompanied by an appreciable shift in national focus and type of activity. Recent actions in Chicago, including a CONFEMEX leadership role in the 2006 marches, suggest that this kind of organization became a significant political actor in the USA even while maintaining its transnational ties to Mexican society.

How is it that many of Chicago's traditionally Mexico-focused HTAs were motivated to take a leading organizational role in US-focused political mobilizations on behalf of immigrant rights? Theories influenced by the transnationalist lens do not effectively explain this turn by HTAs. Because HTAs are largely characterized in this scholarship as transnational organizations focused on Mexico, they are often seen as

CITIES, DIVERSITY AND ETHNICITY

occupying a sociopolitical sphere that is distinct from the host society and its state actors (Goldring 2002; Smith 2006). Although this approach sheds useful light on the influence of Mexican governmental reincorporation projects and long-term campaigns for absentee voting rights in Mexico on the development of HTAs, such studies pay insufficient attention to the US political environment and how it may have influenced HTA activism. Theories of assimilation and political incorporation (Alba and Nee 2003; Mollenkopf and Hochschild 2010), by contrast, while recognizing that the host society exerts a growing influence over immigrant activities, tend to underestimate the potential role of the contemporary sending state in facilitating migrant incorporation into the host society. Furthermore, neither transnational nor assimilation frameworks adequately explore the possibility that host-society political threats might spur migrant mobilization or accelerate political incorporation. Even while growing numbers of scholars argue that assimilation and transnational processes are not opposing but can intertwine in shaping the immigrant experience (Guarnizo 2003; Portes, Escobar, and Radford 2007; Smith 2007; Smith and Bakker 2008), the literature on immigrant politics is only beginning to examine how state actors in both Mexico and the USA might be influencing processes of migrant political behaviour.

Several contributors have started to challenge the often artificial analytic divisions between domestic immigrant politics and diaspora reincorporation politics (Smith 2007; Waldinger 2009). Smith and Bakker's (2008, 167) focus on the 'second face of transnational citizenship', for example, offers several cross-cutting insights: immigrants' political engagement in Mexican and US politics can function simultaneously, as when advocates for expatriate voting rights also participate in US immigrant rights marches; migrants' political capital garnered within the sending country can become a resource in the host society; and state actors at multiple levels can influence these processes. These contributions suggest the utility of a binational approach to migrant associations' growing engagement with US politics.

However, Chicago-based HTAs and their emerging US-focused agendas have been relatively overlooked in the literature, despite the fact that the area has the second-highest number of Mexican HTAs in the USA. An important exception is the work by Escala-Rabadan, Bada, and Rivera-Salgado (2006), which explores the trajectory of growth experienced by both California- and Chicago-based HTAs. Considering HTAs' expanding activities on both sides of the border, this research draws useful attention to the associations' ability to function as political actors, particularly as they have grown to interact with multiple levels of the Mexican government and gradually with US state projects as well. As a result, these authors argue, migrant ethnic and social networks have learned to adapt to a new social and political environment. Yet, involvement in US political networks does not, by itself, explain how Chicago's HTAs came to occupy a leadership role in the 2006 marches. Therefore, a social movement framework might better explore the dynamics of interaction between state actors and immigrant organizations, elucidating more specifically how political opportunities and threats shape the capacities and strategic orientations of HTAs.

A social movement paradigm focused on political processes is well suited to examining the shifting projects of state actors as well as their impacts on migrant organizing over time. In general terms, studies of the mobilizations in 2006 do

143

recognize the threat posed by the Sensenbrenner Bill as a major catalyst of immigrant unity and contention (Cordero-Guzman et al. 2008; Barreto et al. 2009; Benjamin-Alvarado, DeSipio, and Montoya 2009; Pallares and Flores-Gonzalez 2010). Yet there has not been much discussion of *why* the Sensenbrenner threat was catalytic, nor any in-depth exploration of the longer-term political processes that might have shaped how migrant rights organizations came to understand their own political capacities or their potential to influence US immigration politics in 2006.

It is important to recognize, however, a significant analytical challenge posed by this kind of historical approach: the contemporary relationship between state and migrant movement involves multiple state actors. There are at least two dimensions to multiplicity in this particular case. One is that the evolution of Chicago HTAs has been strongly shaped by governmental actors on both sides of the US–Mexican border. Taking the binationality of HTAs seriously – that is, recognizing the puzzle that it poses for elucidating the behaviour of Chicago HTAs in relation to the events of 2006 – means trying to unravel the shifting political strategies of both Mexican and US governmental actors with respect to Mexican migrant/immigrant populations and their organizations in US cities. A further complication, however, is that neither nation's state strategies can be understood monolithically: in each country, different sets of government officials often pursued divergent migrant-related strategies over the past two decades. At certain moments, these divergences become especially striking if we examine the political behaviour of national versus state and local officials; at other moments, certain government officials recalibrate their own political interests and thereby take a new approach, with consequential implications for migrant organizations on the ground. In order to capture such complex and shifting dynamics, then, it is necessary to develop a framework of analysis that traces the evolving political strategies of multiple government actors, over several decades, on both sides of the US–Mexican border.

In the following account, we attempt to understand Chicago HTAs' engagement in US-centred contentious mobilization as the consequence of a multi-step organizational response to different state actors at different moments in time. Employing a binational social movement framework focused on the complex relationship between states and social movement organizations, we examine the political agenda, organizational form and repertoire of action of Chicago HTAs as they have evolved in relation to the shifting political projects of Mexican and US governmental officials at several levels over the course of a decade and a half. Our analysis tracks the trajectory of Chicago's HTAs across three distinct stages: (1) a period of organization building that enlarged the capacity and role of the HTAs as actors in Mexican politics; (2) a post-9/11 moment during which Mexican and US state projects encouraged a mounting HTA focus on US-related activities; and (3) after the passage of the Sensenbrenner Bill in December 2005, a new HTA embrace of US-centred mobilization. Over the long term, we argue, there have been various state projects by different governmental actors that tended to confer substantial political legitimacy on Chicago's HTA federations, giving association leaders the political consciousness and organizational structure to respond to the Sensenbrenner threat by engaging in popular mobilization in the USA.

The research for this paper is drawn from a larger multi-method case study focused on the political involvements of Chicago's Mexican HTAs. The study employs archival research, direct observation and key informant interviews to explore the emergence and development of CONFEMEX, Chicago's HTA confederation. Archival sources include Chicago Mexican consular publications and records, HTA federation and CONFEMEX meeting minutes, newspaper archives, protest flyers and pamphlets. Analysis of recent organizational developments draw from direct observation within the leadership circles of CONFEMEX (2005–07) as well as interviews with past and present HTA federation leaders, Mexican and US government officials, and local immigrant activists. Interviews with former and current HTA leaders encompass ten federations (Aguas Calientes, Chihuahua, Durango, Michoacán, Jalisco, Hidalgo, Zacatecas, Guanajuato, Guerrero and Oaxaca)[1]. Other interviewees were selected because of their involvement with Chicago HTAs over the past 20 years.

Mexico unbound: political-economic transformation and HTA growth up to early 2001

Chicago's HTAs grew dramatically in size and scope of activity in the final decades of the twentieth century. The organizational development of these immigrant HTAs needs to be understood in the context of a far-reaching restructuring in the political economies of Mexico and the USA from the 1970s onwards.

In the US economy, international competition, deindustrialization and corporate deregulation brought about a dramatic reorganization of labour markets (Sassen 1998). Trade liberalization accelerated the country's economic integration with Mexico, and unevenly restrictive immigration laws facilitated low-wage employment opportunities for growing populations of documented and (increasingly) undocumented migrant workers in large US cities (Massey, Durand, and Malone 2002). Meanwhile, Mexico's own economic transformation included a growing reliance on labour export and return remittance flows as mechanisms of national income generation and political stability (Delgado-Wise and Covarrubias 2008). Mexico's developments were also propelled by a profound alteration in the political foundations of the Mexican state. Dominated since the early twentieth century by the *Partido Revolucionario Institucional* (PRI), the Mexican government struggled to re-establish the basis of its legitimacy not only through political liberalization and electoral competition, but also through developing new alliances with important actors (e.g. multinational capital, migrant groups) outside the country (Valdes Ugalde 1996; Cameron and Wise 2004).

Central to Mexico's new state project was a growing level of political attention to its burgeoning migrant population in the USA and the economic contribution of those workers' remittances. Already by the late 1980s and particularly through the 1990s, the Mexican government had initiated various outreach efforts through its consular offices to immigrant HTAs to facilitate their growth, to spur their coalescence into broader state-level federations and to expand their philanthropic community development projects in hometowns in Mexico. After a visit to the city by Mexican President Carlos Salinas de Gortari to galvanize support for free-trade proposals, the Chicago consulate in 1990 began a Program for Mexican Communities Abroad (*Programa de Comunidades Mexicanos en el Exterior*) to promote cultural events that might

CITIES, DIVERSITY AND ETHNICITY

strengthen Mexican identity, stimulate migrant network ties and organizational developments, and coordinate the growing stream of visits by Mexican national government officials and state governors. Encouraged by the consulate, HTAs in Chicago soon began experimental matching programmes geared towards community development in their hometowns; these initiatives evolved into the Three for One (*Tres por Uno*) programme, according to which every dollar a club provided for development was matched by a dollar each from the municipal, state and national governments of Mexico.

For migrants, then, Chicago's HTAs continued to serve as places of refuge and social support. Yet as political attention from the homeland grew, these organizations were also evolving into something more. As one HTA leader observed:

> [Migrants] participate [in an HTA] because it is a form, a mechanism of mental hygiene in order to escape the oppression and the lack of participation in this [US] society.... When you go to the real world... everyone tries to ignore you. They try to ignore your rights and you are a second-class citizen. [Yet from] the moment the *diputados* [Mexican officials] come and they listen to you and respect you, you [begin to] have a certain amount of respect for what you represent as a collective mind. (Interview, former Michoacán federation president, 15 May 2008, Chicago)

Poor migrants had journeyed northward not only because of economic hardship but also because of pervasive political neglect by government leaders in Mexico. Now these migrants were finding themselves worthy of attention and even esteem by those same political notables, imparting a new sense of political purpose to their lives and to their organizations.

Basking in this new attention, Chicago's HTAs began to see themselves as organizations that might develop their own political agendas beyond the traditional community development initiatives. Over the second half of the 1990s, these groups came to see themselves less as fortunate beneficiaries of governmental attention and more as political agents negotiating with Mexican elites over development project implementation and even over the terms of their reincorporation into the homeland. For example, federation and HTA leaders became active advocates for dual nationality rights, granted in 1997 (Fitzgerald 2006), and for absentee voting rights; these activities propelled their organizing role in Chicago's symbolic elections for the Mexican presidency in 1994 and 2000, as noted in *New York Times*, July 1, 2000. (Not until 2005 would certain Mexican nationals residing abroad actually gain absentee voting privileges.) Perhaps more significantly, migrant leaders joined together in 1999 to protest the Mexican government's effort to impose a dramatic increase (from $15 to $400 or higher) on mandated deposits for cars crossing the border from the USA (De la Garza and Hazan 2003, 35). In fact, out of these Chicago protests grew a short-lived coalition of federation and other migrant activists whose chosen name (*Grupo David*) suggests the newly feisty underdog status that HTAs were now embracing in their relations with the Goliath-like Mexican government (CONFEMEX Estatutos, 'Anexo, Historia, Mistica y Metodologia de Trabajo' 2006, 13–14). As a consular official later noted, it was the car tax protest that first enabled the 'clubs to envision their capacity for having effective politics' (Interview, Institute of Mexicans Abroad coordinator, 8 June 2008, Chicago).

Mexican immigrants, then, not only occupied increasingly prominent economic roles in Mexico and the USA over the final decades of the twentieth century, they also drew growing attention from Mexican political elites. Aggressive support for the expansion of Chicago's HTAs, in turn, was increasingly met by a rising political assertiveness on the part of these organizations.

Crosscurrents: post-9/11 politics and the shifting HTA agenda, 2001–05

The years following September 2001 saw dramatic changes in US immigration politics. By ushering in major shifts in the relationship between Chicago's HTAs and various governmental actors, these political changes would also serve to push – and draw – the HTAs deeper into US domestic politics.

The Bush governance strategy in the wake of 9/11 encompassed a national security approach to immigration policy, bringing about a significant chill in Mexico–US governmental relations. The US administration's turn away from bilateral immigration reform soon led Mexico's President Vicente Fox to develop his own efforts to safeguard emigrants – and their remittance flows – in a US domestic environment that was increasingly hostile towards immigrants. Beginning in 2002, he greatly restructured and expanded his government's diaspora programmes with the formation of the Institute of Mexicans Abroad, or *el Instituto de los Mexicanos en el Exterior* (IME). IME oversaw a major overhaul of consular services throughout the USA, and transformed the experimental remittance-based development projects (e.g. Three for One) in various US cities into a nationally structured programme (Smith and Bakker 2008).

Among Mexico's new diaspora-targeted initiatives, the Chicago Mexican Consulate embarked on a number of programmes to facilitate closer ties between local residents and the homeland, while also giving community members greater protection from deportation. Consular efforts were especially evident through the local promotion of the *Matricula Consular de Alta Seguridad*, an upgraded identification card for migrants residing in the USA without documentation. Working in concert with the consulate, HTA leaders promoted the use of the card by their members. The card was soon recognized by local financial institutions, which not only gave undocumented migrants safer access to banking services and easier ways to send remittances to Mexico, but also enabled them to establish credit histories – a mechanism that might prove time-of-residency requirements in future applications for legal status in the USA (Hernandez-Coss 2005, 97–99).

Other activities also drew Chicago's HTAs into the orbit of US domestic concerns. Starting in 2002, Chicago federation and HTA leaders began working with a local Chicago non-profit organization, called *Enlaces America*, to develop new leaders for their organizations and build support for a broader cross-border approach to US immigration reform. This activity culminated the following year in the formation of CONFEMEX, an umbrella organization initially comprising eight of the Chicago-based federations and 175 Midwestern HTAs.

CITIES, DIVERSITY AND ETHNICITY

> All of us were working individually for each [Mexican] state, and we [federation leaders] saw the need to have a common bridge or unity in order to have more impact.... We could not change the laws in Mexico if we were not together, because no one is going to pay attention to us as just one state [federation].... This is where we began to see the need to be in CONFEMEX. (Interview, Durango federation leader, 6 May 2008, Chicago)

CONFEMEX was created by its leaders to stand apart from the guiding hand of the Mexican government and, quite intentionally, embraced from its inception an explicitly binational Mexico–USA focus (CONFEMEX Estatutos, 'Anexo, Historia, Mistica y Metodologia de Trabajo', 13–14).

Despite the post-9/11 national security climate and the expansion of Mexico's emigrant-targeted programmes, Chicago HTAs were beginning to refashion themselves into a more integrated and autonomous organization. One sign of this more independent stance was the decision by CONFEMEX to begin to participate in the interest group efforts surrounding US immigration policy debates. In January 2004, President Bush, facing re-election later in the year, revived proposals for a new immigration policy, and CONFEMEX soon took on an active role in a new coalition, the National Alliance of Latino and Caribbean Communities (NALACC), that advocated for immigration reform on behalf of eighty-five migrant-led organizations from many US cities (Chacón and Shannon forthcoming). A Michoacán federation leader talked about the decision by CONFEMEX to join this US-focused alliance.

> There used to be this conception that, well, the question of immigration reform and all that, we should leave it for the *gringos* [US activists] to do. [But] inWashington there are people speaking who are not migrants, someone else is speaking for us. I believe it is important that the migrants... we are the ones who should speak for us about topics that affect us. The Mexican Americans don't have problems with [legal] papers, they don't have problems of documentation and migratory status. We are the Mexicans. We are the ones that should be speaking for our own people, for our own members. (Interview, Michoacán federation leader, 15 May 2008, Chicago)

An added gravitational pull towards US-related concerns, and one that in the long term would prove quite powerful, came from state-level politics in Illinois. As early as 2002, state and local politicians, including Democratic candidate for governor Rod Blagojevich, had started to take an especially strong electoral interest in Chicago's Mexican immigrants. As Blagojevich looked ahead to his re-election effort in 2006, it was clear that a significant political gesture would be required to mobilize Latino supporters and the expanding immigrant community, noted in *Chicago Reporter*, January 1, 2004. On 19 November 2005, the governor issued with much fanfare a New Americans Executive Order intended to promote immigrant integration through an expanded range of state services to immigrants (such as English classes, citizenship acquisition and increased accessibility to health care) regardless of legal status. Governor Blagojevich tipped Jose Luis Gutierrez, a CONFEMEX leader from the state of Michoacán, to become the director of the Governor's Office of New Americans Policy and Advocacy. Gutierrez's appointment signalled a new kind of public recognition for Chicago's HTAs and for CONFEMEX, and this political connection to state-level government and Democratic Party politics would set the stage for a growing level of US-related interest group and electoral mobilization efforts on the part of federation leaders.

Over the period 2001–05, then, CONFEMEX had continued to grow and change. As a new US political climate encouraged Mexican government officials to develop innovative mechanisms to secure the stability of its Chicago-based migrant diaspora, the city's HTAs developed growing links – through financial integration, immigrant rights activism and state governmental politics – to a diversified arena of US-centred engagement. In the process, the organizations' capacities and political sophistication were significantly enhanced; leaders were becomingly increasingly conversant in the complexities of migrant/immigrant politics on both sides of the border, and the mechanism of confederation had welded together the various state-level federations into a more vertically integrated structure. Just as important, CONFEMEX was developing ties with new state governmental allies in the USA that increasingly complemented its more established political standing south of the border.

'We should give thanks to Sensenbrenner': mobilizing for US immigrant rights

Immigration politics in the USA shifted again with the passage by the House of Representatives of the Sensenbrenner Bill in December 2005. As word of the bill spread, an unprecedented wave of concern and anger rippled through the leadership circles of the Mexican immigrant community of Chicago. After several weeks of uncertainty over how to respond to this threat, CONFEMEX leaders found themselves hosting in February 2006 an unprecedented gathering of migrant and immigrant rights advocates to plan a major protest demonstration. This pivotal step would reposition the confederation at the centre of Chicago's immigrant rights movement, pulling CONFEMEX much more firmly into the mainstream of US politics.

The Sensenbrenner Bill emerged directly from a rightward political resurgence following the Bush re-election in 2004. House Judiciary Chair James Sensenbrenner introduced a bill that incorporated several highly punitive provisions, including making illegal entry into the USA a felony, while also redefining any provision of support by people or organizations to undocumented migrants as a criminal offence (Wayne 2005). The Republican-controlled House of Representatives passed the bill in December 2005 by a vote of 239 to 182, and while its long-term prospects in the Senate were said to be uncertain, the political impacts of the measure in immigrant communities were immediate and considerable, as local activists quickly framed the bill as an assault on the Latino community (Shannon 2007).

It is perhaps telling that Chicago's Mexican immigrant federations felt blindsided, at least at first, by the aggressive thrust of the Sensenbrenner Bill. After all, in spite of post-9/11 measures that tightened the border, the HTAs were experiencing a growing sense of rightful recognition in the USA, in part because of strengthened governmental and inter-organizational alliances. After the initial shock had been absorbed, however, there was anger, along with a new kind of political determination to respond. '[We] got mad: everyone was related to someone undocumented' (Interview, Hidalgo federation leader, 23 June 2008, Chicago).

Precisely where this new determination would take CONFEMEX, however, was not immediately clear. Although Chicago had long been an epicentre for immigrant rights mobilizations (Pallares and Flores-Gonzalez 2010), the HTAs and their federations had not been significant participants in these actions. Durable divisions within the city's Latino community tended to separate transnationally oriented migrant associations from grass-roots organizations that focused on immigrant rights. Even as late as July 2005, CONFEMEX did not officially participate in a pro-immigrant rally that drew tens of thousands of demonstrators to Chicago's Back of the Yards neighbourhood, as noted in *Chicago Sun-Times*, July 2, 2005 and *El Imparcial: La Guia de la Comunidad Mexicana*, July 7, 2005, mainly because its attention was directed towards what seemed to be an historic opportunity to Vote from Abroad in Mexico's upcoming national elections.

Following the House approval of the Sensenbrenner Bill, the political calculus changed. As details of the bill filtered down to HTA leaders in late December 2005, its chilling implications happened to coincide with the growing recognition that the upcoming Mexican elections in February were unlikely to provide the further elevation of south-of-the-border influence that had been long anticipated. CONFEMEX quickly re-examined its agenda, as one federation leader from Michoacán recalls:

We were going with the vote of the Mexicans [in Mexico]. But when we became aware of the fiasco, of the lack of people with [Mexican] electoral credentials, there was great disenchantment and all of that hope we had of being able to have major political weight in Mexico [disappeared]. So then it grabbed our attention: Mexico is very far from here, many kilometers. Here is where we are, here is where we are living, and they are at the point of passing a law that is going to make you a criminal – and you continue thinking about voting in Mexico's next elections? (Interview, Michoacan federation leader, 15 May 2008, Chicago)

Initial fears were not immediately dispelled, yet they were also matched, for many HTA members, by a deep sense of insult and the perception of a new opportunity:

It hit them: This was *so* bad. The proposal... was so discriminatory that we took it personally. Because before, when you heard about such things on television, yeah, sure, but that is happening there in Washington. It is very far away... But when you begin to see that this is going to affect the doctor who treats your brother who doesn't have documents, when you see that it is going to be the teacher who gives classes to your nephew who is undocumented, you say, *"Ah chinga, eso esta mal!'* [Screw this, this is bad!]" We have to change it... I believe there was a certain new level of consciousness. (Interview, Michoacan federation leader, 15 May 2008, Chicago)

For the first time, US-centred concerns rose to the very top of the CONFEMEX agenda.

One immediate measure of the political impact of the Sensenbrenner Bill was that it quickly brought together the two parts of the Latino community organizational field in Chicago working on separate sides of the migrant/immigrant agenda. If, as one study (Cordero-Guzman et al. 2008) persuasively suggests, the 2006 marches

CITIES, DIVERSITY AND ETHNICITY

emerged in part out of a long-developing network of organizational ties, it took a threat as powerful as Sensenbrenner for Chicago's grass-roots organizations to surmount the deep divide between Mexico- versus US-oriented organizing. On 15 February 2006, sixteen leaders from both sides of the Mexico- and US-focused organizing realms attended an ad hoc meeting at Casa Michoacán, the HTA federation's Pilsen headquarters, to plan a rally for the following month. They would soon be known as the March 10th Committee, after the date of this first march (Meeting minutes: 'Resumen de la reunion del comite ad hoc en contra de la HR4437, 15 de febrero del 2006, Casa Michoacán').

Federation leaders recall noting at the time that mobilization could well prove to be an uphill climb. One obstacle was fear: it was unclear whether some HTA members could develop the confidence to participate in what would be a very public event. Leaders from Guanajuato, for example, described how their members expressed concern that the 2006 marches might be a 'conspiracy' to get undocumented immigrants out into the streets so as to more easily round them up for deportation (Interview, Casa Guanajuato co-founder and president, 27 May 2008, Chicago). Yet for other members, the challenge was complacency; the growing political legitimacy achieved by migrants and their organizations over the preceding decade made it hard to believe that the threat posed by Sensenbrenner could actually materialize. Durango leaders, in particular, were concerned about the lack of alarm, and even the outright scepticism, among many of their members. As one noted: '[The law] was bad, but it was worse that people didn't believe it' (Interview, Durango federation co-founder, 6 May 2008, Chicago). Another echoed this concern: '[M]any people ignored the law. A lot of the [member] base ignored it. Many knew it was something dangerous, but not exactly how dangerous it was' (Interview, former Durango federation president, 26 May 2008, Chicago). In any event, it would clearly be up to federation leaders to educate and mobilize the base through workshops, announcements at HTA events, telephone trees and their email listserv.

Certain federations took an especially active role in mobilization. When the Hidalgo federation leaders began to realize the dire implications of the potential law, they quickly immersed themselves in making phone calls to enlist volunteers and to turn out their base. A small federation with a large number of undocumented members, Hidalgo was quickly able to round up eighty volunteers to coordinate security for 10 March, and soon found itself dedicating all of its organizational energies to the marches – to the extent that the federation even suspended its annual Mexico-oriented banquet and cultural festivities. 'We focused 100 per cent on immigrant rights' (Interview, Hidalgo federation president and secretary, 23 June 2008, Chicago). The leaders of other federations also began to mobilize their base, many of them using a list of contacts developed through their recent drive to register Mexican absentee voters (Shannon 2007). In the process, the confederated structure that had been encouraged years earlier by the Mexican government, along with the growing levels of trust that had developed within the larger confederation, ensured that the various federation leaders were able to coordinate their efforts effectively.

The ensuing turnout on 10 March was not only enormous but was also, surprisingly, the result of local effort. Rather than national civil rights organizations or labour unions taking leadership, the Chicago March 10th Committee comprised an unparalleled coming together of local migrant and immigrant organizations that had long faced in two different national directions. The role of CONFEMEX, as a newcomer within Chicago's US-focused protest politics, may have been especially pivotal. 'I just don't see [the marches] happening if [the planning process] was based in any institution other than Casa Michoacán because, you know, it's [an] open environment' (Interview, Illinois Coalition for Immigrant and Refugee Rights board president, 9 January 2009, Chicago). In effect, other Chicago-based organizations saw the HTA confederation as a neutral, trustworthy coalition partner, in part because of its traditionally Mexico-focused agenda.

Launching this early march encouraged CONFEMEX to finally recognize to finally recognize its own growing political power in the USA. As one Durango federation leader wryly noted: 'We woke up.' She continued:

> We should give thanks to Sensenbrenner.... We have changed a little our vision that we had in the beginning that there was nothing more [than] Mexico....We have shown that you are not losing Mexico when you become a [US] citizen. In fact, we are winning as federations.... I think the marches helped us to understand that we can be American citizens and work in two countries. (Interview, Durango federation leader, 6 May 2008, Chicago)

Moving forward, organizational priorities that oriented towards the host state – such as US voter mobilization and interest group advocacy, as well as participation in subsequent marches – would be given equal importance to those focused on Mexico.

Retrospective: the long binational road

Chicago's 10 March mobilizations clearly played a key role in sparking the broader US immigrant rights movement, which fully emerged seven weeks later in the nationally synchronized rallies of 1 May 2006. What has been less clear is how traditionally Mexico-oriented HTAs, which had long avoided contentious politics, came to occupy such an important leadership position surrounding the 10 March events. Why did CONFEMEX respond to the political threat posed by Sensenbrenner by leading protest actions focused on the USA?

Using a social movement approach encompassing both political opportunity and threat, we have argued that long-term efforts by various state actors to build the capacity and political legitimacy of Chicago's HTAs played an important (if frequently unintended) role in preparing those organizations to engage in US-centred contentious politics. We traced this long road to immigrant rights mobilization as a multi-step organizational response to governmental initiatives in both Mexico and the USA that resulted in significant gains in political capital and ambition on the part of these migrant associations. Employing a binational historical framework, we examined how the organizational activities of Chicago HTAs shifted in relation to Mexican and US governmental projects pursued by officials at different levels. Our analysis traced the evolution of Chicago HTAs across three distinct moments: (1) an early moment of organization building supported by Mexican government officials that enhanced the capacity and status of HTAs as actors in Mexican politics; (2) a post-9/11 period in which various Mexican and US state projects spurred an increasing HTA focus on US-related activities; and (3) following the passage of the Sensenbrenner Bill in 2005, a new willingness to consider making US-centred contentious activity an overriding organizational priority. Over time, these various state projects, we have suggested, served to confer significant political legitimacy on CONFEMEX, giving association leaders sufficient confidence, ambition and organizational structure to respond to Sensenbrenner by engaging in concerted popular mobilization in the USA.

This case study provides insights into how certain evolving political conditions can influence the emergence of migrant protest activity. The example of CONFEMEX suggests that even non-contentious organizations may respond to a new political threat with confident mobilization when their prior claims have been extensively validated and supported by powerful state officials. Research has suggested that US cities with long-standing patterns of local governmental encouragement of immigrant incorporation tend to see high levels of political activism by recent migrant groups (Mollenkopf and Sonenshein 2010). In the European context, Chimienti (2011) has found that prior periods of governmental tolerance may facilitate a mobilizing response to new measures of repression. By taking a binational historical approach to the 2006 marches, we have shown how a preceding series of legitimizing actions by various government entities – including state actors whose central realm of authority lies on the other side of a national border – can instil non-contentious migrant organizations with the capacity and confidence to take to the streets, even in the face of a potentially chilling threat. In this respect, evolving transnational political opportunity structures (Ostergaard- Nielsen 2003; Però and Solomos 2010), as well as the divisions that sometimes emerge between national and subnational governmental officials when issues of immigrant rights are at stake (Koopmans 2004; Ellis 2005), can offer migrant associations a shifting array of potential governmental allies.

It is important to recognize that political threats like the Sensenbrenner Bill in the USA have the potential to encourage or discourage engagement in public defiance by vulnerable migrant groups. By retracing the long binational road travelled by Chicago's Mexican HTA federations, we can see how long-term relationships with a complex array of governmental actors may sometimes reshape the political capabilities and agendas of such organizations in unanticipated and – in this case – empowering ways.

Notes

1. The nine federations represented within CONFEMEX as of 2008 were Oaxaca, Michoacán, Zacatecas, Durango, Guerrero, Guanajuato, Hidalgo, Aguas Calientes and Chihuahua. Jalisco was not a member of the confederation.

References

Alba, Richard, and Victor Nee. 2003. *Remaking the American Mainstream: Assimilation and Contemporary Immigration*. Cambridge: Harvard University Press.

Barreto, Matt A., Sylvia Manzano, Ricardo Ramirez, and Kathy Rim. 2009. "Mobilization, Participation, and *Solidaridad.*" *Urban Affairs Review* 44 (5): 736–764. doi:10.1177/10780 87409332925.

Benjamin-Alvarado, Jonathan, Louis DeSipio, and Celeste Montoya. 2009. "Latino Mobilization in New Immigrant Destinations: The anti-HR 4437 Protest in Nebraska's Cities".' *Urban Affairs Review* 44 (5): 718–735. doi:10.1177/1078087408323380.

Cameron, Maxwell A., and Carol Wise. 2004. "The Political Impact of NAFTA on Mexico: Reflections on the Political Economy of Democratization." *Canadian Journal of Political Science* 37 (2): 301–323. doi:10.1017/S0008423904040144.

Chacón, Oscar, and Amy Shannon. forthcoming. "Challenges and Opportunities for Transnational Community Building: Immigrant Organizations as Change Agents." Unpublished manuscript prepared for the Ford Foundation initiative on Transnational Community Building.

Chicago Mexican Consular Materials. 2009. Miscellaneous documents related to Midwest Region HTAs.

Chimienti, Milena. 2011. "Mobilization of Irregular Migrants in Europe: A Comparative Analysis." *Ethnic and Racial Studies* 34 (8): 1338–1356. doi:10.1080/01419870.2011. 566624.

Cordero-Guzman, Hector, Nina Martin, Victoria Quiroz-Becerra, and Nik Theodore. 2008. "Voting with their Feet: Nonprofit Organizations and Immigrant Mobilizations." *American Behavioral Scientist* 52 (4): 598–617. doi:10.1177/0002764208324609.

De la Garza, Rodolfo, and Miryam Hazan. 2003. *Looking Backward, Moving Forward: Mexican Organizations in the US as Agents of Incorporation and Dissociation.* Claremont: The Tomas Rivera Policy Institute.

Delgado-Wise, Raul, and Humberto Marquez Covarrubias. 2008. "Capitalist Restructuring, Development and Labour Migration: The Mexico-US Case." *Third World Quarterly* 29 (7): 1359–1374. doi:10.1080/01436590802386542.

Ellis, Mark. 2005. "Unsettling Immigrant Geographies: US Immigration and the Politics of Scale." *Royal Dutch Geography Society* 97 (1): 49–58.

Escala-Rabadan, Luis, Xochitl Bada, and Gaspar Rivera-Salgado. 2006. "Mexican Migrant Civic and Political Participation in the US: The Case of Hometown Associations in Los Angeles and Chicago." *NorteAmerica* 1 (2): 127–172.

Fitzgerald, David. 2006. "Inside the Sending State: The Politics of Mexican Emigration Control." *International Migration Review* 40 (2): 259–293. doi:10.1111/j.1747-7379.200 6.00017.x.

Fox, Jonathan, and Xochitl Bada. 2009. "Migrant Civic Engagement." Research Paper Series on Latino Immigrant Civic and Political Participation, No. 3. Woodrow Wilson International Center for Scholars, Mexico Institute. Accessed June 17. http://www.wilsoncenter.org/migrantparticipation

Goldring, Luin. 2002. "The Mexican State and Transmigrant Organizations: Negotiating the Boundaries of Membership and Participation." *Latin American Research Review* 37 (3): 55–99. Accessed July 2, 2013. http://www.ime.gob.mx/investigaciones/bibliografias/goldring1.pdf

Guarnizo, Luis Eduardo. 2003. "Assimilation and Transnationalism: Determinants of Transnational Political Action among Contemporary Migrants." *The American Journal of Sociology* 108 (6): 1211–1249. doi:10.1086/375195.

Hernandez-Coss, Raul. 2005. "The US-Mexico Remittance Corridor: Lessons on Shifting from Informal to Formal Transfer Systems." Working Paper No. 47. Washington, DC: World Bank.

Koopmans, Ruud. 2004. "Migrant Mobilisation and Political Opportunities: Variation among German Cities and a Comparison with the United Kingdom and the Netherlands." *Journal of Ethnic and Migration Studies* 30 (3): 449–470. doi:10.1080/13691830410001682034.

Kriesi, Hanspeter. 2004. "Political Opportunity and Context." In *The Blackwell Companion to Social Movements*, edited by David A. Snow, Sarah A. Soule, and Hanspeter Kriesi. Malden: Blackwell, 67–90.

Massey, Douglas S., Jorge Durand, and Nolan J. Malone. 2002. *Beyond Smoke and Mirrors: Mexican Immigration in an Era of Economic Integration.* New York: Russell Sage Foundation.

Mollenkopf, John H., and Jennifer Hochschild. 2010. "Immigrant Political Incorporation: Comparing Success in the United States and Western Europe." *Ethnic and Racial Studies* 33 (1): 19–38. doi:10.1080/01419870903197373.

Mollenkopf, John H., and Raphael Sonenshein. 2010. "The New Urban Politics of Integration: A View from the Gateway Cities." In *Bringing Outsiders in: Transatlantic Perspectives on Immigrant Political Incorporation*, edited by Jennifer L. Hochschild and John H. Mollenkopf. Ithaca: Cornell University Press, 74–92.

Orozco, Manuel, and Michelle Lapointe. 2004. "Mexican Hometown Associations and Development Opportunities." *Journal of International Affairs* 57 (2): 31–49. Accessed July 2, 2013. http://www.thedialogue.org/PublicationFiles/Orozco_final.pdf

Ostergaard-Nielsen, Eva. 2003. "The Politics of Migrants' Transnational Practices." *International Migration Review* 37 (3): 760–786. doi:10.1111/j.1747-7379.2003.tb00157.x.

Pallares, Amalia, and Nilda Flores-Gonzalez, eds., 2010. *Marcha! Latino Chicago and the Immigrant Rights Movement.* Urbana: University of Illinois Press.

Però, Davide, and John Solomos. 2010. "Migrant Politics and Mobilization: Exclusion, Engagements, Incorporation." *Ethnic and Racial Studies* 33 (1): 1–18. doi:10.1080/0141 9870903418944.

Portes, Alejandro, Cristina Escobar, and Alexandra Walton Radford. 2007. "Immigrant Transnational Organizations and Development: A Comparative Study." *International Migration Review* 41 (1): 242–281. doi:10.1111/j.1747-7379.2007.00063.x.

Reese, Ellen. 2005. "Policy Threats and Social Movement Coalitions: California's Campaign to Restore Legal Immigrants' Right to Welfare." In *Routing the Opposition: Social Movements, Public Policy, and Democracy*, edited by David S. Meyer, Valerie Jenness, and Helen Ingram, 259–287. Minneapolis: University of Minnesota Press.

Sassen, Saskia. 1998. *Globalization and its Discontents: Essays on the New Mobility of People and Money.* New York: New Press.

Shannon, Amy. 2007. "Mobilizing for Political Power: Immigrant Marches and their Long-Term Impacts." *Voices of Mexico* 78: 28–32. Accessed July 2, 2013. http://webcache.goo gleusercontent.com/search?q=cache:http://www.revistascisan.unam.mx/Voices/pdfs/7807.pdf

Smith, Michael Peter. 2007. "The Two Faces of Transnational Citizenship." *Ethnic and Racial Studies* 30 (6): 1096–1116. doi:10.1080/01419870701599523.

Smith, Michael Peter, and Matt Bakker. 2008. *Citizenship across Borders: The Political Transnationalism of El Migrante.* Ithaca: Cornell University Press.

Smith, Robert C. 2006. *Mexican New York: Transnational Lives of New Immigrants.* Berkeley: University of California Press.

Valdes Ugalde, Francisco. 1996. "The Private Sector and Political Regime Change in Mexico." In *Neoliberalism Revisited: Economic Restructuring and Mexico's Political Future*, edited by Gerardo Otero, 127–148. Boulder: Westview Press.

Voss, Kim, and Irene Bloemraad, eds., 2011. *Rallying for Immigrant Rights: The Fight for Inclusion in 21st Century America.* Berkeley: University of California Press.

Waldinger, Roger D. 2009. "A Limited Engagement: Mexico and its Diaspora." SelectedWorks of Roger D. Waldinger. Accessed June 17. http://works.bepress.com/roger–waldinger/38

Walton, John. 1993. *Western Times and Water Wars: State, Culture, and Rebellion in California*. Berkeley: University of California Press.

Wayne, A. 2005. "House Panel Approves Legislation Aimed at Illegal Immigration." *CQWeekly*, 3332, Dec 12. Accessed June XX. http://library.cqpress.com/cqweekly/weekly report109-000001998134

Back to the Future: revisiting the contact hypothesis at Turkish and mixed non-profit organizations in Amsterdam

Wahideh Achbari

This paper revisits the contact hypothesis by assessing differences in generalized trust among participants of Turkish non-profit organizations and ethnically mixed organizations in Amsterdam. Most voluntary sector research takes the contact hypothesis at its core and assumes that the concentration of ethnic minorities in non-profit organizations is detrimental to learning generalized trust. These studies assume that diversity within organizations is better for developing generalized norms without examining participation in ethnically homogenous organizations. I address this gap in the literature by analysing the variance of generalized trust among organizations and their participants. I achieve this through the analysis of purposively designed survey data. The findings suggest that a contact mechanism at voluntary organizations is problematic and should not be asserted uncritically.

Introduction

For almost a decade, the argument in favour of multiculturalism in Western Europe has been losing popularity (Vertovec and Wessendorf 2010). Whether we look in policy documents, in journalistic accounts or academic debates, very few seem to argue in favour of the cultural retention of minorities. In the Netherlands, more specifically, the incorporation of ethnic minorities has become the topic of debates around the notions of citizenship and nationhood (Scholten and Holzhacker 2009). These disputes resonate with the old Chicago School assimilationist language in which a simple chain of events was held to be responsible for the accommodation of minorities into the mainstream. As with the old assimilationist debate, integration in the Netherlands is now seen by some policymakers as the end point to the cycle of interethnic contact. Moreover, what is meant by integration is not only participation in socio-economic life, but also adherence to a set of common norms and values (Joppke 2004; Scholten and Holzhacker 2009).

Amsterdam is no exception to the attack on multiculturalism (Uitermark, Rossi, and van Houtum 2005; Vertovec and Wessendorf 2010). Ever since a Dutch man of Moroccan descent murdered Theo van Gogh, a film-maker who fervently criticized Islam, ethnic concentration seems to have become taboo. Civil servants fear subsidizing cultural and religious activities. Instead the local government promotes diversity under the rubric of enhancing 'contact' between majority and minority populations. What risks to be forgotten is that ethno-national organizations might still be contributing to the (political) integration of new and old immigrants – albeit 'by a detour' (Berger, Galonska, and Koopmans 2004). The Chicago School was criticized precisely because it ignored differential routes that minorities take into, for example, the labour market, housing market, the educational system and so on. (Portes and Zhou 1993; Alba and Nee 2005). Not necessarily because minorities do not want to mingle with the majority population, but sometimes because they face discrimination or because they otherwise lack the language skills to participate in social life. In line with the American literature, this differential route is labelled as segmented assimilation by European researchers and acculturation is not seen as the only viable integration route (Vermeulen 2010). To be sure, ethno-national organizations were initially promoted by the local government to facilitate integration (Penninx and Slijper 1999) rather than the result of purposeful self-segregation by minorities.

In what follows below, I compare a segmented[1] form of participation in voluntary organizations with a diverse setting that is now favoured by some policymakers and sections of the Dutch public. I question the assumption that ethnic concentration in voluntary or non-profit organizations should a priori be regarded as problematic and take the view that we should put the 'contact hypothesis' in voluntary organizations empirically to the test. This article thus investigates the effect of the ethnic composition of voluntary organizations on generalized trust and poses the following questions: to what extent does the level of generalized trust differ across Turkish and mixed organizations, and to what extent does it differ across their participants? In addition, do members of mixed organizations self-select into those organizations on the basis of their prior trust levels or are they socialized into trusting individuals due to participation?

The findings suggest that participants of Turkish organizations have overall less generalized trust than participants of mixed organizations. However, I demonstrate that participants of mixed organizations in Amsterdam might self-select into hightrusting organizations, controlling for their length of participation.[2] In addition, the data suggest that generalized trust is consistently better explained by having a higher vocational qualification or a university degree as compared to having no qualifications or having finished primary school. A final finding is that generalized trust seems to be lower among participants who have experienced divorce or been widowed.

Before discussing the results, I will elaborate on the voluntary organizations and generalized trust nexus and which factors generate generalized trust. I focus on the contact mechanism at the organizational level, although many studies have recently focused on ethnic diversity at the neighbourhood level. The research strategy of this study overcomes shortcomings of previous research by oversampling individuals in organizations (see Stolle 1998; Maloney, van Deth, and Roßteutscher 2008). Moreover, voluntary organizations are a small enough setting to investigate the effects of face-to-face contact between ethnically diverse groups on generalized trust. Using multilevel modelling and ordinary least squares regression, I then test if generalized trust is affected by participation in Turkish and mixed voluntary organizations in Amsterdam. Apart from contact between ethnically diverse groups, social success factors can also

CITIES, DIVERSITY AND ETHNICITY

contribute to generalized trust. These will be controlled for in the models below. Finally, I discuss the results and conclude the paper.

Why study generalized trust at non-profit or voluntary organizations?

Generalized trust refers to thin or abstract trust in the cooperativeness of others (Newton 1999b), which is theoretically best conceptualized as an evaluation of the unknown other (Sturgis and Smith 2010). Implications of low levels of generalized trust in a given society are more far-reaching than one could expect at face value. Generalized trust is argued to be a prerequisite of a qualitatively better functioning political and economic system (Putnam 1993; Knack and Keefer 1997; Fukuyama 2001). Based on experimental economics, Sønderskov (2011) argues that people who say that they trust others are cooperators in large-N collective action dilemmas, since they expect others to act similarly. He supports this argument with data in which he finds that people with higher levels of generalized trust are more likely to recycle or donate money to environmental organizations.

A growing body of research emphasizes voluntary organizations as venues where generalized trust is learned (cf. Nannestad 2008; Stolle and Howard 2008). Voluntary organizations are arguably 'schools of democracy' where people become active citizens and learn to adhere to norms of trust (Warren 1999, 2001). However, it has been argued that different types of organizations have varying effects on adherence to generalized trust of their members (Stolle and Rochon 2001; Coffé and Geys 2007; Maloney, van Deth, and Roßteutscher 2008). A corollary to this literature is the assumption that participation in ethno-national organizations induces particularized trust and attitudes, as opposed to generalized trust (Newton 1999b; Putnam 2000; Mutz 2002; Uslaner 2002; Uslaner and Conley 2003; Marschall and Stolle 2004; Theiss-Morse and Hibbing 2005; Paxton 2007).

It is argued that ethno-national organizations bring people together from the same background, and hence would impede the development of norms that transcend the in-group. Participating in organizations that bring together people from dissimilar backgrounds is seen to be conducive towards adhering to generalized trust. These two different set-ups have been labelled as 'bonding' and 'bridging'. Bonding organizations are those that are 'inward looking and tend to reinforce exclusive identities and homogenous groups' (Putnam 2000, 22). Bridging organizations are, however, 'outward looking and encompass people across diverse social cleavages' (Putnam 2000, 22). These assumptions put forward by Putnam, seem to be inherited from the civic republican theories of democracy. Since these theories emphasize an egalitarian public sphere, they sit uneasily with a segmented form of civil society on the basis of identity (see Warren 2001).

Contrary to the above, Putnam (2007) recently asserted that residents of homogenous neighbourhoods have a greater propensity to trust the generalized others. Heterogeneity of environment, on the other hand, would inhibit the development of out-group and even in-group ties, consequently leading to isolation. This type of research assumes that contact with diverse others would explain differences in (generalized) trust, although it was not investigated as such. Instead it is assumed that in ethnically homogenous neighbourhoods people may gather together often; whereas in ethnically heterogeneous neighbourhoods contact is 'constricted', which consequently leads to lower levels of (generalized) trust at that level (Putnam 2007, 144).

Contact mechanism is the socialization effect occurring from interethnic contact (Pettigrew 1998). Social psychologists have initially developed this framework in order to understand the processes behind the development of prejudiced attitudes (Allport 1979; Pettigrew 1998; Pettigrew and Tropp 2006). Most of this research has focused on the conditions as to why successful contact occurs and how it reduces prejudice (Pettigrew 1998; Pettigrew and Tropp 2006; Hewstone 2009). Among these conditions, Pettigrew (1998) finds: (1) equal status among the groups; (2) a common goal between the participants; (3) inter-group cooperation; and (4) institutional support. Small-scale voluntary organizations are therefore seen as optimal sites for inter-group contact to take place. Contact with diverse others is often argued to be conducive to the development of generalized trust (see Putnam 2007). Reduced prejudice is clearly not the same as increased trust, since the former involves decreasing negative emotions towards a specific out-group, whereas the latter requires one to extend a positive emotion towards the unknown other. It is important to note that the social capital literature posits that out-groups can be anyone different to the person in socio-economic and cultural terms. Therefore, there are ample conceptual parallels for the contact mechanism to be theoretically relevant to studies of generalized trust (see Hewstone 2009).

While interethnic contact is assumed to be an important driver of generalized trust, this is rarely examined in connection to ethnic diversity in voluntary organizations (cf. Stolle 1998). For example, Putnam (2007) reaches the above conclusion based on neighbourhood rather than association research, and is therefore not directly contradicting his previous conclusions on the virtuous effect of diversity (bridging) within associations. However, one could extend his argument from neighbourhoods to associations and question whether in-group ties are necessarily detrimental to adherence to generalized trust. The relation between generalized and particularized trust that is sketched by the researchers above does not need to be a zero-sum game. There are two other possible scenarios that research has so far ignored. Not only could participation in ethno-national associations be compatible with the development of generalized trust, but a more optimistic model also suggests that participation in these associations would increase one's level of generalized trust (Rijkschroeff and Duyvendak 2004, 21). To date, a systematic comparison of generalized trust for members of ethno-national associations and mixed associations is lacking in the literature.

Self-selection or socialization?

Stolle's (1998) research put forward the assumption that voluntary association membership would increase one's level of generalized trust, and found that length of membership did not affect generalized trust for members. She concluded that hightrusting people might self-select into membership. She also found that organizations with higher proportions of foreigners had a larger proportion of trusting members. This perspective suggests that engagement in ethnically homogenous associations could impede the development of generalized trust, although no ethno-national organizations are included in this study.

While the self-selection argument seems a straightforward conclusion, earlier evidence points in a different direction. When members and non-members were investigated, some researchers found significant, albeit small differences, in generalized trust (Brehm and Rahn 1997). These researchers suggested that the direction of the relationship runs from joining to trust rather than the other way around (Paxton 2007).

In summary, it is still not entirely clear whether members of voluntary organizations –ethno-national or otherwise – are self-selecting into low- and high-trusting groups or whether associations have socializing effects on their members (Nannestad 2008; Stolle and Howard 2008). At the very least, there is some consensus that socio-demographic characteristics and individual resources, such as educational level, correlate positively with generalized trust. Gender and age are indirectly related to trust since women may find themselves among vulnerable groups in society, and the middle-aged have control over their financial position. In other words, generalized trust is expressed by 'winners in society' (Newton 1999a, 185; see also Whiteley 1999; Putnam 2000; cf. Uslaner 2002, 112–113) and could thus be explained by individual-level processes.

As the discussion above has shown, there are different mechanisms at work behind the generation of generalized trust, and by separating different levels of analysis we can specify them at the appropriate level. In what follows, I will focus on the contact mechanism at the organizational level, but also examine individual-level explanations. On the basis of the literature reviewed above, which assumes the contact mechanism to be at work in voluntary organizations, we should expect the following:

(1) The variance in generalized trust among organizations is better explained by the mixed ethnic composition of the organization rather than individual characteristics.
(2) Controlling for participants' socio-demographic characteristics and resources, the longer they are active in a mixed organization, the higher their level of generalized trust.

Research design and measures

To demonstrate whether generalized trust is affected by the ethnic composition of voluntary organizations, I will draw on data collected in 2009 and 2010 in Amsterdam by visiting non-profit organizations or circulating questionnaires via their board.[3] The originality of this approach lies in the multilevel structure of the data. We can thus distinguish between individual- and organizational-level variances in generalized trust in order to single out the contextual effect of ethnic composition in associations. Using multilevel modelling enables contextual analysis and allows for the results to be generalized to other organizations (Steele et al. 2008). In studies where a random sample of the population is asked to name their membership of different types of organizations, contextual effects are in fact being ignored, since there are no data available on other participants of the same organization (see e.g. Coffé and Geys 2007; Paxton 2007; Howard and Gilbert 2008).

The design of this study is a comparative case study with an embedded large *N*. It is a case study, since the results refer only to a specific population: participants in Turkish organizations and mixed organizations in Amsterdam. This population is, however, representative of a key situation. If we consider the Turkish and mixed organizations as *critical* or *crucial* cases (Yin 1994, 40, 54; Gerring 2007, 115–122), they meet the necessary condition for testing the contact hypothesis, namely exposure to interethnic contact. Hence by comparing these two settings, we would be able to generalize whether the contact mechanism or rival explanations are better accounts. If we do not find evidence for the contact mechanism, we would be less likely to find theoretical support for this mechanism in other ethno-national organizations or mixed organizations.

What about contact outside voluntary organizations, which might distort the results for the Turkish participants? Although interethnic contact is obviously not solely confined to voluntary organizations, Turkish minorities have the least amount of contact outside their group during leisure time compared to other ethnic groups, with about 70% reporting no contact (Dagevos and Gijsberts 2005; van den Broek and van Ingen 2008). Even the majority of the second generation says that they have contact only with other Turkish minorities (Dagevos 2005, 75–61; Dagevos and Gijsberts 2005, 26–96). Eighty per cent report that their best friend or marriage partner is of Turkish descent (van der Houwen, Kloosterman, and te Riele 2010, 188). Finally, since the Turkish community is very well organized (Fennema and Tillie 1999, 2001; Vermeulen 2005), they often fall back on their own group for cultural, sport and political activities.

The situation might be different at work or in schools. However, the existence of 'black schools' in which the majority of the students are from a minority background can also reduce opportunities for interethnic contact in the formative years of the pupils (Vervoort, Scholte, and Scheepers 2011). This, of course, has long-term effects for forging friendship ties during adulthood.

Selection of organization and participants

In autumn 2009 and spring 2010, I surveyed the organizations. I created a stratified random sample from a database where information about 15,000 (non-profit) organizations is stored (Vermeulen, Brünger, and van de Walle 2009). This information, in turn, is derived from the Registry of the Chamber of Commerce in Amsterdam. Many organizations record their credentials in order to be eligible for funding. Registration is often associated with greater transparency about the mission of the organization and who is involved in its activities. The selection of participants was at random, since I visited events when they happened and the participants were not informed of my visit in advance.

The researchers who compiled the database above also recorded the ethnicity (country of birth) of the board members. When 30–50% of an organization's board are born in a country other than the Netherlands, the organization is characterized as mixed. This enabled me to make two groups of organizations: an ethnically mixed group and the Turkish group. However, even though the board members of the organization could be from different backgrounds, the participants' background could be from a single ethnic group. Before surveying the participants, I made sure that the mixed organizations actually had diverse participants through interviewing one of the board members. I asked them to estimate the percentage of participants from different ethnic backgrounds, which group constitutes the majority and the relative proportion of each minority group in the organization. The majority group could thus be of any ethnic background. With this information, I created a diversity score for each organization (see also Putnam 2007; Agirdag, van Houtte, and van Avermaet 2011). Often it was straightforward to calculate this as the majority of the members were from Dutch descent and there was only one minority group in the organization. In a very few cases there were more than one minority group in the organization. In those cases I added the proportion of the smaller groups together to calculate the diversity score.

Within each group (Turkish and mixed) I narrowed down the selection towards different activities of the organizations, such as sports and culture, in order to include enough participants with different socio-demographic characteristics. Within each group I have chosen different types of associations (see Table 1), but across groups I aimed at including a similar set. The logic is to have enough variation in age, gender, income and educational level. However, later I had to introduce a snowball method to complement the stratified random sample. This was because some organizations were disbanded or, due to non-response, the sample would not contain a certain type of organization. Moreover, the sampling frame did not include theoretically interesting organizations such as parent teacher associations or those that had been recently established. The snowball method was based on information from the internet and from informants in the council and other organizations.

In total, I aimed at sampling forty organizations with an average of ten responses within each in order to be able to properly separate organizational and individuallevel effects (Maas and Hox 2005).

Variables

The *dependent variable* was measured using the standard question: 'Generally speaking would you say that most people can be trusted or that you need to be careful

Table 1. Types of sampled organizations.

	Turkish	Mixed
Cultural	2	3
Elderly	2	
Political	2	
Religious	5	3
Sports	2	4
Women	3	3
Youth	4	1
Neighbourhood group		4
Social work		1
Parent teacher association		1
Total	20	20

in dealing with people?' (World Values Survey 1990, 7).[4] I adopted the European Social Survey's (2002, 6) eleven-point answer format in which 0 represents 'cannot be too careful' and 10 'most people can be trusted'. The overall mean of generalized trust is 5.5 with a standard deviation of 1.94. Moreover, its frequency distribution resembles a bell-shaped normal distribution.

Ethnic composition, the key *independent variable*, is a binary measure that takes two values: mixed versus Turkish. In the latter case, diversity was low and ranged between 0 and 5%. Only three organizations had a diversity score of 1–5%. The other seventeen had a diversity score of 0%. There were 199 participants from twenty Turkish organizations in the sample. In mixed organizations, the level of diversity was more than 15% and reached 80%. In this group, 213 participants from twenty organizations were included in the sample. In total, there were forty organizations with an average response of ten participants each (SD = 4.5, range four to twenty responses). Length of participation (M = 5.8, SD = 5.7) was measured in the number of years and months that one has been active. As the ethnic composition of some organizations has only become mixed in recent years, the length of participation for those participants was capped at ten years. I also created an interaction term between the type of organization and the length of participation (length of participation at mixed organization, M = 1.8, SD = 3.1).

Finally, based on the available literature on generalized trust, the following list of individual-level *control variables* was included in the analysis: gender, age, divorced/ widowed, employment status, household income and educational attainment. The ratio of men was slightly higher to women: 59% compared to 41%. However, the age bands of twenty-four and younger, twenty-five to thirty-four, thirty-five to forty-four, forty-five to fifty-four, and participants older than fifty-five were relatively equal, with 18–22% of the sample in each band. In contrast, only 13% of the sample comprised participants who had lost their partner through divorce or who had been widowed. Similarly, 16% of the participants were unemployed due to long-term illness or were searching for a job. Household income was measured as net monthly income in euros, with the categories of minimum wage (€1,000 or less), modal income (€1,700), twice modal (€3,200) and more than twice modal (+€3,200). The majority of the respondents (34%) had a modal household income of around €1,700 per month. This was followed by people with less than €1,000 per month (29%). Then 27% of the respondents had an income twice the model income (€3,200) and only 10% had a household income above €3,200. Educational attainment took three categories: no qualification or finished primary school; low vocational degree or a secondary school degree; and high vocational or university degree. The last two categories were relatively equal with 37% and 41%, respectively, while the first category comprised of 22% of the sample.

The findings

Before discussing the findings, I will first give an overview of the organizational characteristics of the Turkish and mixed groups and their activities. This is necessary in order to contextualize the findings and also to demonstrate why a comparison between these two groups will shed light on the contact mechanism and its relation to generalized trust. Apart from four mixed organizations, all other organizations have a formal board registered at the Dutch Chamber of Commerce. These four organizations still operate under a formal structure by having a president or a coordinator and a few people who assist them in the daily management. The size of the organizations varies between ten and 1,200 members. However, across the Turkish and mixed organizations, the size distribution is similar.

Like many other organizations, Turkish organizations are very versatile in their activities, because they usually fill a void for people who are otherwise segregated from voluntary organizations. Among other things, their activities range from sports, cultural gatherings, neighbourhood barbeques, debates, religious festivities to social work for which they only attract Turkish minorities. In contrast, mixed organizations' primary missions are surprisingly not to bridge ethnic gaps. This is because the ethnic composition of the organizations is often de facto mixed. For example, most sports organizations attract a mixed membership due to the ethnic composition of a neighbourhood.

Although most Turkish organizations organize activities in neighbourhoods where different ethnic groups can take part, these are mostly yearly one-off events, such as religious festivities, street parties, barbeques, or debates around political events or at election times. They do not provide durable contact with ethnically diverse others to their participants on a regular basis. In contrast, eight mixed organizations actively promote interethnic contact as their primary mission. This is then reflected in the composition of their membership, board and volunteers that they recruit. Four of these organizations were either founded by second-generation immigrants or were formerly ethno-national organizations. They actively promote contact during projects that are often more than one-off events. All other mixed organizations, although not set up to actively promote contact, still regularly bring participants together during their events.

Partitioning variance in generalized trust

Now I turn to the analysis of generalized trust. As argued in the previous section, a single-level model ignores contextual effects. That is why I start partitioning variances at the organizational and participant levels. As we can see in Table 2, organizations vary 4% in their participant's generalized trust scores.[5] This model is significant at an 8% level. Second, the variance estimate at the organizational level is significant at 17%, which indicates that with such a small organizational-level variance we need many more organizations to pick up a statistically significant effect size. Social science data with high contextual effects will typically attribute less than 40% of the variation in their data to higher levels (Snijders and Bosker 1999, 151–152). Organizations thus differ very little in generalized trust scores in comparison to the participants. This is because organizational variance is relatively small (4%) compared to participant-level variance (96%).

However, we have to explore further the effect of ethnic composition on generalized trust in a multilevel model, because it is possible that between-group differences may only then be revealed. Still, this small level of variation between organizations in the generalized trust levels of their participant questions the extent to which we can explain their differences by the environment that they are in.

CITIES, DIVERSITY AND ETHNICITY

Table 2. Variance components model of generalized trust for participants of Turkish and mixed organizations in Amsterdam, 2009–10.

	Estimate	SE
Fixed effect		
Intercept	5.495	0.095
Random *effect variances*		
Organizational level	0.164	0.120 ($p = .17$)
Participant level	3.592***	0.264
Variance partition (%)		
Organizational level	4	
Participant level	96	
-2 log-likelihood deviance	1714 − 1711 = 3 (df = 1) $p = .0833$	
Number of participants	412	
Number of organizations	40	

*** $p \leq .001$

Ethnic composition: mixed versus Turkish

In Table 3 I have added the first variable to an empty random intercept model in order to differentiate between a mixed and a homogenous environment in voluntary organizations. Thus we can assess the mean difference in generalized trust by including the ethnic composition of an organization into the model. By adding this level-two variable to the model, the variance at the organizational level drops to 1%.[6] The model change is significant, although the estimate of organizational-level variance is highly insignificant this time. This again means that with such a small variation between organizations, we need a much larger sample of organizations to pick a significant effect size. Therefore, the first hypothesis that differences in generalized trust can be attributed to the mixed ethnic composition of an organization can be rejected. Next, the length of participation is added in model 2. This variable also does not change the model much. Organizational variance drops to 0.6% and the model change is significant. Unsurprisingly, the estimate of the organizational variance is insignificant again. Finally, in model 3, I differentiate between the length of participation in mixed organizations compared to that in Turkish organizations. This variable (or cross-level interaction term) does not improve the model and is insignificant. As expected, the organizational variance does not change, nor does its significance level improve.

The results of these models seem to suggest that an organization's ethnic composition has very little bearing on generalized trust. Generalized trust seems not to be enhanced when there is more than one ethnic group present in non-profit organizations. On the contrary, the results suggest that people with higher trust levels might self-select into ethnically mixed organizations. The multilevel structure of the data barely explains differences in generalized trust. Consequently, we can safely differentiate the effect of ethnic composition in voluntary organizations from other factors in a single-level regression model and assess the relative importance of each variable in order to assess the second hypothesis.

Table 3. Fixed and random effects models of generalized trust for participants of Turkish and mixed associations in Amsterdam, 2009–10.

	Model 1		Model 2		Model 3	
	Estimate	SE	Estimate	SE	Estimate	SE
Fixed effect						
Intercept	5.171	0.141	4.939	0.202	4.978	0.217
Ethnic composition:						
Mixed (reference = Turkish)	0.619***	0.198	0.718***	0.212	0.618*	0.294
Length participation			0.030	0.019	0.025	0.021
Length participation x ethnic composition (reference = length participation x Turkish organization)					0.022	0.044
Random effect variances						
Organizational level	0.037	0.089	0.025	0.089	0.020	0.088
Participant level	3.620***	0.265	3.657***	0.272	3.659***	0.272
Variance partition (%)						
Organizational level	1		0.6		0.5	
Participant level	99		99.4		99.5	
-2 log-likelihood deviance	1711 − 1703=8 (df = 1)*		1703 − 1652 = 51 (df = 1)**		0	
Number of participants	412		399		399	
Number of organizations	40		40		40	

* $p \leq .05$, *** $p \leq .001$

Controlling for socio-demographic factors and resources

Table 4 summarizes the relative importance of each factor: participation in mixed versus Turkish organizations; length of participation in addition to the interaction term between these when controlling for socio-demographic factors and resources.

Overall, model 1 is significant at the 5% level, whereas models 2 and 3 are significant at the 1% level. As we might have expected from the multilevel model, type of organization is a significant predictor of generalized trust. Moreover, it has substantively the largest effect size. In model 3, I add the interaction term length of participation in a mixed organization. Theoretically, the contact mechanism is corroborated when this variable is significant and has a higher effect size than the variable mixed ethnic composition. On the contrary and as already been discussed in the multilevel model, this interaction term is insignificant. This suggests that length of participation in mixed organizations does not have any substantive weight in explaining differences in generalized trust. It might be that higher-trusting individuals self-select into mixed organizations.

In sum, this study finds better support for a self-selection mechanism in explaining generalized trust attitudes of participants of mixed and Turkish organizations in Amsterdam. This is because a mixed ethnic composition has the highest effect size in the last two models when the length of participation and other factors are controlled for. Therefore, the second hypothesis based on the contact mechanism is also refuted. Next, having a higher vocational or university degree as opposed to having no qualifications or having finished primary school has the second largest effect size. Then having lost one's partner through divorce or being widowed has a negative effect and is significant at the 5% level. Having an income between €1,001 and 1,700 as compared to less than €1,000 is significant at the 10% level. Finally, it is interesting to note that in earlier models, being fifty-five and older had the largest effect size (0.187) in explaining generalized trust. However, once the ethnic composition of an organization and the interaction effect is added, being middle-aged loses its significance.

Discussion and conclusions

Across generalized trust studies, there is a general pattern: individual-level variable educational attainment is consistently a significant predictor (Huang, Maassen van den Brink, and Groot 2009). This study, which has built on previous work, also found strong evidence for individual-level factors as discussed above rather than for organizational variation. Moreover, the variance partition showed that the majority of variance in generalized trust (96%) is clustered at the individual level of analysis. A self-selection mechanism seems best to explain differences between participants. That is to say, participants of mixed organizations seem to join these organizations on the basis of higher prior held generalized trust attitudes. Next, having a higher vocational qualification or university degree compared to no qualifications or having finished primary school seems to contribute to generalized trust. Then, participants who have lost their partner through divorce or who have become widowed are less likely to trust others. These findings support the 'winner in society' theory that people with a relatively better socio-economical position have higher trust levels (Newton 1999a, 185).

Table 4. Fixed effects models of generalized trust for participants of Turkish and mixed associations in Amsterdam, 2009–10.

Variables	Model 1		Model 2		Model 3	
	B (SE)	β	B (SE)	β	B (SE)	β
Gender (reference = men)	0.101 (0.208)	0.026	−0.093 (0.222)	−0.024	−0.002 (0.227)	−0.001
Age (reference = 24 and younger)						
25–34	0.342 (0.302)	0.075	0.149 (0.310)	0.033	0.144 (0.312)	0.032
35–44	0.115 (0.329)	0.023	0.012 (0.329)	0.002	−0.112 (0.337)	−0.023
45–54	0.537 (0.331)	0.110	0.416 (0.332)	0.085	0.236 (0.347)	0.048
55–70+	−0.906 (0.337)	0.187**	0.633 (0.354)	0.131†	0.371 (0.374)	0.076
Divorced or widowed (reference = married or cohabiting; never been married)	−0.799 (0.318)	−0.141*	−0.783 (0.316)	−0.139*	−0.804 (0.315)	−0.142*
Unemployed or sick (reference = in paid job; retired; doing unpaid or voluntary work)	0.001 (0.286)	0.000	0.026 (0.285)	0.005	0.092 (0.286)	0.018
Net household income (€)						
1,001–1,700	0.424 (0.259)	0.105	0.529 (0.261)	0.132*	0.495 (0.261)	0.123†
1,701–3,200	0.139 (0.270)	0.033	0.231 (0.271)	0.055	0.137 (0.274)	0.033
More than 3,200 (reference = 1,000 or less)	0.450 (0.365)	0.075	0.472 (0.362)	0.079	0.470 (0.361)	0.078
Educational attainment						
Secondary vocational training and pre-university	0.162 (0.286)	0.042	0.044 (0.288)	0.011	0.012 (0.289)	0.003
Higher vocational degree or university (reference = no education or primary school)	0.699 (0.296)	0.180*	0.533 (0.302)	0.138$	0.589 (0.303)	0.152*
Ethnic composition						
Mixed (reference = Turkish)			0.557 (0.232)	0.147*	0.738 (0.247)	0.195**
Length participation (centred)					0.028 (0.024)	0.080
Length participation (centred) x *ethnic composition* (reference = length participation (centred) x Turkish organization)					0.053 (0.046)	0.078
Intercept	4.747		4.699		4.760	
	$R^2 = 0.068$*		$R^2 = 0.083$**		$R^2 = 0.095$**	

†$p \le .10$, * $p \le .05$, ** $p \le .01$, $n = 360$

Since organizational variance in generalized trust attitudes is so low (4%), it is highly unlikely that contact with ethnically diverse others in voluntary organizations socializes one to become more trusting of strangers. However, most research assumes that voluntary organizations socialize their participants into trusting people, but fails to adequately address this question since the structure of their data does not allow for the distinguishing between participants' and organizational variance in generalized trust. Most studies fail to sample organizations and their participants; instead they rely on surveys that sample individual households.

A limitation of the present study might be the design, which only included Turkish organizations. However, it might be unlikely to find evidence for this mechanism among other voluntary organizations, if we regard Turkish and mixed organizations as critical cases. Insignificant variances at the organizational level might also seem to weaken the findings. Nevertheless, we might also question whether confirming the statistical significance of the results justifies the collection of more data. Finally, the results seem to suggest that high-trusting individuals are selfselecting into mixed organizations. Stolle's (1998) study reached a similar conclusion when examining generalized trust for participants of different types of voluntary organizations in the USA, Germany and Sweden (see also Uslaner and Brown 2005). Ultimately, however, we need longitudinal panel data, which should show whether careful individuals are not opting out of mixed organizations.

As argued before, the data suggest that participants of mixed organizations seem to have self-selected themselves into those organizations on the basis of their higher trust levels. Controlling for length of participation, participants of mixed organizations are not more trusting. This implies that the context in which interaction takes place, namely the presence of diverse ethnic groups or conversely ethnic homogeneity in voluntary organizations, is unlikely to affect generalized trust. Thus a contact mechanism, through bridging and bonding ethnic ties, in voluntary organizations seems not to explain differences in generalized trust. This is not so surprising, since the voluntary sector literature suffers from the same shortcomings as the earlier versions of contact theory. That is to say, most of these studies only predict that 'positive contact effects will occur, not how and why' (Pettigrew 1998, 80).

Acknowledgements

I thank MTEM Ltd., Prins Bernhard Cultuur Fonds, Stichting Vrijvrouwe van Renswoude and Research Foundation Flanders (FWO grant number G.0022.12) for their generous funding of this project. I am greatly indebted to Floris Vermeulen and the Institute for Migration and Ethnic Studies in Amsterdam for their support during the fieldwork. I would also like to thank two anonymous reviewers of this journal and Benny Geys for their helpful comments on earlier drafts.

Notes

1. In the current migration literature, segmented assimilation is applied to different social mobility routes that children of immigrants take (for a review, see Vermeulen 2010). I use the term 'segmented' more loosely to mean segregated.
2. Controlling for length of participation to address the self-selection concern should probably be seen as a start, but it may be insufficient. Unfortunately, panel data – which would

be required to do more in this direction – were not available. This is clearly an avenue for future research.

3. Participants usually filled out a questionnaire in Turkish, Dutch or English, depending on their fluency in either of the languages. If they requested to be contacted later, I would send them a link to a web-based questionnaire. Occasionally, when the board found that my visit would disrupt the event, I circulated questionnaires via them. I instructed the board member to give the questionnaire to a diverse set of participants or to all participants.

4. Recently there has been debate about the validity of the generalized trust question. Sturgis and Smith (2010; cf. Delhey, Newton, and Welzel 2011) demonstrated that some people refer to known others when answering the question. To overcome this bias, in the questionnaire I first posed questions on trust about specific groups (such as different ethnic groups, one's family, etc.) before asking the generalized trust question. By doing so, the respondents became aware of the fact that 'most people' in the generalized trust question refers to an unknown person.

5. I used the software MLWin for the analysis (Steele et al. 2008).

6. The results do not change when the continuous diversity score is entered into the models.

References

Agirdag, Orhan, Mieke van Houtte, and Piet van Avermaet. 2011. "Ethnic School Context and the National and Sub-National Identifications of Pupils." *Ethnic and Racial Studies* 34 (2): 357–378. doi:10.1080/01419870.2010.510198.

Alba, Richard D., and Victor Nee. 2005. *Remaking the American Mainstream: Assimilation and Contemporary Immigration.* London: Harvard University Press.

Allport, Gordon W. 1979. *The Nature of Prejudice.* Cambridge, MA: Addison-Wesley.

Berger, Maria, Christian Galonska, and Ruud Koopmans. 2004. "Political Integration by a Detour? Ethnic Communities and Social Capital of Migrants in Berlin." *Journal of Ethnic and Migration Studies* 30 (3): 491–507. doi:10.1080/13691830410001682052.

Brehm, John, and Wendy Rahn. 1997. "Individual-Level Evidence for the Causes and Consequences of Social Capital." *American Journal of Political Science* 41 (3): 999–1023. doi:10.2307/2111684.

Coffé, Hilde, and Benny Geys. 2007. "Participation in Bridging and Bonding Associations and Civic Attitudes: Evidence from Flanders." *Voluntas: International Journal of Voluntary and Nonprofit Organizations* 18 (4): 385–406. doi:10.1007/s11266-007-9048-2.

Dagevos, Jaco. 2005. "Gescheiden werelden? De etnische signatuur van vrijetijdscontacten van minderheden." *Sociologie* 1 (1): 52–69. doi:10.1347/sogi.1.1.52.64110.

Dagevos, Jaco, and Mérove Gijsberts. 2005. *Uit Elkaars Buurt.* Den Haag: Sociaal Cultureel Planbureau.

Delhey, Jan, Kenneth Newton, and Christian Welzel. 2011. "How General Is Trust in "most People"? Solving the Radius of Trust Problem." *American Sociological Review* 76 (5): 786–807. doi:10.1177/0003122411420817.

European Social Survey. 2002. "Source Questionnaire (Round 1, 2002)." Accessed July 24. http://www.europeansocialsurvey.org/index.php?option_com_docman&task_doc_download&gid_5&itemid_80.

Fennema, Meindert, and Jean Tillie. 1999. "Political Participation and Political Trust in Amsterdam: Civic Communities and Ethnic Networks." *Journal of Migration and Ethnic Studies* 25 (4): 703–726. doi:10.1080/1369183X.1999.9976711.

Fennema, Meindert, and Jean Tillie. 2001. "Civic Community, Political Participation and Political Trust of Ethnic Groups." *Connections* 24 (1): 26–41.

Fukuyama, Francis. 2001. "Social Capital, Civil Society and Development." *Third World Quarterly* 22 (1): 7–20. doi:10.1080/713701144.

Gerring, John. 2007. *Case Study Research: Principles and Practices*. Cambridge: Cambridge University Press.

Hewstone, Miles. 2009. *Living Apart, Living Together? The Role of Intergroup Contact in Social Integration*. Göttingen: Max Planck Institute for the Study of Religious and Cultural Diversity.

Howard, Marc Morjé, and Leah Gilbert. 2008. "A Cross-National Comparison of the Internal Effects of Participation in Voluntary Organizations." *Political Studies* 56 (1): 12–32. doi:10.1111/j.1467-9248.2007.00715.x.

Huang, Jian, Henriëtte Maassen van den Brink, and Wim Groot. 2009. "A Meta-Analysis of the Effect of Education on Social Capital." *Economics of Education Review* 28 (4): 454–464. doi:10.1016/j.econedurev.2008.03.004.

Joppke, Christian. 2004. "The Retreat of Multiculturalism in the Liberal State: Theory and Policy." *The British Journal of Sociology* 55 (2): 237–257. doi:10.1111/j.1468-4446.2004.00017.x.

Knack, Stephen, and Philip Keefer. 1997. "Does Social Capital Have an Economic Payoff? A Cross-Country Investigation." *Quarterly Journal of Economics* 112 (4): 1251–1288. doi:10.1162/003355300555475.

Maas, Cora J. M., and Joop J. Hox. 2005. "Sufficient Sample Sizes for Multilevel Modeling." *Methodology* 1 (3): 86–92.

Maloney, William A., Jan W. van Deth, and Sigrid Roßteutscher. 2008. "Civic Orientations: Does Associational Type Matter?." *Political Studies* 56 (2): 261–287. doi:10.1111/j.1467-9248.2007.00689.x.

Marschall, Melissa J., and Dietlind Stolle. 2004. "Race and the City: Neighbourhood Context and the Development of Generalized Trust." *Political Behavior* 25 (2): 125–154. doi:10.1023/B:POBE.0000035960.73204.64.

Mutz, Diana C. 2002. "Cross-Cutting Social Networks: Testing Democratic Theory in Practice." *American Political Science Review* 96 (1): 111–126. doi:10.1017/S0003055402004264.

Nannestad, Peter. 2008. "What Have We Learned about Generalized Trust, if Anything?." *Annual Review of Political Science* 11 (1): 413–436. doi:10.1146/annurev.polisci.11.060606.135412.

Newton, Kenneth. 1999a. "Social and Political Trust in Established Democracies." In *Critical Citizens: Global Support for Democratic Government*, edited by Pippa Norris, 169–187. Oxford: Oxford University Press.

Newton, Kenneth. 1999b. "Social Capital and Democracy in Modern Europe." In *Social Capital and European Democracy*, edited by Jan van Deth, Marco Maraffi, Kenneth Newton, and Paul Whiteley, 3–24. London: Routledge.

Paxton, Pamela. 2007. "Association Memberships and Generalized Trust: A Multilevel Model across 31 Countries." *Social Forces* 86 (1): 47–76. doi:10.1353/sof.2007.0107.

Penninx, Rinus, and Boris Slijper. 1999. *Voor Elkaar? Integratie, Vrijwilligerswerk en Organisaties van Migranten*. Amsterdam: Universiteit van Amsterdam, Institute for Migrationand Ethnic Studies (IMES).

Pettigrew, Thomas F. 1998. "Intergroup Contact Theory." *Annual Review of Psychology* 49 (1): 65–85. doi:10.1146/annurev.psych.49.1.65.

Pettigrew, Thomas F., and Linda R. Tropp. 2006. "A Meta-Analytic Test of Intergroup Contact Theory." *Journal of Personality & Social Psychology* 90 (5): 751–783. doi:10.1037/0022-3514.90.5.751.

Portes, Alejandro, and Min Zhou. 1993. "The New Second Generation: Segmented Assimilation and its Variants." *The Annals of the American Academy of Political and Social Science* 530 (1): 74–96. doi:10.1177/0002716293530001006.

Putnam, Robert D. 1993. *Making Democracy Work: Civic Traditions in Modern Italy.* Princeton, NJ: Princeton University Press.

Putnam, Robert D. 2000. *Bowling Alone: The Collapse and Revival of American Community.* New York: Simon & Schuster.

Putnam, Robert D. 2007. "E Pluribus Unum: Diversity and Community in the Twenty-First Century the 2006 Johan Skytte Prize Lecture." *Scandinavian Political Studies* 30 (2): 137–174. doi:10.1111/j.1467-9477.2007.00176.x.

Rijkschroeff, Rally, and Jan W. Duyvendak. 2004. "De omstreden betekenis van zelforganisaties." *Sociologische Gids* 51 (1): 18–35. doi:10.1347/sogi.51.1.18.30374.

Scholten, Peter, and Ronald Holzhacker. 2009. "Bonding, Bridging and Ethnic Minorities in the Netherlands: Changing Discourses in a Changing Nation." *Nations and Nationalism* 15 (1): 81–100. doi:10.1111/j.1469-8129.2009.00350.x.

Snijders, Tom A. B., and Roel J. Bosker. 1999. *Multilevel Analysis: An Introduction to Basic and Advanced Multilevel Modeling.* London: Sage.

Sønderskov, Kim Mannemar. 2011. "Does Generalized Social Trust Lead to Associational Membership? Unravelling a Bowl of Well-Tossed Spaghetti." *European Sociological Review* 27 (4): 419–434. doi:10.1093/esr/jcq017.

Steele, Fiona, William Browne, Harvey Goldstein, Jo-Anne Baird, and Sally Thomas. 2008. "University of Bristol Learning Environment for Multilevel Methodology and Applications (LEMMA)." Accessed July 24. http://www.bristol.ac.uk/cmm/research/lemma/.

Stolle, Dietlind. 1998. "Bowling Together, Bowling Alone: The Development of Generalized Trust in Voluntary Associations." *Political Psychology* 19 (3): 497–525. doi:10.1111/0162-895X.00115.

Stolle, Dietlind, and Marc M. Howard. 2008. "Civic Engagement and Civic Attitudes in Cross-National Perspective: Introduction to the Symposium." *Political Studies* 56 (1): 1–11. doi:10.1111/j.1467-9248.2007.00714.x.

Stolle, Dietlind, and Thomas R. Rochon. 2001. "Are all Associations Alike? Member Diversity, Associational Type, and the Creation of Social Capital." In *Beyond Tocqueville: Civil Society and the Social Capital Debate in Comparative Perspective*, edited by Bob Edwards, Micheal W. Foley and Mario Diani, 143–156. Hanover, NH: University Press of New England.

Sturgis, Patrick, and Patten Smith. 2010. "Assessing the Validity of Generalized Trust Questions: What Kind of Trust Are We Measuring?". *International Journal of Public Opinion Research* 22 (1): 74–92. doi:10.1093/ijpor/edq003.

Theiss-Morse, Elizabeth, and John R. Hibbing. 2005. "Citizenship and Civic Engagement." *Annual Review of Political Science* 8: 227–249. doi:10.1146/annurev.polisci.8.082103.104829.

Uitermark, Justus, Ugo Rossi and Henk van Houtum. 2005. "Reinventing Multiculturalism: Urban Citizenship and the Negotiation of Ethnic Diversity in Amsterdam." *International Journal of Urban and Regional Research* 29 (3): 622–640. doi:10.1111/j.1468-2427.2005.00614.x.

Uslaner, Eric M. 2002. *The Moral Foundations of Trust.* Cambridge: Cambridge University Press.

Uslaner, Eric M., and Mitchell Brown. 2005. "Inequality, Trust, and Civic Engagement." *American Politics Research* 33 (6): 868–894. doi:10.1177/1532673X04271903.

CITIES, DIVERSITY AND ETHNICITY

Uslaner, Eric M., and Richard S. Conley. 2003. "Civic Engagement and Particularized Trust: The Ties that Bind People to their Ethnic Communities." *American Politics Research* 31 (4): 331–360. doi:10.1177/1532673X03031004001.

van den Broek, Andries, and van Ingen, Eric. 2008. "Sociale contacten in de vrije tijd", In *Het dagelijks leven van allochtone stedelingen*, edited by Andries van den Broek and Saskia Keuzenkamp, 101–124. Den Haag: Sociaal Cultureel Planbureau.

van der Houwen, Karolijne, Rianne Kloosterman, and Saskia te Riele. 2010. "Contacten tussen bevolkingsgroepen." In *Sociale Samenhang: Participatie, Vertrouwen en Integratie*, edited by H. Schmeets, 183–196. Den Haag: Centraal Bureau voor de Statistiek.

Vermeulen, Floris F. 2005. "The Immigrant Organising Process: The Emergence and Persistence of Turkish Immigrant Organizations in Amsterdam and Berlin and Surinamese Organisations in Amsterdam, 1960–2000." PhD thesis, The University of Amsterdam.

Vermeulen, Floris F., Martijn Brünger, and Robert van de Walle. 2009. *Het Maatschappelijk Middenveld in Amsterdam en in de Stadsdelen, 2002–2007. Aantallen, Typen, Netwerken, (Bestuurs) leden en de Relatie met de Lokale Overheid*. Amsterdam: Instituut for Migration and Ethnic Studies (IMES), Universiteit van Amsterdam.

Vermeulen, Hans. 2010. "Segmented Assimilation and Cross-National Comparative Research on the Integration of Immigrants and their Children." *Ethnic & Racial Studies* 33 (7): 1214–1230. doi:10.1080/01419871003615306.

Vertovec, Steven, and Susanne Wessendorf. 2010. "Introduction: Assessing the Backlash against Multiculturalism in Europe." In *The Multiculturalism Backlash: European Discourses, Policies and Practices*, edited by Steven Vertovec and Susanne Wessendorf, 1–31. Abingdon: Routledge.

Vervoort, Miranda H. M., Ron H. J. Scholte, and Peer L. H. Scheepers. 2011. "Ethnic Composition of School Classes, Majority–Minority Friendships, and Adolescents' Intergroup Attitudes in the Netherlands." *Journal of Adolescence* 34 (2): 257–267.

Warren, Mark E. 1999. *Democracy and Trust*. Cambridge: Cambridge University Press.

Warren, Mark E. 2001. *Democracy and Association*. Princeton, NJ: Princeton University Press.

Whiteley, Paul F. 1999. "The Origins of Social Capital." In *Social Capital and European Democracy*, edited by Jan van Deth, Marco Maraffi, Kenneth Newton, and Paul Whiteley, 25–44. London: Routledge.

World Values Survey. 1990. "1990 Questionnaire." Accessed July 24. http://www.worldvalu essurvey.org/wvs/articles/folder_published/survey_1990/files/root_q_1990.pdf.

Yin, Robert K. 1994. *Case Study Research: Design and Methods*. 2nd ed. Thousand Oaks, CA: Sage.

The early history of migration and settlement of Yemenis in Cardiff, 1939–1970: religion and ethnicity as social capital

Jody Mellor and Sophie Gilliat-Ray

Utilizing Putnam's concept of bonding social capital, this article explores the under-researched topic of the history of migrant men's reproduction of social capital in Cardiff, Wales. Drawing upon a series of oral history interviews with a respected imam of more than fifty years, and informed by existing research on Muslim migrants, we explore both the advantages and disadvantages of community relationships between Yemeni men in relation to trust, reciprocity and interpersonal well-being. By examining these complex bonds, this article contributes to the literature on religious and ethnic social networks by challenging the assumption that migrants always benefit from social resources (Wilson 1978; Shah 2007), and offers an alternative account of religiously underpinned social capital to those of studies of majority ethnic Christians in North America (Smidt 2003). Uniquely, this article also points to the divergences between religious and ethnic capitals in the context of Yemeni migrants' social resources during 1939–1970.

Introduction

We explore the formation and deployment of the social resources of Yemeni migrants living in SouthWales from 1939 onwards by examining the memories and experiences of a single person, Sheikh Saeed, a respected, long-serving imam (Gilliat-Ray 2010), and by drawing on several important historical studies. These include Ansari's (2004) historical work, which provides a broad understanding of Muslim migration and settlement in the UK, and Halliday's (2010) exploration of Yemenis residing in British cities. These are supplemented by historical studies of Welsh migration including Aithie (2005), O'Neill (2001) and Sinclair (1997).

To explore the significance of social capital we explore the extent to which faith- and ethnic-based networks provided a tight-knit, supportive environment for Yemeni seafarers in the early history of migration to Cardiff. Drawing on Putnam's concept of bonding capital, our attention focuses upon the strong community spirit fostered by our interviewee, Sheikh Saeed, as well as the two previous Yemeni sheikhs in Cardiff (al-Hakimi and Hasan Ismail), who – through a system of community rights and reciprocity – ensured that Yemenis in Cardiff were provided with emotional, financial and practical support. However, we also explore the negative aspects of bonding social capital. In particular, we focus on the heavy responsibilities of Yemeni men and the sanctions in place to ensure that duties towards community members were fulfilled. We also point to the ways in which strong close-knit ethnic and religious ties closed down the potential for the development of bridging capital.

As Halliday (2010) suggests, Cardiff's Yemenis enjoyed very close links with fellow countrymen in several cities such as Birmingham and South Shields. However, in this article we focus specifically on relationships between Yemenis in Cardiff because it is the local, dayto- day interactions that we are interested in here. Moreover, as an imam of the Yemeni mosque, Sheikh Saeed interacted predominantly with other Yemenis and his accounts centred on the experiences and memories of this ethnic group in particular. Our data focus upon three decades, starting at the beginning of the Second World War. Although the history of Muslims in Cardiff can be traced much earlier than this (Gilliat-Ray and Mellor 2010), we start in 1939 with our participant's arrival in Cardiff as a young boy. Our research ends at around 1970, following the decline of the maritime industry in South Wales and at a time when Butetown was undergoing full-scale redevelopment.[1]

Local context

Cardiff was once one of the biggest ports in the UK and in 1900 was the largest exporter of coal in the world (Ansari 2004). Several studies have highlighted the experiences of Yemeni and Somali migrants who made up the first relatively permanent migrant Muslim communities in the port cities of Cardiff, South Shields, London and Liverpool, but of these ports, Cardiff is the most important in terms of Yemeni migration (Halliday 2010). During this early history of migration, the Yemeni community in the UK consisted almost entirely of men who worked as seafarers. There were very few Yemeni-born women, partly because the national government encouraged women to stay at home due to concerns that remittances coming into the country would reduce (Halliday 2010). According to the 1911 census, there were around 700 settled black people in Cardiff (Evans 1980). Numbers reached their peak in the mid-1930s and even during the Second World War, at a time when many Yemenis returned home, it is estimated that 1,500 Yemeni seamen were in Cardiff (Little 1972). According to Sinclair (1997), the foreign seamen working out of Cardiff during the war were economic migrants, involved in sending remittances to family.

Sheikh Ali al-Hakimi arrived in Cardiff in 1936 and one of his most notable achievements was to organize the purchase of the Nur al-Islam mosque, which also held an Arabic political printing press (Halliday 2010). Al-Hakimi's deputy in the Allawi Society was Sheikh Hasan Ismail, who had been resident in Cardiff for a number of years. However, although there were close bonds between the Yemenis in Cardiff, as Halliday (2010) notes, from 1949, religious, sectarian and political divisions developed between Yemenis from the north and south. The dispute in Cardiff centred on al-Hakimi, Hasan Ismail and the Nur al-Islam mosque. Whereas al-Hakimi and a small number of followers aimed for the reform and unification of Islam, Hasan Ismail and most of the Cardiff community – who were loyal to traditional Yemeni beliefs – were opposed to this (Halliday 2010). There was a disagreement over leadership of the mosque and the problem was only resolved when

CITIES, DIVERSITY AND ETHNICITY

Hasan Ismail and his followers established a separate space, a zawiya, of which Hasan Ismail was sheikh (Halliday 2010).[2]

He remained in Cardiff until 1956 and soon after, Sheikh Saeed, his adopted son, was appointed as his replacement (Halliday 2010). Although some of the conflicts between the two Yemeni factions were reported in the local press, there is little evidence to suggest that the white Welsh population in Cardiff met with or spoke to black or Arab residents on a day-to-day basis. The Yemeni population, alongside other migrants in Cardiff, mainly resided in Tiger Bay, an area that became renowned for being both exotic and dangerous, and such representations – which both fascinated and unsettled the white Welsh residents – rested partly upon the sexual relationships between male migrants and white Welsh women that were widely reported in the South Wales Echo and the Western Mail newspapers (Halliday 2010). These local knowledges and myths about the docklands area and its residents, which were perpetuated by racial and class prejudices, were left unchallenged partly due to the segregation between the two groups. Such representations were compounded by the rising levels of unemployment in the maritime industry after the Second World War, for which white Welsh unemployment was understood as the consequence of the arrival of the large migrant workforce (O'Neill 2001).

Oral history

Between 2004 and 2009 we conducted a series of five oral history interviews with Sheikh Saeed, in English, as part of a research project exploring the history of migration to and settlement in South Wales. In 2011 Sheikh Saeed died in Cardiff, aged eighty-one, after five decades of serving the Muslim community in the city. Originally born in South Shields to a British mother and a Yemeni seafaring father, he arrived in Cardiff having been adopted by Sheikh Hassan Ismail shortly after the death of his father, who was killed at the beginning of the Second World War. At the age of sixteen, he travelled to the Yemen, along with Sheikh Hasan Ismail, to receive his religious training and ten years later, Sheikh Saeed became the spiritual leader of Cardiff 's Yemeni community. Sheikh Saeed was the most prominent figurehead of Islam in Cardiff until his death, playing a leading role in organizing the construction of the South Wales Islamic Centre, on Alice Street, and becoming the first Welsh Muslim to serve as a chaplain to a civic leader (Gilliat-Ray 2011).

The five oral history interviews were conducted and fully transcribed by the authors. One of the strengths of oral history is that it allows an exploration of the ways in which macro social structures interact with the opportunities and experiences of individuals, enabling an effective interrogation of ongoing processes (Becker 2002). As Bornat (2004, 44) argues, oral history gives 'access to the methods and theories of more than one discipline and a balanced approach ensures that no one emphasis predominates.' One concern about relying upon archival data only may be that the voices of individuals are left largely unexplored, but by utilizing both oral history and secondary sources we can explore more fully the history of Yemeni social networks in Cardiff. In drawing upon one person's account, the issue of general-izablity must be considered. Here, we approach this kind of analysis with caution about what can (and cannot) be claimed, and generalizability is not something that

177

this article aims for. Instead, we use the perspective of a long-standing imam to begin to analyse the significance of ethnic and religious capitals in South Wales. Becker's (2002) standpoint suggests that each oral history should contribute equally to an understanding of the 'whole picture', but in contrast, we argue that our interviews with the sheikh are particularly significant to an investigation of local processes of community development and change. According to Sheikh Saeed, virtually all the Yemenis who worked out of, or resided in, Cardiff between 1939 and 1970 were deceased at the time of fieldwork, or had returned to the Yemen, making this group particularly hard to reach.

Even if we had managed to elicit accounts from other local Yemenis, it is unlikely that they would have such an eclectic knowledge of community development. Despite being a factory worker for much of his life, the sheikh's religious knowledge gave him a degree of moral and religious authority relative to other local Yemenis. The sheikh's ability to speak English and Arabic fluently and his relatively stable residence in Cardiff (as compared to the transient seafarers around him) meant that he assumed a representative role, almost by default. Our purpose here is to facilitate discussion and debate, but we do not aim to offer the last word on this history. By relying upon the account of one person, these recollections should not be read as complete or as 'truth'. Narrative research (Plummer 1995) is crucial here in understanding the way in which the telling of this particular story may contribute to ethnic and religious boundary making and the education of young Muslims. Important, too, is the deeply personal nature of storytelling, the way that accounts are necessarily intertwined with self-identity. Perception is always subjective and memories involve 'bias, partiality, silence, some revelation and much forgetting' (Bornat 2004, 34). In particular, there is a danger that conflict is downplayed in oral history, considering that many Muslims understand negative talk about others (especially the deceased) to be disapproved of in Islam. Nevertheless, the account is not wholly personal and needs to be understood in relation to Sheikh Saeed's position in the community, relative to those around him. The outcome of the inevitable imbalance of power between him and the wider community raises political and methodological questions about representation and the likely divergence in perspective between our participant, as a community leader, and other Yemenis in Cardiff. Our data and our understanding of Yemeni community life in Cardiff will have been coloured by this divergence. This issue, although a perennial one, has been critically evaluated in some depth by Burlet and Reid (1998), who in their study of the Bradford disturbances of 1995, noted the problematic position of community leaders as local representatives, especially when these so-called leaders work at the interface between their community and local power and authority structures. They noted that such leaders obscure the 'diversity of voices present within minority communities' (Burlet and Reid 1998, 273) and that 'the actions and opinions of male "community" members are often generalized and objectified as representative of the total community in the public sphere' (Burlet and Reid 1998, 273). We are mindful of the inevitably partial and individual views of the sheikh in the account that follows.

Social capital

We define social capital as networks of communities and families that involve the transmission of resources, knowledges and practices. Although historically, concepts of social capital were used to analyse the positions of elite groups (Bourdieu 1984), there is a growing interest in how social capital is deployed by poor groups living in socio-economically deprived neighbourhoods (McGrellis 2010; Mellor 2010). Social networks are a central part of the migration process, for instance by providing information about employment openings abroad (Gamburd 2009). On arrival in the host society, networks are particularly important to individual well-being and often individuals from low socio-economic backgrounds, whether migrants or not, rely heavily upon the support of family and friends to help 'cope with poverty, unemployment and wider processes of social exclusion' (Forrest and Kearns 2001, 2141).

Putnam (2000) emphasizes the values of trust, reciprocity and cooperation, and his concepts of bonding and bridging capital are a particularly useful framework for understanding the diverse forms of networks mentioned by our participant, Sheikh Saeed. According to Putnam (2000), 'bonding' social capital – which is regarded as closed and inward-looking – allows the development of networks of trust between homogenous communities, whereas 'bridging' social capital is characterized by its outward-looking nature and allows bonds to be created between heterogeneous groups. However, the work of social capital theorists has often implicitly assumed that poor families are responsible for their own marginalization by failing to create networks of support (Gillies 2006). Tight-knit minority ethnic and religious communities have been represented by government discourses as problematic because of the way in which bridging social capital is regarded as a way to escape poverty. This assumption problematically places blame on disadvantaged communities for their positions but we would argue that poverty and discrimination influences an individual's ability to maintain ties.

The concept of ethnicity as social capital – which is defined as the values and beliefs that form a central part of an ethnic group's organizational structure – has been used to explain how ethnicity can result in advantageous outcomes for some communities (Zhou 2005). For instance, Zhou's research explains how particular minority groups do very well in education markets in the USA despite coming from low socio-economic backgrounds. However, Shah's (2007) research emphasizes the way in which structural inequalities impact upon trajectories and opportunities for social mobility and while ethnic capital can facilitate social mobility, it does not render social inequalities unimportant. Moreover, ethnic capital does not necessarily enable positive results for everyone at all times. Research has shed light on the negative outcomes of social capital for some minority ethnic community members and minority ethnic men, especially elders and religious leaders, have often been represented as the 'winners' of social ties (Wilson 1978; Burlet and Reid 1998). However, gendered differences in the nature of involvement in community settings (Lowndes 2000) suggest a much more complex scenario. Much is known about the vital role of women in promoting a sense of community and maintaining ties with friends and kin (Goulbourne et al. 2011). For instance, Lowndes (2000) highlights how caring for children broadens women's community networks. However, in communities with very few women, it is not clear whether social networks suffer as a consequence of this absence. Research on class and social mobility has been strongly influenced by Bourdieusian concepts and while Bourdieu (1984) wrote very little about ethnicity, his work is useful in understanding how social capital is both an outcome and exacerbation of structural inequalities. Bourdieu's work has been used by contemporary theorists (Ball 2003; Devine 2004) to emphasize the way in which some families with low levels of economic or cultural capital can deploy social resources to bolster opportunities for social mobility.

As Shah (2007) suggests, the potential of ethnic capital may be enhanced or lowered by the complex interplay between ethnicity, religion and gender. However, with the exception of Karner and Parker (2008) – who found that religiously inflected social capital facilitated local networks – there has been very little research on religiously based social capital in the UK, even by theorists working on ethnic capital. In the USA, it has been noted that religious capital 'far exceeds the level of social capital produced through other means' (Smidt 2003, 217), evidence for which can be seen by the large number of volunteering organizations and charities that are attached to religious institutions (Nemeth and Luidens 2003). Yet, while people of faith are more likely to be civic orientated, this does not necessarily mean that faith communities have broad social networks (Campbell and Yonish 2003). Much of the literature on faith and social capital in North America has focused upon networks as experienced by white American Christians (Smidt 2003) and little is known about religiously underpinned social capital in relation to migrants and minority ethnic groups. This is with the exception of Levitt and Lamba-Nieves (2011, 16) whose work on social remittances and community development suggests that the migrants take 'a strong commitment to work for the collective good through active social, political and religious organisations with them to the US' (see also Harris 2003). There has been little attention on possible differences between ethnic and religious capitals, although Smidt (2003) suggests that religious capital may be more durable than social capital generated through more secular sources because many people of faith consider that giving one's time for good purposes is a requirement of their faith.

In the remainder of this article, we focus upon both a series of oral history interviews with our participant, Sheikh Saeed, and secondary evidence presented by Ansari (2004) and Halliday (2010) and others, in order to examine the ethnic- and religious-based social networks of Yemenis in Cardiff from the Second World War onwards. Paying attention to the advantages of these social networks, we highlight the significance of the system of community obligations and rights that ensured that Yemeni migrants had access to accommodation, food and emotional support. We also explore the negative aspects of social capital in relation to the opportunities and experiences of the Yemeni community, noting the disadvantages of close-knit bonding capital. First, however, in order to offer an understanding of social networks during the early history of Muslim migration, we interrogate the differences between the concepts of religious and ethnic capitals.

CITIES, DIVERSITY AND ETHNICITY

Religious and ethnic capitals

In the following sections, we distinguish between religious and ethnic capitals, noting which types of capital were formed at the prayer room or mosque, and which were maintained at non-religious locales such as the place of employment or boarding house. Importantly, it was religion as social capital – rather than ethnic capital – that was the driving force behind community formation and maintenance. One of the most important individuals in the history of Islam in Cardiff was Sheikh al-Hakimi. As a disciple of the founder of the Allawi Shadhilli Sufi order, he promoted networks between Yemeni Muslims in particular in order to provide opportunities for the continuation of this group (Halliday 2010). Through the establishment of the Allawi Society, al-Hakimi was largely successful at institutionalizing the religious activities of Yemenis in the UK (Ansari 2004). However, although religious capital can explain the rapid community formation and strong tight-knit bonds, ethnic resources were not unimportant, as we go on to indicate. There were, of course, Muslim migrants of other ethnic groups living in the Cardiff docklands at the time, particularly Somalis, Bengalis, Pakistanis and Malays (O'Neill 2001; Ansari 2004) and Sheikh Saeed told us that he assisted diverse ethnic groups if they came to his mosque. Nevertheless, perhaps because of a shared language, culture, traditions and home country, the Yemeni community were closer to each other than to Muslims from other ethnic groups, as demonstrated by our participant's account. We are therefore cautious of confirming Karner and Parker's (2008, 523, original emphasis) observation that Islam necessarily provides 'social capital capable of bridging ethnic divisions within the umma'.

At times, religious and ethnic capital intersected. As opposed to the general trend in the USA – where individuals become slowly involved in congregations by attending coffee mornings and membership classes – for Yemenis in Cardiff, ethnic and religious networks were very closely connected in a community in which most daily activities were shared. The following section explores the ways in which ethnic and religious capitals enhanced the Yemeni community's social trajectories. We argue that the community benefited from the knowledge and time of a dedicated imam who was devoted to the well-being of the local Muslim population. Moreover, the prayer rooms (and later mosque) were the 'hub' of the community in which the men met several times a day for prayers. The indirect consequence of meeting together in this safe space was the opportunity to discuss politics and community problems as a group. The religious imperative of giving to charity also provided the means by which the Yemeni community survived during times of crisis. In relation to ethnic capital, community members created a 'home from home', working together on a reciprocal basis by offering traditional Yemeni skills in the absence of financial resources.

Positive aspects of ethnic- and religious-based social capital

First, religious capital exerted a positive force on the Yemeni migrants' life chances in that the imam was in charge of the spiritual guidance and well-being of the community. According to Sheikh Saeed, the Yemeni community 'was very strong. We were hundreds and hundreds and hundreds of followers' (original emphasis).

CITIES, DIVERSITY AND ETHNICITY

Community links were reinforced when al-Hakimi founded the Zaouia Islami Allawouia Religious Society of the United Kingdom (Ansari 2004). Our participant indicated that he, along with the two previous sheikhs, set up social organizations for those in need of emotional or financial support, offered mediation to disputes between community members and had acted as advocate for the Muslim community. Some examples of Sheikh Saeed's work include representing the community in arguing against the dissection of dead bodies by medical staff and lobbying council staff for land for the mosque.

According to our participant, the sheikhs were also responsible for organizing events and classes for children born into the community. It is traditionally women who are responsible for their children's religious education and for passing on the 'mother tongue'. However, most Yemeni migrants married white Welsh women who were unable to help with their children's Arabic or Islamic education. In a community almost completely devoid of Yemeni women, the sheikhs worked hard to try to ensure that the community was not disadvantaged by this absence. For example, several men ran classes and events for children, such as choirs and youth clubs, as well as Arabic and Islamic classes. Sheikh Saeed recalls being part of the choir as a small boy: 'There was about fifteen of us [in the choir]. And when they had the festivities they used to get us fifteen [boys].' By becoming closely involved with a traditionally woman-centred activity such as childcare, the Yemeni men's social resources were promoted by these wider networks of sociability (Lowndes 2000). We corroborate the earlier observations of Levitt and Lamba-Nieves (2011) that such events can instil a logic of self-help, a commitment to community as well as promoting leadership and teamwork skills.

Second is the importance of dedicated rooms or buildings for prayer in exerting a positive influence on the trajectories of the Yemeni community in Cardiff. Establishing religious facilities on first arrival in the UK gave Muslim community members – whether permanently settled in Cardiff or otherwise – a place to pray and, by extension, an opportunity to form closer bonds with fellow Muslims, particularly as men would meet for prayers several times a day, work permitting. Working alongside other Muslims to create Islamic institutions was not only considered a cultural tradition (Levitt and Lamba-Nieves 2011) but a requirement of the faith. The level of determination to establish appropriate prayer facilities is clear from Sheikh Saeed's account:

> I thank the Yemenis very much because the first thing they did, when they got into the town or a city, was to look for a place for worship. The first thing they did. Maybe just a front room of somebody's house. And as the community got larger, so they started to buy bigger properties, and then they started to buy shops and turning them, convert them into mosques. (Sheikh Saeed original emphasis)

For Yemenis, these 'safe spaces' (Furbey et al. 2006) served as the hub of community social networks. Halliday's (2010, 40) description of the atmosphere in the zawiya in Cardiff, which he visited in the 1970s, indicates that the mosque was indeed the centre of community life: 'In the zawiya building there was a reading-room where a half dozen or so Yemeni men read Islamic books and newspapers from Arab states;

CITIES, DIVERSITY AND ETHNICITY

some who were retired spent all day there, in between prayers.' Finally, religion as social capital was important in creating positive resources for the migrants because of the community ethos of giving to charity and helping sick and needy neighbours. Most major world religions emphasize the religious imperative of practising active citizenship (Wuthnow 1997) and our participant emphasized the Islamic command that asks that Muslims have a concern for the social good, although he did not quote any specific religious texts.

Throughout Sheikh Saeed's accounts was the emphasis that destitute individuals have a legitimate claim on the community, and he told us that this was a message that he tried to pass on through his religious teachings. These close community ties are similar to the reciprocal giving and taking within the British Pakistani briraderi system (Bolognani 2009). For instance, the mosque was used as a base to pool resources to ensure a more equal allocation during the period of food rationing:

> We had to...bear the rationing; one egg a week [laughs]. If you finished your sugar, that's it, no more sugar. We were okay, you know, because our men used to go to sea, and seamen had plenty...Plenty of sugar, plenty of tea. Plenty galore, you know, because the men used to bring it in and give it to the mosque. So anybody that came into the mosque, if they didn't have a cup of tea: come to the mosque and you'll get a cup of tea. (Sheikh Saeed)

These tight-knit bonds provided emotional support, particularly for the casualties of the bombings. It was common for seafarers working out of UK docks to be killed or injured. Sheikh Saeed himself benefitted from the generosity of the Yemeni community as a boy following the death of his father, who was killed while working as a seafarer at the start of the Second World War. Our participant told us how Hasan Ismail became his adopted father after meeting him during a trip to his home town in the north-east of England:

> [he] said "who's this boy?", and they said, "well his father's just been killed and er he's a Yemeni boy" and that's it: "he's an orphan". So he said "do you think his mother would allow me to take him to Cardiff with me and teach him and bring him up?" (Sheikh Saeed)

Similar to the experiences of the first generation of male migrants from Pakistan, as described by Bolognani (2009), Sheikh Saeed told us how earlier migrant Yemenis in Cardiff – who could not yet rely upon 'chain migration' – used to provide necessary financial support as well as friendship to fellow countrymen. This was important in helping to find suitable housing, considering the reluctance of white proprietors to take in foreign lodgers (Ansari 2004). In cases where a Yemeni seafarer had nowhere to sleep, the generosity of Yemeni boarding house keepers is clear in the work of Aithie (2005, 189):

> [boarding house owners] provided food cooked by Islamic law, and offered rooms for the five daily prayers ... The lodging house owner would also help in finding work with their links with the seamen's agents in Aden and would even lend money or extend

credit to sailors waiting to find work. Some lodging houses even sent money back to Yemen on behalf of seamen.

Sheikh Saeed's account also indicated that there were such high levels of trust that it was common for boarding house owners to lend money to unemployed seafarers. The extent of these obligations was such that every member of the entire community was in some way involved in the 'infrastructure of exchange of favors', where those who offer help accrue more 'social credit' to be called upon when needed (Smidt 2003, 23). Often, Yemeni sailors who had become on-shore permanent settlers eventually joined together with friends to purchase inexpensive accommodation and, despite the growing social decline and urban decay in the docklands areas (Sinclair 1997; O'Neill 2001), Yemenis preferred to stay in a locality known for its extreme deprivation in order to ensure their own safety (for an account of the 1919 riots, see Fryer 1984).

Alongside the importance of religious capital, ethnic capital was also significant in exerting a positive influence on Yemeni migrants' life chances. By relying upon systems of trust, where each person contributed time or an individual skill to reciprocate favours, Yemenis in Cardiff managed to survive on very little money, especially during times of unemployment. For instance, although most of the men worked primarily in the maritime industry, several had trained 'back home' in skills such as Yemeni traditional medicine (Halliday 2010), cuisine or tailoring. As Sheikh Saeed told us, the community 'just lived as they lived in the Yemen. Once you've shut your front door, you're in Arabia', managing to recreate a home from home in the docklands of Cardiff. One member of the community was an expert in traditional Yemeni medicine and in Sheikh Saeed's words, he 'used to send for the plants from the Yemen, send them over here, mix them up and make medicine from them. And people benefited from it.' At a time when overt racial discrimination was rife, these traditions reinforced a shared ethnic identity (Ansari 2004).

However, the social resources deployed by Yemeni men did not always result in positive outcomes for all. As Smidt (2003, 215) suggests, 'bonding social capital without bridging social capital can be counterproductive' and we emphasize the ways in which social capital is fundamental to the reproduction of hierarchies (Bourdieu 1984). In the following section we examine the negative aspects of religious and ethnic capitals that at times served to limit the advancement of Muslims in Cardiff, paying attention to the way in which tight-knit bonds exacerbated Yemeni unemployment and committed members to contribute to religious infrastructures. We suggest that at times, these social networks worked to tie individuals further into exclusory practices, rather than helping them to overcome structural barriers. Negative aspects of ethnic- and religious-based social capital Due to the heavy burden of responsibility placed on the men's shoulders in return for the high levels of informal support, religious capital was often a negative resource. The level of donations channelled into Cardiff's Islamic institutions was phenomenal relative to the earnings of unskilled migrants who were also sending remittances and sometimes supporting a family in Cardiff. It is possible that the lack of enterprise in the Yemeni community was related to the amount of money donated to the mosque. According to our participant's account, regardless of personal circumstances, community members were required to donate cash to the mosque at the sheikh's demand. Here, Sheikh Saeed

CITIES, DIVERSITY AND ETHNICITY

gives an example of what Sheikh Hasan Ismail expected from each Yemeni man in Cardiff:

> The Sheikh used to say to them, "I want £100 from every one of you". I remember one old man, he had a half a dozen children ... He had a motorbike and he used to go from house to house, selling this stuff he made and that's all the income he had like, you know. And when the Sheikh said to him, "I want £100 from you" he said "okay, here's ten shillings, I owe you ninety-nine" [laughs] and he brought the ten shillings and ten shillings until he'd paid it. (Sheikh Saeed)

Although Sheikh Saeed did not mention the significance of honour, Wilson's (1978) research on South Asians in Britain indicated that upholding the family's reputation is highly important for men. Many religious institutions police practices of giving, using 'formal and informal sanctions when these expectations are violated' (Nemeth and Luidens 2003, 108). It is hard to imagine how such a payment for a large family on a very low income was possible, but the threat of losing community respect or support was a strong enough motivation to ensure that each person paid their share.

Second, Yemenis in Cardiff were negatively affected by tight-knit religious bonds at times of internal disagreements. For Muslims living in a host society, the loss of networks can be felt much more intensely when the community is also segregated from the wider society (Lloyd-Evans and Bowlby 2000). The arguments about the ownership of the Nur al-Islam mosque (O'Neill 2001; Gilliat-Ray and Mellor 2010) in the 1940s were likely to have established boundaries, curtailing the freedom to conduct specific religious practices, as Sheikh Saeed himself indicated. Furbey et al. (2006) note that religious buildings play an important role in linking communities together, but in this case, internal arguments became centred on the mosque, making it difficult for the two groups to remain united through shared religious beliefs.

At times, ethnic capital also exerted a negative impact on Yemeni migrants in Cardiff. Strong-knit ethnic ties limited opportunities for bridging capital, working to close down possibilities for social mobility. One important example of this is employment. Sheikh Saeed told us that Yemenis had carved out a reputation for being reliable, hard-working seafarers: 'Yemenis worked hard ... working at sea was the only work Yemenis knew how to do' (original emphasis). Through co-ethnic networks, community members found employment at sea, but this niche worked against seeking alternative sources of employment in the absence of broader networks during the decline of the South Wales maritime industry. Like MacDonald and Marsh's (2006) respondents, the majority of the Yemeni community were in essence trapped in unemployment or temporary, low-level work, with very few opportunities for social mobility. As Ansari (2004, 99) notes, Yemeni migrants:

> had relatively little social contact with whites. Much of their working lives was spent on ships away from their seaport bases, with the result that they developed few contacts in the dock areas they shared with white men when they returned from work.

Moreover, working alongside co-ethnic members often diminished employment prospects because for those who could rely upon friends' and colleagues' interpretation skills, there was often little incentive to improve their English language skills (Halliday 2010) or to become familiar with local Welsh culture and traditions. This was a problem that plagued a later group of Yemenis working on a factory floor in Birmingham in the 1970s (Halliday 2010).

Although Sheikh Saeed's account emphasized harmonious relationships between Muslims and Christians, especially during religious festivals, these occasions have not been explored in any of the literature on the history of Muslims in Cardiff and we are therefore left wondering how significant these interchanges were in enhancing other Yemen migrants' lives. In fact, romantic relationships with white Welsh women were one of the only opportunities for Yemenis to interact with the local white population of Cardiff. While these white Welsh brides did exert some integrative force by becoming 'key intermediary figures between the sailors and the local community' (Aithie 2005, 190), we would question the extent of this influence. Considering the public distain towards white women and their Yemeni partners, mixed-ethnic marriages often led to a relationship breakdown between the women and their parents (Collins 1951), fuelling inter-ethnic fervour rather than quelling it. Moreover, these relationships would not have enhanced opportunities for enterprise or employment because these women were typically from poor families, possibly suffering from network poverty themselves.

Conclusion

Most research on religious social capital has found that people with faith are more likely to be civically minded, but this does not necessarily mean that faith communities have broad social networks. Wuthnow's (1997) and Coleman's (2003) research on Christian congregations in the USA has reported that religious capital may in fact encourage faith communities to be more inward looking and this is corroborated by our research. Yet, it seems that the Yemeni community of Cardiff – as minorities living in a hostile host society – demonstrated even stronger bonding capital than white Christian groups in North America. In this historical context, Yemeni migrants' resources were specifically channelled into community members' pockets, rather than other local groups. These close bonds limited the transformative potential of the social capital generated; yet, for a small, marginalized community living through a difficult period, the Yemeni migrants proved remarkably resourceful.

This community formed in general a cooperative group, structured through interdependent responsibilities and rights and a strong immersion in faith- and ethnic-related community events. We have argued that the marginal status of the Yemenis influenced the forms that social capital could take. These close networks were an unintended consequence of the Sheikhs' aims to establish religious institutions in the host society. This community participation had both positive and negative results for individuals. In terms of the advantages that communities brought, we explored the emotional and financial support and camaraderie that helped new migrants survive on a day-to- day basis. However, we also pointed to negative aspects, especially the ways that community support came hand in hand with responsibilities. Members of the Yemeni community in Cardiff did not routinely come into contact with diverse networks and it is possible that this community organization

CITIES, DIVERSITY AND ETHNICITY

was partly responsible for this isolation. Yet, we have intended to demonstrate how the Yemeni community benefited from strong ties, even when these resources also closed down routes for social mobility. In pointing to the negative aspects of social capital as experienced by Yemeni migrants, this article has diverged from the emphasis of recent research that has positioned older men, including religious and community leaders, as benefiting from community networks (Burlet and Reid 1998; Shah 2007).[3]

Uniquely, we have also attempted to explore the differences as well as the parallels between religious and ethnic capital in relation to the way in which these forms of social capital influenced Yemeni migrants' life chances. Previous work has emphasized the significance of ethnicity as social capital, while the role of faith has received much less attention. This absence is particularly striking considering the growing importance of revivalist Islam and the distinction between 'culture' or 'ethnicity' and 'religion' (Bolognani 2009). In light of these recent developments, our approach of analysing faith alongside ethnicity as social capital may be useful for those researching Muslims' networks. We have argued, however, that the nature of social networks is such that it is often impossible to separate groups as either wholly 'ethnic' or 'religious' in focus and, overall, this article contributes to an understanding of the processes by which ethnicity and faith interconnect in relation to social networks.

Acknowledgements

We would like to acknowledge the generous support of Cardiff University's Innovation and Engagement Committee, which provided funding for the research upon which this paper is based. We would also like to thank the anonymous reviewers of this paper who provided very useful comments. This paper is dedicated to Sheikh Saeed Hasan Ismail (1930–2011).

Notes

1. There is very little contemporary research on Yemeni migration to the West, with the exception of Sarroub's (2001) work on Yemeni American girls in the USA.
2. Sheikh Saeed describes the zawiya as a mosque for Sufis that provides a welcoming space for chanting, singing and Sufi rituals. He distinguishes the zawiya from other mosques that require silence: 'in a zawiya they chant ... if they did that in a mosque they would throw them out. You know, disturbing them.' Halliday (2010, 156, f. n. 11) defines the zawiya as 'literally a corner or nook', 'used in Sufi Islam to denote a small mosque where a religious order has its centre.'
3. While one might consider an imam to enjoy a particularly powerful position within the community, in practice Sheikh Saeed's account suggests that he conducted his work at the mosque in the spirit of humility and self-sacrifice. He did not receive payment for his religious duties and, as a young man, combined night shifts as a factory welder with his work at the mosque. Many Muslims would agree that it would be wrong for an imam to use his position to become socially or economically mobile.

References

Aithie, Patricia. 2005. *The Burning Ashes of Times: From Steamer Point to Tiger Bay.* Bridgend: Seren.

Ansari, Humayun. 2004. *The 'Infidel' Within: Muslims in Britain, 1800 to the Present.* London: Hurst.

Ball, Stephen J. 2003. *Class Strategies and the Education Market: The Middle Classes and Social Advantage.* London: Routledge.

Becker, Howard. 2002. "The Life History and the Scientific Mosaic." In *Qualitative Research Methods*, edited by Darin Weinberg, 79–87. Blackwell: Oxford: Blackwell.

Bolognani, Marta. 2009. *Crime and Muslim Britain: Culture and the Politics of Criminology among British Pakistanis.* London: I.B. Taurus.

Bornat, Joanna. 2004. "Oral History." In *Qualitative Research Practice*, edited by Clive Seale, et al., 327–43. London: SAGE.

Bourdieu, Pierre. 1984. *Distinction: A Social Critique of the Judgement of Taste.* London: Routledge & Kegan Paul.

Burlet, Stacey, and Helen Reid. 1998. "A Gendered Uprising: Political Representation and Minority Ethnic Communities." *Ethnic and Racial Studies* 21 (2): 270–287. doi:10.1080/014198798330016.

Campbell, David, and Steven Yonish. 2003. "Religion and Volunteering in America." In *Religion as Social Capital: Producing the Common Good*, edited by Corwin Smidt, 87–106. Waco, TX: Baylor University Press.

Coleman, John. 2003. "Religious Social Capital: Its Nature, Social Location and Limits." In *Religion as Social Capital: Producing the Common Good*, edited by Corwin Smidt, 33–48. Waco, TX: Baylor University Press.

Collins, Sydney F. 1951. "The Social Position of White and 'Half-caste' Women in Coloured Groupings in Britain." *American Sociological Review* 16 (6): 796–802. doi:10.2307/2087506.

Devine, Fiona. 2004. *Class Practices: How Parents Help Their Children Get Good Jobs.* Cambridge, MA: Cambridge University Press.

Evans, Neil. 1980. "The South Wales Race Riots of 1919." *Llafur: Journal of the Society for the Study of Welsh Labour History* 3 (1): 5–29.

Forrest, Ray, and Ade. Kearns. 2001. "Social Cohesion, Social Capital and the Neighbourhood." *Urban Studies* 38 (12): 2125–2143. doi:10.1080/00420980120087081.

Fryer, Peter. 1984. *Staying Power: The History of Black People in Britain.* London: Pluto Press.

Furbey, Rob, et al. 2006. *Faith as Social Capital: Connecting or Dividing?* Bristol: Policy Press.

Gamburd, Michele Ruth. 2009. "Advocating for Sri Lankan Migrant Workers: Obstacles and Challenges." *Critical Asian Studies* 41 (1): 61–88. doi:10.1080/14672710802631152.

Gilliat-Ray, Sophie. 2010. *Muslims in Britain: An Introduction.* Cambridge: Cambridge University Press.

Gilliat-Ray, Sophie. 2011. "An Iconic Welsh Figure in the History of Islam." Click on Wales, 15 May. Accessed March 11. http://www.clickonwales.org/2011/05/an-iconic-welsh-figure-in-the-historyof-islam

Gilliat-Ray, Sophie, and Jody Mellor. 2010. "'Bilad al-Welsh' (Land of the Welsh): Muslims in Cardiff, South Wales: Past, Present, and Future." *The Muslim World* 100 (4): 452–475. doi:10.1111/j.1478-1913.2010.01331.x.

Gillies, Val. 2006. "Working Class Mothers and School Life: Exploring the Role of Emotional Capital." *Gender and Education* 18 (3): 281–293. doi:10.1080/09540250600667876.

CITIES, DIVERSITY AND ETHNICITY

Goulbourne, Harry, et al. 2011. *Transnational Families: Ethnicities, Identities and Social Capital.* London: Routledge.

Halliday, Fred. 2010. *Britain's First Muslims: Portrait of an Arab Community.* London: I.B. Taurus.

Harris, Fredrick. 2003. "The Ties that Bind and Flourish: Religion as Social Capital in African-American Politics and Society." In *Religion as Social Capital: Producing the Common Good*, edited by Corwin Smidt, 121–138. Waco, TX: Baylor University Press.

Karner, Christian, and David Parker. 2008. "Religion Versus Rubbish: Deprivation and Social Capital in Inner-city Birmingham." *Social Compass* 55 (4): 517–531. doi:10.1177/00377686 08097236.

Levitt, Peggy, and Deepak Lamba-Nieves. 2011. "Social Remittances Revisited." *Journal of Ethnic and Migration Studies* 37 (1): 1–22. doi:10.1080/1369183X.2011.521361.

Little, Kenneth. 1972. *Negroes in Britain: A Study of Racial Relations in English Society.* 2nd ed. London: Kegan Paul.

Lowndes, Vivien. 2000. "Women and Social Capital: A Comment on Hall's 'Social Capital in Britain'." *British Journal of Political Science* 30 (3) 533–537. doi:10.1017/S0007123400 210223.

Lloyd-Evans, Sally, and Sophie Bowlby. 2000. "Crossing Boundaries: Racialised Gendering and the Labour Market Experiences of Pakistani Migrant Wives in Britain." *Women's Studies International Forum* 23 (4): 461–474.

Macdonald, Robert, and Jane Marsh. 2006. *Disconnected Youth? Growing up in Britain's Poor Neighbourhoods.* London: Palgrave Macmillan.

Mcgrellis, Sheena. 2010. "In Transition: Young People in Northern Ireland Growing Up in, and Out of, Divided Communities." *Ethnic and Racial Studies* 33 (5): 761–778. doi:10.1080/01419870903318177.

Mellor, Jody. 2010. "Ethnicity as Social Capital: Class, Faith and British Muslim Women's Routes to University." In *Classed Intersections: Spaces, Selves, Knowledges*, edited by Yvette Taylor, 73–94. Aldershot: Ashgate.

Nemeth, Roger, and Donald Luidens. 2003. "The Religious Basis of Charitable Giving in America: A Social Capital Perspective." In *Religion as Social Capital: Producing the Common Good*, edited by Corwin Smidt. Waco, TX: Baylor University Press.

O'Neill, Dan. 2001. *Tiger Bay and the Docks: The Story of a Remarkable Corner of the World.* Derby: Breedon Books.

Plummer, Kenneth. 1995. *Telling Sexual Stories: Power, Change and Social Worlds.* London: Routledge.

Putnam, Robert D. 2000. *Bowling Alone: The Collapse and Revival of American Community.* New York: Simon and Schuster.

Sarroub, Loukia. 2001. "The Sojourner Experience of Yemeni American High School Students: An Ethnographic Portrait." *Harvard Educational Review* 71 (3): 390–415.

Shah, B. 2007. "Being Young, Female and Laotian: Ethnicity as Social Capital at the Intersection of Gender, Generation, 'Race' and Age." *Ethnic and Racial Studies* 30 (1): 28–50. doi:10.1080/01419870601006520.

Sinclair, Neil. 1997. *The Tiger Bay Story.* Cardiff: Bute town History & Arts Centre.

Smidt, Corwin. 2003. "Religion, Social Capital and Democratic Life: Concluding Thoughts." In *Religion as Social Capital: Producing the Common Good*, edited by Corwin Smidt, 211–222. Waco, TX: Baylor University Press.

Wilson, Amrit. 1978. *Finding a Voice: Asian Women in Britain.* London: Virago.

Wuthnow, Robert. 1997. *The Crisis in the Churches: Spiritual Malaise, Fiscal Woe.* New York: Oxford University Press.

Zhou, Min. 2005. "Ethnicity as Social Capital: Community-based Institutions and Embedded Networks of Social Relations." In *Ethnicity, Social Mobility and Public Policy: Comparing the USA and UK*, edited by Glenn Loury, Tariq Modood, and Steven Teles, 131–159. Cambridge: Cambridge University Press.

Index

Note: Page numbers in *italics* represent tables
Page numbers in **bold** represent figures
Page numbers followed by 'n' refer to notes

acculturation 158
Achbari, W. 3, 157–74
Agyeman, J. 93
Albanian Kosovars 2–3, 108–20
Albhai-Brown, Y. 94
Allawi Shadhili Sufi order 176, 181
Allawi Society 176, 181
alternative identity 119
ambivalence: identity 94
American dream 126
Americo Bank: Latino entrepreneurs 133, 134, 136
Amsterdam, Turkish and mixed-non-profit organizations 3, 157–71; characteristics of organizations studied 164–5; Dappermarkt 5–6, 14; measuring trust 158; Turkish minorities 162
Anderson, B. 116
Ang, I. 94
anonymity 80
Ansari, H. 180–5
anti-immigrant sentiments (Belgium) 2, 37–52; actual and perceived diversity 43–4; characteristics of scale 41, *42*; competition for resources 37–8; control variables 42–3; data and methods 40–1; descriptive statistics of variables 43, *44*; effect of different diversity-related community-level parameters 49, *49*; hypotheses 40; immigrant concentration 37; independent variables 41; literature 38–40; measuring 41; media 43; multi-level findings and interpretations 45–6, 49–50; multi-level model for perceived percentage non-Belgians 44, *45*; multi-level regression models for anti-immigrant sentiments 46–9, *47–8*; perceived size 51;

self-selection 50; statistics 41; study method 43
anti-immigrant sentiments (Italy) 59
anti-immigration: political parties 7
anxiety: status 87
Asian entrepreneurs 126
Askins, K.: and Parks, J. 2, 91–107
assimilation 75; Chicago School 157; economic saliency 118; ethnic identity 109; ethnicity 119; processes 108; segmented 158, 170n; spatial 87; theory 126–7, 136, 143
assumed ethnicity: New York City 2–3, 108–20
assumed ethnicity study: cultural opportunity 116–18; identity entrepreneurship 118–19; Little Italy 110–20; overview 110–11; performativity opportunity 113–16; structural opportunity 111–13
asylum seekers 99
Australia: Census data (2011) 78, *79*, 82; discrimination 85; diversity 76; immigration for nation building 76; Scanlon-Monash Index of Social Cohesion (SMI) 75, *see also* Greenburb; Melbourne; Northburb
authenticity 11; identity 110
avoidance: mutual 11

back-stage identity 110
banks: Latino community 133–4
barriers: low entry 6, 11–12
Becker, E. 2–3, 108–23
Becker, H. 178
Belgium *see* anti-immigrant sentiments (Belgium)
Bell, R.: and Hopper, R. 119
Bhabha, H. 94
bias: perception 178

INDEX

Birmingham (UK) 1, 176, 186
black: term 94
black and minority ethnic (BME) 94–5
blacking up 120
Blagojevich, R. 148
Blalock, H. 40
Bologna 2; carers 64; citizenship rights 65; council for migrants 65–6; cultural diversity 64; demographic change 64; hospitable city 67–8; integration narratives 63–6; migrants and criminality 66; migrants as economic resources' narrative 63–5; narrative constructions of integration 56–70; national context 59; participating migrant narrative 65–6; security threat narrative 66
Bolognani, M. 183, 187
bonding 170; capital 186; organizations 159
bonding social capital concept (Putnam) 175, 179, 184
Border Protection, Antiterrorism and Illegal Immigration Control Act (US, 2005) 140, 141, 144, 149
Bornat, J. 177–8
boundaries: ethnicities 119
boundary-making: identity 94; terminology 92
Bourdieu, P. 180
bridging 170; organizations 159
briraderi system 183
British identity 24
Bulmer, M.: and Solomos, R. 1–3
Burlet, S.: and Reid, H. 178, 179
business resource: diversity 63
business-friendly policy 59
businesses: Chinese community 126
businesss: Korean community 126

Çağlar, A.: and Glick Schiller, N. 23, 30
capital: ethnic 179, 180, 181–6; human 59; human-cultural 69; political 58, 142, *see also* social capital
Cardiff: history of Muslims 176; Muslim community 181; Nur al-Islam Mosque 176, 185; Yemeni community 3, 175–87; Yemeni seamen 176
carers: Bologna 64
categorizations 92
Census: Australia (2011) 78, *79*, 82; England and Wales (2011) 24
Centre on Dynamics of Ethnicity (CoDE) 24
chain migration 183
chain settlement-pattern 82
change: urban 33
charity 183
Chicago: immigrant rights march (2006) 140–53; Mexican Consulate 147

Chicago School: assimilation 157; criticism 158; race relations 1
Chicago's Mexican HTAs (hometown associations) 3, 140–53; changes since 9/11 and agenda (2001–5) 147–9; creation 148; development 144; political capital 142; political-economic transformation and growth (–2001) 145–7
childcare 96
Children's Centres (England) 91–105
Chinatown 17
Chinese community: businesses 126
citizenship 23, 33, 58; population records 52n; religion 183; rights (Bologna) 65; transnational 143
city: collective 24, 27–30; dimensions 24; intimate 24, 30–3; symbolic 24–7
city-making 23
civil rights movement: Mexican Americans 127
Clarke, J.: and Speeden, S. 93
class: analysis 94; middle 81; social 92; social mobility 180; working 81
cohesion: community 21, 74–87, 92; social 15, 75–8
Coleman, J. 186
Colic-Peisker, V.: and Robertson, S. 2, 74–90
collective city 24; street perspectives 27–30
collective identity: Sweden 69
colour-blind discourse 95
communities: development 180; faith 186; imagined 75, 116; Korean 126; Latino 125; meanings 2; policy 57–8; spirit 175; visible 94; women 179
community cohesion 21; concept 75–8; local 85, *85*; and social change (Melbourne) 74–87; United Kingdom (UK) 92
community leaders: disapproval of negative talk 178
competition: actual and perceived 40; inter-group 37, 39
CONFEMEX (Confederacion de Federaciones Mexicanos) 140–53
connectedness: social 74
consuming cultures 79–80
contact: interethnic 160; intergroup 39
contact hypothesis: Turkish and non-profit organizations in Amsterdam 157–71
contact theory 39; diverse others 161
cosmopolitan entrepreneurial migrant narrative: Malmö 62–3
cosmopolitan identities 17
credit: social 184
criminality 66
criminalization 150
crisis: multiculturalism 7

INDEX

Cruz, J. 131, 135
Cuban migrants 138n
cultural capital: human 69
cultural diversity: Bologna 64; meaning 5
cultural hegemony 37
cultural opportunity 116–18
cultural subordination: minorities 11
culture: consuming other 79–80

Dappermarkt (Amsterdam) 5–6, 14
de Vroome, T.: and Hooghe, M. 2, 37–55
deception: through implication 119
democracy schools 159
demographic change 64
densification 80
deprivation: ethnic diversity overlay 25–6, **25**; ethnic minorities 25
difference: indifference to 11; visible 95
discourse: colour-blind 95; racial 92
discrimination: Australia 85; Latino entrepreneurs 136; racial 184
discursive practices: markets and diversity 13
dispersion: spatial 76
diversity: Australia 76; business resource 63–5; cultural 5, 64; innovation 7; managing 76; measuring 163–4; perception 37–51; policies 7; positive 86; prizing 118; promoting contact 158; public opinion 13–14; social 13; street markets 1, 5–18; within minority communities 178, *see also* super-diversity

economic dynamism 86
economic engagement 17
economic exchange: regulation 10
economic globalization 25
economic resources: Bologna 63–5; Malmö 64; migrants 68
economy: informal 6, 8; and society 6; society and street markets 16–18
education programmes: unemployed migrants 62
elective affinity 116–17
Elias, N.: and Scotson, J.L. 99, 103
Emilia Romagna 67; migrant representation 59, *see also* Bologna
employed migrant narrative: Malmö 61–2
employment: generation 8; integration 62; network-based 112; social capital 60
England: childcare 96; Children's Centres 91–105; ethnic spread 24; riots (2001) 74
enterprise: ethnic 125; lack 184
entrepreneurial migrant narrative: Malmö 62–3
entrepreneurs: Asian 126; individualism and meritocracy 126, *see also* Latino entrepreneurs

entrepreneurship 68; identity 118–19
equal opportunities 59
ethnic: term 93
ethnic capital 179; potential 180; and religious capital 181–6
ethnic concentration 157
ethnic enterprise 125
ethnic fragmentation 82–5
ethnic identity: alternative 119; assimilation 109; constructing 93–6; narratives 91–105; paradox 109; shared 184; study methodology 96–8
ethnic minorities: deprivation 25; groups 93
ethnic other 93
ethnic philanthropy: mobility 137
ethnic preservation 109
ethnic pride 87
ethnic social capital: positive and negative aspects 181–6
ethnic solidarity 124; Latino entrepreneurs 124, 137
ethnic spread: England and Wales 24
ethnicities: boundaries 119
ethnicity: assimilation 119; assumed 2; -based assumptions 101–4; contested representations 93–4; migrants 109; mobilization 3; more than 94–6, 105; social capital 179
ethno-national organizations: promotion for integration 158
ethnocentrism 50
ethnography: urban super-diversity 23–4
Eurocentrism 8
European Social Survey (ESS) 41
exchange 21
exclusion 94

faith 180; communities 186
Flanders 40
Florida, R. 7
Foundation Center: report (2011) 125
Fox, V. 147
Franzosi, R. 60
front-stage identity 110

Gans, H. 81
generalized trust: ethnic composition of group 166; fixed and random effects models 16, *167*; learning 157–71; partitioning variance 165; research design and measures 161–4; research organizations 162–3, *163*; research variables 163–4; self-selection 168, 170; socio-demographic factors and resources 168; socio-economical position 168; validity of questions 171n; variance components

INDEX

model 165, *166*; voluntary organizations 159–61; why study 159–61; winner in society 168
gentrification 14, 22, 86; Northburb 78–81
gentrifiers 77
Gilliat-Ray, S.: and Mellor, J. 3, 175–90
giving back: Latino entrepreneurs 129, 135–6
Glick Schiller, N.: and Çağlar, A. 23, 30
globalization 13; economic 25
goal orientation: middle classes 81
Goffman, E.: *The Presentation of Self in Everyday Life* 108–10, 113, 116, 119
Greenburb (Melbourne) 75; anomie and ethnic tension 77; Census data (2011) 78, *79*, 82; chain settlement-pattern 82; disconnect with recent Muslim settlers 83; immigration and ethnic fragmentation 82–5; invasion-succession 82; job prospects 84; Muslim non-Muslim interaction 84–5; positive diversity 86
group categorizations: political capital 58
group conflict theory 49, 50; out-group size 39–40
group threat 37; theory 38
Guarnizo, L.E.: and Smith, M.P. 23
Gutierrez, J.L. 148

Hacking, I. 94
al-Hakimi, Sheikh Ali 175, 176, 181, 182
Hall, S. 2, 21–36
Halliday, F. 175–7, 180–2, 184, 186, 187n
hegemony: cultural 37
Hiebert, D.: Rath, J. and Vertovec, S. 1, 5–18
hierarchies of power 23
hometown associations *see* Chicago's Mexican HTAs (hometown associations)
honour: Yemeni community 185
Hooghe, M.: and de Vroome, T. 2, 37–55
Hopper, R.: and Bell, R. 119
housing costs: rising 80
human capital 59
human-cultural capital 69
hybrid identity 23

identity: alternative 118; ambivalence 94; boundary-making 94; British 24; collective 69; concealment 110; entrepreneurship 118–19; ethnic 91–105, 109, 119, 184; fluid 23; front-stage 110; hybrid 23; Muslim 95; national 68–9; needs and interest based 93; personality 100; religious 114, 121n
identity construction: ambivalence and ethnicity 98–101
identity entrepreneurship: assumed identity study 118–19

imagined communities 75, 116
imam duties 187n
immigrant concentration: anti-immigrant sentiment 37
immigrant mobilization: state strategies 142–5
immigrant rights: Chicago march (2006) 140–53; USA 149–52
immigrants: criminalization 150; cutting links when economically assimilated 126; Latino 125
immigration: nation building 76; post 9/11 USA policy147
inclusion: socio-economic 12
income: fixed 86
incorporation: modes 23
independent retail 29
Indices of Deprivation 25
individualism: entrepreneurs 126
inequality 25; social 179
informal economy 6, 8
innovation: diversity 7
Institute of Mexicans Abroad (IME) 147
integration 7, 15, 102; employment 62; language barriers 103; local and national narratives 67–9; Netherlands 157; perception 85; perceptions and practices 70; processes 108; stories 58
integration narratives: Bologna 63–6; construction study method 60; constructions of (Malmö) 56–70; local and national 67–9
interaction: public 10, 62
interethnic contact 160
intergroup contact 39
intimate city 24; interior perspectives 30–3
invasion-succession 76, 77, 82
Islam: criticism 157; Western values 76, *see also* Muslims
Islamophobia 92
Ismail, Sheikh Hasan 176, 185
Italian Americans 116
Italy: anti-immigration sentiments 59; Emilia Romagna 59, 67; immigration and integration (Law 189/2002) 59; migration (Law 286/1998) 59; national identity 69, *see also* Bologna

Kaplan, T. 60
Karner, C.: and Parker, D. 180
Korean community: businesses 126

labour market: segregation 77
labour shortages 63
Lamba-Nieves, D.: and Levitt, P. 180, 182
language 182; proficiency 21, 63; skills lack 186

INDEX

Latino Alumni Association 131, 132
Latino communities 125
Latino Education Fund 132
Latino entrepreneurs: Americo Bank 133–4, 136; assimilating and giving back 136–7; building ethnic social structures 131–5; data and methods 127–8; discrimination 136; educational philanthropy 131; ethnic solidarity 124, 137; firm ownership 127; giving back 129; giving back motivations 135–6; increase 124; inspiring 129; leveraging capital 134; Los Angeles 125; mobility narrative 130; philanthropy 124–38; previous research 125–7; scholarships 131; social capital agents 129–30; struggle and sacrifice 135
Latino immigrants: enterprise 125
learning: generalized trust 157–71; tolerance 11
Levitt, P.: and Lamba-Nieves, D. 180, 182
Little Italy: assumed identity study (NYC) 2–3, 110–20; out-migration 111
local and national integration narratives 67–9
locality 23; practised 27
locality fit: Rye Lane 19
London: deprivation and ethnic diversity overlay 25–6, **25**; independent retail 29; Indices of Deprivation 25; migrant population 24–5; Peckham street super-diversity 21–35; *see also* Rye Lane
Los Angeles: Latino entrepreneurs 125
Lowndes, V. 179, 182

McKenzie, R.D. 76
Maisel, R. 11
Malmö 2; cosmopolitan entrepreneurial migrant narrative 62–3; employed migrant narrative 61–2; engine of growth 67–8; integration policy 59; narrative constructions of integration 56–70; national context 58–9
marginalization 76; social mobility 17
markets: regulations 14; sociability of exchange 11; spaces of contact 11; spatiality 12, 14; temporality 12, 27, *see also* street markets
markets and diversity 7–8; conceptual and political complications 15; continuity and change 12–14; demarcating 8–10; discursive practices 13; methodological complications 15–16; new relationship 13–14; old and generic relationship 12–13; rules of engagement 12–13, 16; social diversity 13
Mas Giralt, R. 92, 94
media: anti-immigrant sentiments 43
Melbourne: immigration statistics 75; social change and community cohesion 74–87, *see also* Greenburb; Northburb

Mellor, J.: and Gilliat-Ray, S. 3, 175–90
mentorship programmes 62
meritocracy: entrepreneurs 126
Mexican Americans: civil rights movement 127; *mutualista* organizations 127, *see also* Chicago's Mexican HTAs (hometown associations)
middle classes: goal orientation 81
migrants: ethnicity 109; flexible resource 59; London population 24–5
migration: family support 100; mass 14; place-making 23
minorities: cultural subordination 11; ethnic 25, 93
minority: term 94
minority ethnic group: construction 93
mixed marriages 186
mobility: ethnic philanthropy 137; Latino entrepreneurs narrative130; Northburb 80; social 17, 125, 179, 180; spatial 86
mobilization: ethnicity 3; immigrant 142–5
Morris, N. 94, 99
multicultural precinct (Northburb) 79
multiculturalism 15; crisis 7; losing popularity 157; rejecting 69, 74; Sweden 59; targeting 105; United Kingdom (UK) 91–2
multilingualism 63
Muslimness: racialization of 92
Muslims: Cardiff community 181; Greenburb settlers 83; identity 95; Islam 76, 157; label and war on terror 92; networks 187; non-Muslim interaction 84–5; radicalization 87
mutual avoidance 11
mutualisms: Rye Lane 31
mutualista organizations: Mexican Americans 127

narratives: construction of integration 56–70; cosmopolitan entrepreneurial migrant (Malmö) 62–3; employed migrant (Malmö) 61–2; ethnic identity 91–105; Latino entrepreneurs mobility 130; local and national integration 67–9; and policy communities 57–8; policy-making 56–70; security threat (Bologna) 66; structure elements 60
nation building: immigration 76
National Alliance of Latino and Caribbean Communities (NALACC) 148
National Council of La Raza 127
national identity: political change 68–9
national and local integration narratives 67–9
nativist populist movements 7
neighbourhood cycle 76–7

INDEX

neighbourhoods: transitional 87
neo-liberalism 15
Netherlands: integration 157, *see also* Amsterdam
networks 179; bridging 87; social 186
New Americans Policy and Advocacy 148
New York City: Little Italy assumed ethnicity study 2–3, 108–20
Nietzsche, F. 119–20
niqab 84–5
Northburb (Melbourne): Census data (2011) 78, *79*; densification and anonymity 80; gentrification and socio-economic polarization 78–81; gentrifiers 77; mobility 80; multicultural precinct 79; population 78–9; rising housing costs 80; social mix 80; Socio-Economic Indexes for Areas (SEIFA) 79, 88n; yuppies 77, 80–1
Norton, M.I.: *et al.* 95, 104
Nur al-Islam mosque (Cardiff) 176; ownership dispute 185

openness 11
opportunity: cultural 116–18; equal 59; performativity 113–16; political 141; structural 111–13
oral history 177
Ordinary Streets project 34
orphans 183
Othello: racialized caricature 120
other: ethnic 93; visible 83, 85
othering 92
otherness 11
out-groups: size and group conflict theory 39–40; social capital 160
outsider 99
outsiderness 95

Pardy, M. 11
Parker, D.: and Karner, C. 180
Parks, J.: and Askins, K. 2, 91–107
participating migrant narrative: Bologna 65–6
passing 110, 118, 119
Peckham (London) 21–35; tale of two 29, *see also* Rye Lane
pensioners 86
people of colour 94
people-orientation: working-classes 81
perception 22; anti-immigrant sentiment 37–52; bias 178; distorted 39; diversity 37–51; integration 85; unfairness 86
performativity opportunity 113–16
personality: identity 100
philanthropy: ethnic 137; Latino entrepreneurs 124–38

place: street markets 7
place-making: migration 23
policy communities: and narratives 57–8
policy-making: local and national 57; narratives 56–70
political capital: Chicago's Mexican HTAs 142; group categorizations 58
political change: national identity 68–9
political correctness 93, 95
political opportunity structure 141
political parties: anti-immigrant 7
pooling resources 183
pop-up shops 33
population: Northburb (Melbourne) 78–9; records 52n
populist movements: nativist 7
Portes, A. 77, 87
positive diversity 86
poverty: escaping 179
power: hierarchies 23; relations 60
prejudice: reducing 161
Presentation of Self in Everyday Life, The (Goffman) 108–10, 113, 116, 119
pride: ethnic 87
processes: social 125
profit 11
public interaction 62; street markets 10
public opinion: diversity 13–14
Putnam, R.D. 175, 179

Quintero, M. 133–4

race: contested representations 93–4
race relations 95; Chicago School 1
racial discourse: social class 92
racial discrimination 184
racial disturbances: UK (2005) 92
racialization of Muslimness 92
racialized caricature: Othello 120
racism 94
radicalization: Muslims 87
reciprocating favours 184
refugees 99
regeneration strategies 62
regulation 11; economic exchange 10
regulations: markets 7, 14
Reid, H.: and Burlet, S. 178, 179
religion: citizenship 183
religion and ethnicity: social capital 124–38
religious capital: and ethnic capital 181–6; USA 180, 186
religious identity: concealing 114, 121n
religious social capital: positive and negative aspects 181–6
remittances: social 180

INDEX

reputation: loss 185
residential segregation 103
retail: independent 29
Rex, J. 1
rights: citizenship 65; civil 127; immigrant 140–53
riots: England (2001) 74
Rivera family 131
Robertson, S.: and Colic-Peisker, V. 2, 74–90
Romero, G. 132
Rye Lane (Peckham): changing face of buildings 30–1; deprivation – a different perspective 30; economic practices 28; hybrid retail interior 31, **32**; hybridity 31–2; land use plan 30; locality fit 19; map of origins and convergence 27–8, **28**; mutualisms 31; organizational logic 30; origin of proprietors 21, 27–8, **28**; perceptions 22; real estate changes 26; regeneration plans 22, 29; regulations 33; shop interiors 31; subletting 31–3; survey of independent proprietors 27–8

Saeed, Sheikh 177, 180–7; oral history 177–8
safe spaces 182
Samers, M. 93
Scanlon-Monash Index of Social Cohesion (SMI) 75
scholarships 131
Scotson, J.L.: and Elias, N. 99, 103
Scuzzarello, S. 2, 56–73
security threat narrative (Bologna) 66
segmented assimilation 158, 170n
segregation: interaction 39; labour market 77; residential 103
self-selection: trust 160–1
semantic grammar 60
Sensenbrenner Bill (US, 2005): opposition to 140, 141, 144, 149
September 11th terrorist attack (2001) 76, 87, 92, 144, 147–9, 153
Shah, B. 179, 180
signifiers 94
Sites, W.: and Vonderlack-Navarro, R. 3, 140–56
Smidt, C. 180, 184
Smith, M.G. 11
Smith, M.P.: and Guarnizo, L.E. 23
sociability of exchange: markets 11
social capital 67; bonding 175, 179; bridging and bonding 179; defined 179; depletion 74; employment 60; ethnicity 179; faith 180; gendered differences 179; Latino entrepreneur agents 129–30; out-groups 160; religion and ethnicity 124–38; religiously

based 180; social mobility 87; Yemeni community (Cardiff) 175–87
social change 88n; concept 76
social change and community cohesion (Melbourne) 74–87; study method 78
social class 92
social cohesion 15; concept 75–8; policy 76
Social Cohesion Indicators in Flanders (SCIF) 40
social connectedness 74
social credit 184
social diversity 13
social inequalities 179
social mixing 76
social mobility 17, 125; class 180; ethnic capital 179
social networks: faith communities 186
social processes 125
social remittances 180
socialization: trust 160–1
society: and economy 6; street markets and economy 16–18
socio-economic fragmentation 74
Socio-Economic Indexes for Areas (SEIFA) 79, 88n
socio-economic polarization 78–81
Soja, E. 23
solidarity: ethnic 124, 137
Solomos, R.: and Bulmer, M. 1–3
South Wales Islamic Centre 177
spaces: safe 182
spaces of contact: markets 11
spatial assimilation 87
spatial dispersion 76
spatial mobility 86
spatiality: markets 12, 14; street markets 9–10
Speeden, S.: and Clarke, J. 93
status anxiety 87
stereotyping 11, 92
Stolle, D. 160, 170
stories: integration 58; power relations 60, *see also* narratives
street markets: describing 9; diversity 1, 5–18; economy and society 16–18; intellectual context 11–12; low entry barriers 6, 11–12; public interaction 10; regulation 7, 10; role of place 7; spatiality 9–10
streets: urban ethnography 2
structural opportunity 111–13
subletting 31–3
subordination: cultural 11
super-diverse city 33–4
super-diversity 6, 91, 92; London street 21–35; trans-ethnography 33–4

INDEX

Sweden: collective identity 69; multiculturalism 59; national stories 69; welfare 59, *see also* Malmö

symbolic city 24; macro perspectives 24–7

targeting: multiculturalism 105

tax revenues 60

television: anti-immigrant sentiments 43

temporality: markets 12

terminology: boundary making 92; inconsistencies 94

terror: war on 92

terrorism: September 11th attack (2001) 76, 87, 92, 144, 147–9, 153

Thomas, W.I.: and Thomas, D.S. 85

tolerance: learning 11

training programmes: unemployed migrants 62

trans-ethnography: super-diverse city 33–4; super-diversity street 21–35

transnational citizenship 143

tribalism 99, 104

trust: Yemeni community 183–4, *see also* generalized trust

Turkish organizations: Amsterdam 3, 157–71

unemployment 62

unfairness: perception 86

United Farm Workers 127

United Kingdom (UK): community cohesion 92; complex migration and diversity 91; map showing northeast region 97; multiculturalism 91–2; narratives of ethnic identity 91–105, *see also* England; London; Wales

United States of America (USA): Albanian Kosovars 110–11; immigrant rights 149–52; immigrant rights marches 141; immigration policy (post 9/11) 147; Little Italy assumed identity study (NYC) 2–3, 110–20; people of colour 94; race and ethnicity 95; religious capital 180, 186; *see also* Latino entrepreneurs

urban anonymity 74

urban change 33

urban economies: development 7

urban ethnography: streets 2

urban super-diversity 21–35; ethnography 23–4

Vallejo, J.A. 3, 124–39

van Gogh, Theo 157

Vertovec, S. 21

visibility: other 83, 85

visible communities 94

visible difference 95

Vlaams Belang party 51

voluntary organizations: democracy schools 159; generalized trust 159–61

Vonderlack-Navarro, R.: and Sites, W. 3, 140–55

Wales: ethnic spread 24, *see also* Cardiff; Yemeni community

war on terror 95; Muslim label 92

Weber, M. 13, 116

welfare 59

Western Union Money Transfer 32

Western values 76

whereness 23

white flight 76

whiteness 93, 98–9

women: childcare and community networks 180; community 179

working-classes: people-orientation 81

Wuthnow, R. 186

Yemeni community (Cardiff) 3, 175–87; absence of broader networks 185; charity 183; childcare 182; creation of Islamic institutions 182; ethnic ties 185; honour 185; inter-ethnic fervour 186; lack of enterprise 184; lack of language skills 186; language 182; loss of network 185; mixed marriages 186; negative aspects of ethnic and religious based social capital 184–6; orphans 183; pooling resources 183; positive aspects of ethnic and religious based social capital 181–4; racial discrimination 184; reciprocating favours 184; representations 177; safe spaces 182; social credit 184; South Wales Islamic Centre 177; trust 183–4

yuppies 77, 80–1

zawiya 177, 182, 187n

Zhou, M. 179

Zukin, S. 86